HUME'S THEORY OF MORAL JUDGMENT

ARCHIVES INTERNATIONALES D'HISTOIRE DES IDÉES

INTERNATIONAL ARCHIVES OF THE HISTORY OF IDEAS

131

WALTER BRAND

# HUME'S THEORY OF MORAL JUDGMENT

# HUME'S THEORY OF MORAL JUDGMENT

## A Study in the Unity of
### *A Treatise of Human Nature*

WALTER BRAND

Kluwer Academic Publishers

Dordrecht / Boston / London

Library of Congress Cataloging-in-Publication Data

Brand, Walter.
    Hume's theory of moral judgment : a study in the unity of A
  treatise of human nature / Walter Brand.
        p.   cm. -- (International archives of the history of ideas =
  Archives internationales d'histoire des idées ; 131)
    Includes bibliographical references and index.
    ISBN 0-7923-1415-8 (alk. paper)
    1. Hume, David, 1711-1776. Treatise of human nature.   I. Title.
  II. Series: Archives internationales d'histoire des idées ; 131.
  B1489.B73   1992
  128--dc20                                                  91-31385

ISBN 0-7923-1415-8

*For my parents*

# Contents

# Preface

This study offers an overall interpretation of Hume's *Treatise of Human Nature*. I have emphasized throughout the dialectic between associationism and a theory of critical judgment – the "combat" of Book I – which continues in Books II and III and with no apparent winner. A theory of critical judgment is first worked out in Book I under what Hume calls "general rules." The theory explains how unreasonable judgments may be made reasonable and is made use of again in Book III to correct partial evaluations. Two sorts of general rules compete for prescriptive claims and two sides of human nature, the untutored and the more cultivated and reflective, contribute to science and morality.

I was first introduced to the philosophy of David Hume by Annette Baier when she conducted a seminar on the *Treatise* at the Graduate Center of The City University of New York. Much of the enthusiasm I have sustained for Hume has been due to the teachings of Professor Baier and to the conversations I have had with her. I have profited from the encouragement and suggestions of Nicholas Capaldi just prior to beginning the work. Charles Landesman, Martin Tamny, and Stephan Baumrin read earlier versions of the manuscript and offered many constructive criticisms. Joram Haber was readily available to hear out my ideas. I am grateful to my wife, Marianne, and children, Anna and Aaron, for their patience and support throughout the project.

# Acknowledgement

Quotes of Hume, David: A Treatise of Human Nature. Edited with an Analytical Index by L.A. Selby-Bigge, M.A. Oxford, Oxford at The Clarendon Press. First Edition 1888; reprint edition Oxford: Oxford at The Clarendon Press, 1964 are reprinted with kind permission of the Oxford University Press.

# Introduction

My aim in this book is to provide a consistent interpretation of David Hume's moral philosophy without being overly comprehensive or unduly restrictive. Readers of Hume by and large agree that extracting consistency from the *Treatise*[1] is problematic. While praising Berkeley's real concern for consistency, John Passmore describes Hume as a "philosophical puppy-dog, picking up and worrying one problem after another, always leaving his teethmarks in it, but casting it aside when it threatened to become wearisome."[2] Selby-Bigge has similar remarks in his introduction to the *Enquiries*.

> His pages, especially those of the *Treatise*, are so full of matter, he says so many different things in so many different ways and different con-nexions, and with so much indifference to what he has said before, that it is very hard to say positively that he taught, or did not teach, this or that particular doctrine ... This makes it easy to find all philosophies in Hume, or, by setting one statement against another, none at all.[3]

Admittedly, the *Treatise* is amply supplied with evidence which would seem to support these claims. The first difficulty occurs in the opening sentences of Book I. Perceptions are exhaustively divided into "two distinct kinds" which, Hume continues, differ in "degrees of force and liveliness." The two-fold manner in which Hume formulates the difference has been seen by Norman Kemp Smith as incompatible.[4] If we try to save Hume from the charge by turning to the text, we run into a further difficulty. For Hume thinks that no sharp discernment is required to grasp the difference, and he quickly dismisses the matter as being too obvious to warrant a discussion (EU18,T1).

Kemp Smith also finds it easy to draw our attention to another apparent inconsistency. In Book II, the impression of self plays an indispensable role in the generation of sympathy, whereas Hume, in Book I, is unable to find such an impression, "and so by implication the admission is made that the explanation of sympathy attempted in the *Treatise* cannot be maintained."[5] It is at least clear, however, that Hume attributes a great deal of importance to the principle of sympathy for his account of the passions and the moral sentiment. If Kemp Smith's allegation can be upheld, much of Hume's work in Books II and III can be dismissed as resting on an untenable principle.

The interpreter is faced with yet another apparent inconsistency if "reason" is given a univocal reading throughout. In Book I, Hume is at pains to establish that our most fundamental beliefs are not acquired by reason. In Book II, Hume wants to show that reason alone cannot cause action and part of what Hume means by "reason" is belief in matters of fact. So even if it turned out that belief alone could cause action, it wouldn't follow that reason causes action.[6]

Again we find Hume explicitly denying a substrate theory of material objects, and yet he speaks so freely about qualities inhering in subjects when discussing pride (T279). And Antony Flew thinks he has found an inconsistency in Hume's claim that motives are the ultimate objects of valuation together with his other claim that tendencies of actions have the greatest influence on our moral sense.[7]

Enough has been said in support of Selby-Bigge and Passmore. No doubt, hunters of inconsistency will find their calling in Hume. But for all that can be said about the muddle and confusion which so plague readers of the *Treatise*, one cannot fail to notice an overall unity which runs through all three Books. Hume was concerned to write a work that had "coherence in the parts and evidence in the whole" (TXIII). The author of the *Abstract*, presumably Hume, credits the *Treatise* with having an "air of singularity" (T643). Section I of the first Enquiry declares that all the principles of the mind are mutually dependent and can be reduced to more general principles by a skillful naturalist (EU15). "We find in the course of nature, that tho' the effects be many, the principles, from which they arise, are commonly but few and simple" (T578). While the understanding and the passions form a "complete chain of reasoning," Book II, "Of the Passions," has "laid the foundation" for Book III, "Of Morals" (T646). The principle of the association of ideas, which fills the pages of Book I, reappears throughout Book II in accounting for the indirect passions. The moral philosophy of Book III depends upon the psychology of sympathy, which occupies so much space in Book II and is "exactly correspondent to the operations of the understanding" of Book I (T320). Addressing himself to those who have converted "reading into an amusement," Hume allows that Book III is to some extent independent of Books I and II, but the more serious reader will find that "our reasoning concerning morals will corroborate whatever has been said concerning the understanding and the passions" (T455). The much neglected but vitally important doctrine of "general rules" is applied throughout to belief, passion and moral judgment.

While Passmore recognizes in Hume surface and perhaps real inconsistency, he recognizes as well the unity in his work, "dominated by a single over-riding intention."[8] As set forth in the Introduction to the *Treatise*, Hume's primary aim was to establish "the science of man" according to the method of observation and experiment. It was Hume's conviction that a proper understanding of human nature is required before any advancements are to be made in the sciences, "since they lie under the cognizance of men, and are judged of by their powers and faculties." Once having gained an understanding of human understanding "we may everywhere else hope for an easy victory." The *Treatise*, it may fairly be said, is a study of human knowledge, "of the ideas we employ, and of the operations we perform in our reasonings" (TXiX).[9]

It should be clear by now that the interpreter of Hume is faced with the two-fold problem of deciding upon the proper scope of his or her subject matter and the method by which the subject matter is to be treated. First, a few words on method. If we are to learn anything from Hume, we must give him a fair reading, even in the face of contradictory claims. If, for example, he appeals to an impression of self but claims also that he is unable to find such an impression, we must look for alternative explanations which he might have consistently adopted. Now this seems to be the proper method of treating a great philosopher. We assume that contradictory claims are only apparent contradictions and that further qualifications and refinements are forthcoming. Without adopting this attitude, we might as well leave the *Treatise* unread, except perhaps as a matter of historical interest.

Throughout I confine my attention to Hume's views about moral judgment as he presented them in *A Treatise of Human Nature*. Though I make occasional references to Hume's later works, *An Enquiry Concerning Human Understanding and An Enquiry Concerning the Principles of Morals*, the present work aims to clarify Hume's theory of moral evaluation as set forth in the *Treatise*. The question of whether Hume's ideas about moral evaluation are to be judged by the *Treatise* or the second *Enquiry* raises an interesting and controversial question.[10] But I have chosen to stay clear of the controversy, and nowhere do I claim that Hume's final word on the subject of morality is represented in his *Treatise*. It is at once obvious, however, that Hume, in the *Treatise*, presents his views both about philosophy in general and moral philosophy in a far more rigorous and closely argued manner than what he offers in the Enquiries. Hume's views in the latter works are clearly and elegantly presented, but the subtle analysis, probing inquiries and acute examinations which characterize the *Treatise* are no longer evident. With all its difficulties and apparent inconsistencies, it is the *Treatise* which remains a philosophical work of the first rank and which has earned Hume his reputation as one of the great thinkers.[11]

I now turn my attention to the subject matter of the present work. The fundamentals of Hume's moral theory may be summed up by the following claims:

1. Reason alone cannot motivate the will to action (T413).
2. Reason alone cannot prevent a passion or emotion from motivating the will (T415).
3. The distinction between good and evil does not arise from reason alone (T457).
4. Sympathy, or fellow feeling, is the primary source of the distinction between good and evil (T618).

Since, according to Hume, these claims are closely interrelated (T457), a consideration of any one, without giving due consideration to the others, must sever the organic connections within Hume's complete theory of morality. In what follows, however, I have chosen to concentrate on the evaluative side of Hume's moral system, and I have less to say about his theory of motivation, moral motivation and the connections between judgment, motivation and action. Commentators have criticized Hume for failing to link his account of the sympathetic judgment with motivation. Approval and disapproval, it is said, do not involve a disposition to act in one way rather than another.[12] Since the method of correcting immediate and often biased judgments is a "fundamentally thoughtful procedure,"[13] the resultant judgment is incapable of motivating action. Although I do not focus attention on the place of motivation in moral judgment, I hope to show that my interpretation of Hume on the subject of evaluation does not imply that Hume's impartial spectator is incapable of action. That Hume admits reason or reasoning into his account of judgment does not violate his claim that "reason alone" cannot motivate the will to action.

We notice that the above statements are in keeping with Hume's general program in the *Treatise*. Statements 1, 2 and 3 reflect Hume's scepticism with regard to the claims of reason in morality, while statement 4 is an attempt to construct a moral theory compatible with the results of this scepticism. Here, as elsewhere, Hume's most unmitigated scepticism gives way to a positive theory. Hume argues that 2 is an inference from 1, and 3 is an inference from 1 and 2 (T414,457). The sympathetic judgment, therefore, the primary source of moral distinctions, cannot arise *solely* from reason. Judgments of approval and disapproval do not rest exclusively on an inference of reason, either causal or demonstrative. I argue throughout that Hume leaves room in his theory for the workings of reason in the evaluation of character, and I try to show the close tie that holds between reason and sympathy in moral judgment. Accordingly, Part One of the present work will be devoted to an exposition of Hume's ideas about human reason, and Part Two will be an attempt to integrate Hume's teachings about reason with the theory of sympathy and the moral judgment.

In Book III, Hume appeals to the theory of sympathy in order to explain how the "artificial" virtue of justice develops and why justice becomes a virtue. Sympathy is again called upon to explain our approvals and disapprovals of the "natural" virtues. All the virtues come to be approved of through the medium of sympathy or "the communication of passions, from one thinking being to another." But we soon find that sympathy is not enough to establish a coherent, "stable" and "general" system of morality in which persons may agree on their evaluations (T591).

Sympathetically acquired pains and pleasures vary in emotional intensity according to a number of factors Hume regards as irrelevant from a "general point of view" (T582). We sympathize more with persons near to us in space and time than we do with those remotely placed, more with family and friends than with strangers, and more with persons whose qualities of character have a tendency to our benefit. But notwithstanding variations in the sympathetic judgment, the same qualities are praised or blamed independently of their tendency to self interest and regardless of their spatio-temporal location. "The sympathy varies without a variation in our esteem" (T581). How can a principle which explains the source of bias and faction in our evaluations serve also as the foundation of morality? How can the fluctuations of sympathy be reconciled with the stability of esteem? And how does sympathy re-enter into the account of the correction of the immediate sympathetic judgment? Hume's answer to these problems lies at the heart of his moral theory.

The present state of scholarship has either downplayed, ignored or criticized Hume's account of how the immediate sympathetic judgment develops into the impartial evaluation of character. This is due in part to the fact that Hume, in Book III, does not enter into a sustained discussion of what the correction of moral sentiments involves. It is my aim to offer such a discussion on Hume's behalf. I will argue that Hume's position on moral judgment in Book III is a direct outcome of his theory of belief and general rules in Book I. The theory of general rules is an essential component of Hume's overall theory of belief. It explains Hume's well known distinction between natural and reflective belief and will similarly explain the difference between the immediate sympathetic response and the reflective moral judgment. The theory of general rules explains Hume's wavering attitude between descriptivism and prescriptivism, and serves also to show Hume's vacillating position between scepticism and naturalism. In what follows I hope to show that the theory of general rules provides the best interpretation of Hume's theory of moral judgment. My overall aim is to provide a defensive account of Hume's fundamental position that reason and sympathy are necessary to establish a universal and impartial system of moral sentiments.

# PART ONE

# Hume's Analysis of Reason

The purpose of this section is to examine Hume's conception of human reason. From the outset, we need an adequate account of what Hume thinks reason is, what he thinks it does and what he thinks reason ought to do before we can appreciate his later claims about the pretensions of reason in the moral sphere.

Among these claims, there is one which occurs toward the end of Book III and which clearly exhibits Hume's view of the relation of reason and passion in moral judgment. Hume wants to show that changes in the intensity of the sympathetic judgment may be corrected by adopting a "steady and general point of view" (T582). What stands in need of correction is the immediate sympathetic judgment, all too often biased. The result of the corrective method yields impartial moral judgments as seen from the viewpoint of an impartial spectator (T581). The method of correction, therefore, arbitrates between partial and impartial viewpoints. Unfortunately, the reader is left with only a few remarks on what is involved when the corrective method lands us in the general point of view.

Commentators recognizing this gap in explanation have drawn consequences which would undermine Hume's moral theory. It is often claimed that Hume simply did not succeed in developing an explanation of the correction of moral sentiments.[1] If the claim is correct, Hume would not have been able to advance beyond his account of "uncultivated" moral nature (T488). We recall that Hume could not find the first virtuous motive to acts of justice and concluded that one's primitive ideas about morality, "instead of providing a remedy for the partiality of our affections, do rather conform themselves to that partiality" (T489). What must therefore become of the artifices; justice, property and promise-keeping, to name a few? The whole of Book II can be seen as a causal account of the natural bias inherent in the passions. Book III aims to remedy or, at least, redirect the more "rude" propensities (T479). The view that Hume failed to provide an account of the correction of unreflective moral sentiments needs to be revised if Book III is to continue the development of morality from the partial to the impartial evaluation of character.

In looking at Hume's ideas about human reason, I pay close attention to what he says in Book I and do not emphasize his discussion of reason in Books II and III in that I offer no close analysis of the sections "Of the influencing motives of the will" and "Moral Distinctions not deriv'd from Reason." Do we need another discussion of the passage "Reason is, and ought only to be the slave of the passions," or do we need yet another interpretation of what "seems altogether inconceivable," of how an "ought" statement can be deduced from an "is" statement (T415,469)? In a sense we do, for there is no widespread agreement among commentators on what exactly Hume had in mind in these passages. In another sense, we might do better to clarify the disagreements, or perhaps to resolve them, by looking to other sections of the *Treatise* where reason is discussed. I found that Hume's teachings in Book I offer further insight into his ideas about the role of reason in morality in Books II and III. Commentators have offered close analyses of the two sections I have mentioned.[2] There is good reason for this. The sections are closely tied in Hume's thought and comprise an important part of the moral epistemology. The former section examines the roles of reason and passion in motivation, the latter section examines the roles of reason and passion in the discernment of moral value. Together they raise the question of what roles reason and passion play in motivating an action according to the evaluation of it. It is not until Part III of Book III that Hume finally confronts the question.

In the first several sections of Part III, Book III, we find scattered comments about a "general" viewpoint, an "inalterable" standard, "stable" judgments and the correction of immediate appearances by an act of reflection (T581,602). As I see it, these bits of text point to a rich aspect of Hume's moral epistemology which receives its full treatment in Book I. The sections I have in mind introduce the theory of general rules which has received little attention from commentators on Book I and less attention from those writing on the moral theory. If we are to piece together Hume's sketchy comments about an impartial spectator, we must first look to Book I in order to appreciate the theory of general rules and learn the difference between the judicial judgment and the judgment of prejudice (T146).

# CHAPTER ONE

# Reason and Imagination

## DISTINCTIONS OF REASON

Toward the end of his discussion on abstract ideas, Hume introduces, almost as an afterthought, the "distinction of reason." Few commentators have appreciated the importance of the distinction despite its repeated application throughout the *Treatise*. Hume, however, would like to include it among the "elements" of his philosophy (T13).

Stanley Tweyman has taken Hume's suggestion seriously by applying the distinction to the moral theory. According to Tweyman, the distinction of reason is the only sense of reason[1] discussed by Hume for correcting the immediate sympathetic response to every and any change in the vivacity of ideas. While I think that Tweyman's position is useful and suggestive, the distinction is certainly not the only sense of reason employed by Hume for correcting biased points of view. I argue throughout that our "adherence" (T374) to general rules with regard to moral and factual reasoning provides the key to an understanding of Hume's account of the generation and correction of erroneous judgment. As I see it, the distinction of reason provides insight into Hume's views on the different "aspects" (T25) of judgment – content and vivacity – but wanes in comparison with the influence general rules have on establishing the "authentic" (T150) judgment of fact and the "standard of merit and demerit" (T583). But since the importance of the distinction is usually overlooked, it is worthwhile to consider Hume's comments on the distinction, on the "abstraction without a separation" (T43). Let us now turn to the text.

Perceptions are divided into simple and complex impressions and ideas. A perception is simple if it can no longer be distinguished or separated into parts (T2). All complex perceptions may be distinguished into the parts which compose them. "Whatever objects are different are distinguishable, and whatever objects are distinguishable are separable by the thought and imagination (T18). Since no two perceptions are "perfectly inseparable" (T10), the imagination may separate the parts of complex perceptions. But since simple perceptions lack parts, the imagination can go no further in separating and distinguishing. The imagination always reaches a limit in the separation of its ideas (T27).

Although simple perceptions do not admit of distinctions in terms of parts, they are susceptible to distinctions of reason. To illustrate, Hume asks us to consider a white globe. The color is neither different nor separable from the form (T18). But if we observe a black globe and a white cube and compare them with the white globe, "we find two separate resemblances, in what formerly seemed, and really is, perfectly inseparable" (T25). By comparing the black sphere with the white sphere and the white cube with the white sphere, we attend to different "aspects" of a simple perception whose "parts" are indistinguishable (T2).

One is immediately confronted with the question of how resemblance can be made compatible with simplicity. According to Meinong, Hume's thesis that inseparables can come to be separated remains an insuperable difficulty. If figure and color are the same, "then it remains a riddle how color comes to be distinguished at all, be it through the most complicated mental operation."[2] Passmore, too, finds the whole business puzzling. It is nonsense to claim that "an idea can have various distinguishable characteristics without any sacrifice of its simplicity."[3]

If the charge that simplicity is not compatible with resemblance can be upheld, most of the *Treatise* rests on a simple logical error. Throughout, Hume freely appeals to relations which allow for the "connection" and "comparison" among simple ideas (T13). Though cause and effect is a "natural" connecting relation, it is included among the "philosophical" relations since resemblance is "implied in" this relation (T15). The inference from an impression to an idea cannot be made unless remembered conjunctions are recognized as resembling. Without resemblance, no philosophical relation can exist "since no objects will admit of comparison, but what have some degree of resemblance" (T14). Also, in Book II, Hume claims that the passions are simple impressions associated only by resemblance (T217, 283).

Meinong's objection reduces to the question, how are distinctions of reason possible? Passmore suggests that distinctions of reason are possible only among complex ideas. Both would hold that to distinguish any quality from a simple idea implies loss of its simplicity. The objection is sound provided it rests on the following assumption. $X$ resembles $Y$ in point of $C$ where $C$ is a characteristic $X$ and $Y$ have in common. $X$ and $Y$ consist of $C$ together with the remaining qualities $Q$ which differentiate them. $C$ and $Q$

are different, distinguishable and separable. So *X* and *Y* are not simples. However, the objection assumes a position Hume rejects in the *Appendix* to the section on abstract ideas. Hume argues that different simple ideas may resemble each other without it being necessary that "the point or circumstance of resemblance should be distinct or separable from that in which they differ."

> Blue and green are different simple ideas, but are more resembling than blue and scarlet; tho' their perfect simplicity excludes all possibility of separation or distinction (T637).

Qualities admit of resemblance, Hume holds, "without having any common circumstance the same."

In accord with Meinong and Passmore, Hume thinks that if the resemblance between two simple perceptions is explicable in terms of a common characteristic, then it must have been distinguished from the characteristic which differentiates them. Hume's key claim is that simplicity is logically incompatible with separation. It "excludes all possibility of separation." Simple perceptions lack parts. They "admit of no distinction or separation." Their "very nature" excludes the possibility of composition (T637). Only complex perceptions can be distinguished into parts. "What consists of parts is distinguishable into them, and what is distinguishable is separable" (T27). How, then, is it possible, Hume rhetorically asks, for the imagination to separate the parts of a simple perception if the perception is not distinguishable into parts? Hume's meaning is that it is impossible to conceive a "clear and distinct idea" (T43) of a simple perception that consists of separable parts.

> A person, who desires us to consider the figure of a globe of white marble without thinking on its colour, desires an impossibility (T25).

If it were possible to form the idea of a separable simple, the parts separated would be common qualities or quantities which resembled some simples and differed from others (T637). But Hume's point is that a quality or quantity cannot be abstracted from the precise degree of a quality or quantity. We cannot abstract from the precise degree of a particular shade of red a color quality – redness – that resembles other varying shades of red.[4]

Hume argues against Locke's view that ideas can be made general "by separating from them the circumstances of time and place and any other ideas that may determine them to this or that particular existence" (Tl7).[5] If we try to abstract qualities from determinate qualities, we run into the following dilemma.

The abstract idea of man represents men of all sizes and all qualities; which 'tis concluded it cannot do, but either by representing at once all possible sizes and all possible qualities, or by representing no particular one at all. Now it having been esteemed absurd to defend the former proposition, as implying an infinite capacity in the mind, it has been commonly infer'd in favour of the latter; and our abstract ideas have been suppos'd to represent no particular degree either of quantity or quality (T18).

Hume's attack runs roughly as follows:

1. All ideas of quantity and quality are precisely determinate in respect of degree.
2. The precise degree of any quantity or quality does not differ from the quantity or quality itself.
3. The point of resemblance between two simple perceptions is neither distinct nor separable from the point of difference.
4. Two simple perceptions resemble one another without having any quantity or quality in common.

As Hume presents the dilemma, either an abstract idea of $X$ represents $x$'s of all quantities and qualities or $X$ represents no particular quantity or quality at all. The critics are unwittingly caught by the second horn of the dilemma. "Our abstract ideas have been supposed to represent no particular degree either of quantity or quality" (T18). Hume generously acknowledges the error as one "commonly inferred." The assumption I have attributed to Passmore and Meinong states that, for example, a white sphere and white cube have a quality in common distinct from the precise shades belonging to each. But Hume insists that the sphere and cube do not have a color quality distinct from their degrees which resembles other white objects of varying degrees. It is impossible to imagine a quality without imagining it as determinate in respect of degree (T18). Difference stands on the same footing as resemblance. The resemblance which holds between a cube and a sphere is greater than the resemblance holding between a cube and an egg. The cube and egg differ to a greater degree than the cube and sphere. But the difference between them cannot be analyzed in terms of a figure quality distinct from their precise shapes (T637). Accordingly, then, by an established principle of metaphysics, "that whatever the mind clearly conceives includes the idea of possible existence," (T32) it is impossible for a quantity or quality to exist in separation from a precisely determinate quantity or quality. Perceptions represented by a general term are not alike in respect of any precise quality or quantity which are common to them all.

We note resemblance, then, between simple perceptions by a distinction of reason, "an abstraction without a separation" (T43). The resemblance which holds between two perceptions is "discoverable at first sight" and recognized by intuition. "The resemblance will first strike the eye, or rather the mind" (T70). But upon a closer reading, the recognition of resemblance is not quite so immediate as Hume would have us believe.

Let us return to Hume's example of the colored figures. By comparing the black sphere with the white sphere and the white cube with the white sphere, we discover two points of resemblance, figure and color, while also admitting their inseparability. Although figure and color are considered together, they may be viewed in different "aspects" when given a "partial consideration" (T25). When it is "commonly infer'd" that abstract ideas do not represent any particular degree of quantity or quality, the inference Hume has in mind is clearly not a "reasonable" inference (T143).[6] What happens is that we mistakenly believe we are considering only the figure of the white sphere, but actually our idea is of figure and color. The imagination confuses the way complex ideas are decomposed into parts with the way it views different aspects of simple ideas. So we come to believe that the viewing of aspects *is* the consideration of parts. Hume would claim that these two operations of imagination are falsely believed to be the same because they are accompanied by similar sensations (T417).

> Wherever the actions of the mind in forming any two ideas are the same or resembling, we are very apt to confound these ideas, and take the one for the other (T61).

Given the belief that we are considering the "parts" of a complex idea when what we are actually doing is "tacitly" attending to different "aspects" of simple ideas, the belief follows that an aspect of a simple idea is separable from the idea itself. A quality of no precise degree is abstracted from a precise degree of a quality and is thought to be separable from the precise degree, because we believe we are separating the parts of a complex idea. Resemblance, then, boils down to noticing hidden transitions of imagination when the attention shifts from one aspect of a simple perception to another.

Once settled in the reader's mind, the distinction of reason remains useful throughout as an explanatory device. In his brief discussion, Hume has touched upon the way different mental states or operations come to be identified. But the full impact of his remarks will later be felt when he accounts for the belief in an external world. The imagination performs different operations when breaking down complex ideas and when attending to aspects of simple ideas. Nevertheless, it is believed that figure can be considered independently of color. The act of imagination in considering the parts of complex ideas resembles that act of imagination when attending to aspects of simple ideas (T205). But since it is also believed that separation in terms of parts is incompatible with simplicity, we attempt to conceal the contradiction by positing the existence of common qualities and quantities. For much the same reason, we fill the gaps in a series of interrupted, resembling perceptions with unperceived existences.

As there is only a distinction of reason between figure and figure colored, so there is only a distinction of reason between impressions and ideas. Hume repeatedly states that impressions and ideas differ only in terms of force and vivacity. Ideas are "exact representations" of impressions, "nor is there any circumstance of the one, which is not to be found in the other." Perceptions differ "only in degree, not in nature" (T3). Later in the *Treatise*, Hume would put the matter beyond dispute. Different degrees of force and vivacity are "the only particulars that distinguish them" (T319). The doctrine extends to other basic distinctions. Thus, vivacity distinguishes ideas of memory from ideas of imagination, conception from belief, understanding from imagination and, generally, thinking from feeling.

Commentators have been disturbed by Hume's claim that degrees of vivacity constitute two kinds of perception, as if kind and degree were incompatible.[7] Since the distinction is reduced to degree alone, Hume admits borderline cases, "in sleep, in a fever, in madness" (T2, EU17). Forceful ideas approach impressions, dull impressions approach ideas. The trouble lurks in the fact that occasionally they cannot be distinguished. Ideas can be taken for impressions and impressions taken for ideas. But if vivacity were the sole basis for the distinction, errors would not arise. All lively or dull perceptions would simply be impressions or ideas as such. No further appeal could be made in order to account for mistakes in identification.[8]

The critic has raised an objection which involves two distinct issues. The first issue raises doubts as to the compatibility of degree and kind. The second issue is a request for a paradigm which could clearly delineate the boundaries of mental states. By such an appeal, the misidentification of closely resembling mental states could be overcome. But the second issue cannot be resolved by insisting that varying degrees of vivacity, even at the extremes of the continuum, are incompatible with two kinds of perception. For even if they were compatible, which Hume thinks they are, the recognition of Humean kinds could not provide that paradigmatic touchstone the critic is asking for. Every perception has its two distinct aspects, in Hume's words, "feeling and thinking" (T2). After explaining the difference in terms of "degrees of force and liveliness," Hume establishes his first principle in the science of human nature.

> All our simple ideas in their first appearance are deriv'd from simple impressions, which are correspondent to them, and which they exactly represent (T4).

Simple ideas are exact representations of their antecedent impressions. "The component parts of ideas and impressions are precisely alike" (T319). All the aspects which comprise a simple impression are exactly copied in its subsequent idea. The exact representation Hume speaks of cannot be construed in terms of vivacity. Although it is true that degrees of vivacity are resembling, the resemblance cannot be understood as an exact representation. What Hume has in mind is the nature of a simple perception, its component aspects, its content. The content of a simple idea, consisting of all its inseparable aspects, is derived from the precisely resembling content of its preceding impression. The impression, however, does not discharge all of its vivacity to its corresponding idea. The reduction of vivacity suffered through the derivation, therefore, constitutes the sole difference between impressions and ideas.

Hume refers to a "perfect idea" as one stripped of all vivacity (T8). But, in fact, all impressions and ideas are perceptions of sensation (T373,416). Vivacity and content are inseparable aspects of all simple perceptions. Only with "precision" can they come to be distinguished (T373). Thus, by comparing ideas having resembling contents but differing in vivacity with ideas differing in content but having resembling degrees of vivacity, a distinction of reason is performed between two inseparable aspects of perception, thought and feeling.[9] We are able, then, to distinguish vivacity from content, feeling from thinking, impressions from ideas, and assign to each a general term to mark the difference (T22). There is no incompatibility between differentiating kinds of perception by degree.

But the second issue raised by Kemp Smith and others cannot be settled by this reconciliation. The common failure to distinguish closely resembling mental states cannot be discerned, let alone corrected, by appealing to various kinds, be it vivacity or content, impression or idea. The critic who has lost hope of reconciling kind with degree would have it that were such a reconciliation possible, it would provide a basis for distinguishing adjacent perceptions on the vivacity continuum. But here the critic goes wrong by enriching Hume's ontology with such beings as languid and lively common properties. Keeping to the figure of a continuum, the most lively impressions are at one end, the dullest ideas at the other, with misidentification most likely to occur at the midrange. To avoid such error, one could appeal to the languid as such and the lively as such, and so come to recognize that the perception in question was only as if it were of one kind but was in fact of the other. But the varying degrees of vivacity to which impressions and ideas are subject, we recall, are not to be explained in terms of common characteristics.

The difficulty in distinguishing resembling perceptions is introduced with the theory of ideas but frequently recurs down through the closing sections of the *Treatise*. Kemp Smith has hit upon an important issue which cuts across the entire *Treatise* but has an especially direct bearing on the ethics. Hume will argue that variations in the intensity of sympathetically acquired pains and pleasures are not coordinate with genuine moral judgments. We falsely identify vivacity with value and thus, for example, find it difficult to condemn those we love or praise those we hate. How do we overcome the tendency to attribute merit or demerit solely on the basis of sympathetic vivacity?

As mentioned earlier, Tweyman claims that the kind of reason Hume employs for correcting immediate sympathetic judgments is the distinction of reason. While I agree with Tweyman that Hume, in Book III, does not clearly explain what is involved in adopting an impartial standpoint,[10] it is clear that Hume, in Book I, presents a rich and complex procedure for the correction of immediate factual judgments, and that the same procedure is then extended to Book III for the correction of immediate moral judgments. As an example of the sort of obscurity we find in Book III regarding the correction of unreflective moral judgments, Hume writes:

> Here we are contented with saying, that reason requires such an impartial conduct, but that 'tis seldom we can bring ourselves to it, and that our passions do not readily follow the determination of our judgment. This language will be easily understood, if we consider what we formerly said concerning that *reason*, which is able to oppose our passion; and which we have found to be nothing but a general calm determination of the passions, founded on some distant view or reflection (T583).

He goes on to make passing remarks about "general rules of morality," "stable" judgments and "steady and general points of view" but is much too brief in explaining what he has in mind. Without returning to Book I, as Hume suggests, in order to "consider what we formerly said," Hume's sparse comments on the establishment of an impartial moral judgment remains unintelligible.

It seems that Tweyman has overlooked Hume's suggestion and so has lost sight of his elaborate work on general rules. As a result, he sees the distinction of reason as the only ordering faculty[11] which corrects the immediacy of sympathetic loves and hatreds. But a close reading of the sections "Of unphilosophical probability" and "Of scepticism with regard to reason" in Book I reveals the complete theory of general rules, the correction of one sort of rule by another – achieved by a "reflex act of the mind" – and a subsequent "opposition" between general rules (T148,182). I shall have a great deal more to say about general rules in the chapters to come. For the present, I claim that Hume's theory of general rules in Book I, which functions to correct the immediate feeling of belief (T630), is extended to the moral theory in Book III, where general rules function to correct the immediate feeling of love or hatred (T329). At this point, it is worthwhile to continue with Hume's overall analysis of reason. I hope to show that the various psychological propensities Hume speaks of throughout underlie his theory of general rules very early in the *Treatise*.

### THE DIVISION OF REASON

In the next few sections it will become clear that Hume's Great Divide[1] of reason into knowledge of relations and factual beliefs reduces to certain psychological tendencies, "trivial suggestions of the fancy" (T267). What Hume calls "the operations of human understanding" (T463) will be found to rest on nothing more than a mechanical response to sense stimuli (EU55). The same propensity which accounts for our idea of mathematical equality and our belief in an external world will also be responsible for all causal inference. Hume's talk of reasonableness will be understood as arising from the "frivolous properties of our thought" (T504). Once reason has been stripped of all its "supposed pre-eminence," its "eternity, invariableness, and divine origin," and reduced to "trivial suggestions" of imagination, Hume's later arguments in Book II against giving preference to reason over passion are a foregone conclusion. There is little sense in speaking of a "combat" of passion and reason once it is learned that "the principle which opposes our passion, cannot be the same with reason" (T415).

What initially characterizes Hume's Fork[2] is equivocation on the term "relation." Two ideas may be related by a connecting principle, "a gentle force," whereby the imagination associates one idea with another. The connecting principle, Hume makes clear, is not to be regarded as an inseparable connection. "Where-ever the imagination perceives a difference among ideas, it can easily produce a separation" (T10). As the imagination may separate different simple ideas, so it may arbitrarily unite them, independently of any connecting principle. Such unions provide the opportunity for comparing ideas, which is the second sense of "relation" Hume has in mind (T13).

The discussion proceeds by listing seven kinds of philosophical relations:

resemblance, identity, relations of time and place, proportion in quantity or number, degrees in any quality, contrariety and causation (T69). Further refinements emerge when the relations are divided into two classes: relations that cannot change provided that the ideas compared do not change, and relations that can change even when the relata do not change. Hume illustrates as follows. The equality holding between the angles of a triangle and two right angles cannot change provided that our idea of a triangle does not change. The relation between its angles and 180° would change if our idea of a triangle changed from a three-sided to a four-sided figure.

But the distance between two objects may change without involving any change in the objects or their ideas. Along with relations of time and place, Hume includes identity as a changeable relation even when the relata do not change. Two objects that are specifically identical (T258) may be numerically different (T69).[3] Finally, since the relation of causation is not discovered by comparing ideas, it too may change even when the relata do not change. "An object, seemingly like those which we have experienced, may be attended with different or contrary effects" (T69, EU35).

Four of the above relations constitute knowledge, those which involve the comparing of ideas for the discovery of abiding relations (T79). Three of these relations – resemblance, contrariety and degrees in quality – are immediately apprehended by intuition "without any enquiry or reasoning" (T70). Only those invariable relations holding between units of number or extension are the proper objects of demonstration. Thus, for Hume, knowledge in the strictest sense is attainable only within the area of the mathematical sciences, where we "carry on a chain of reasoning to any degree of intricacy, and yet preserve a perfect exactness and certainty" (T71). The remaining three relations – time and place, identity and causation – are changeable relations, independent of their relata, and therefore do not constitute knowledge.

Hume does not regard the recognition of identity and spatio-temporal relations as reasoning of any sort "since in none of them the mind can go beyond what is immediately present to the senses" (T73). They are more appropriately described as acts of perception. Only in the case of causation do we reason about "existences and objects that we do not see or feel" (T74). Although causation involves thought and reasoning, the reasoning involved is sharply distinguished from demonstrative reasoning, the former yielding belief, the latter knowledge.

The contrast between changeable and abiding relations corresponds to the two operations of understanding, the comparing of ideas and the inferring of facts (T463). The function of understanding is to judge. Only the judgments of understanding have a reference to truth (T415). We have, therefore, two kinds of truth corresponding to the two operations of understanding.[4]

> Reason is the discovery of truth or falsehood. Truth or falsehood consists in an agreement or disagreement either to the real relations of ideas, or to real existence and matter of fact (T458).

True judgments are made when invariable relations are found to hold between fixed ideas or when they affirm that some fact has existed, exists or will exist.

In the first *Enquiry*, geometry, algebra and arithmetic are the demonstrative sciences which admit of perfect certainty (EU25). From Hume's examples, we understand that he takes equality to be the fundamental concept of mathematics. Propositions which affirm that equality holds between numbers or figures "are discoverable by the mere operation of thought."

> Though there never was a circle or triangle in nature, the truths demonstrated by Euclid would for ever retain their certainty and evidence (EU25).

Truths of fact, the second object of reason, amount to no more than belief. The denial of any fact, however incredible, is not inconceivable "because it can never imply a contradiction" (EU25). And since the denial or affirmation of a fact is conceived with the same clarity of thought, that fact may or may not exist (T43). But it is impossible to deny the truth of a demonstration since the denial is inconceivable and hence contradictory (T95). We are determined to recognize demonstrative truths by an "absolute necessity." The propositions of demonstration are, therefore, necessary or impossible. There is no middle ground. Either one knows that $P$ is $Q$, in which case $P$ is $Q$ necessarily, or one knows that $P$ is not $Q$, in which case $P$ is $Q$ is impossible. "'Tis either irresistible, or has no manner of force" (T31). But necessity and impossibility are modalities not applicable to matters of fact. For to believe that $P$ is not $Q$ is no less conceivable than to believe that $P$ is $Q$. The denial of either belief, therefore, does not imply a contradiction. No proposition asserting fact is demonstrable. "Whatever is may not be" (EU164).

Hume's division of reason distinguishes a priori from a posteriori knowledge. Truths of intuition and demonstration are known a priori "by the mere operation of thought." Truths of fact, as resting on causal reasoning, "arise entirely from experience" (EU27). The distinction is marked by the way truths come to be verified.[5] Resemblance, contrariety and degrees in quality are "discoverable at first sight." The certainty achieved by one act of intuition seldom requires a second examination (T70). Similarly, the conclusion of a mathematical demonstration does not require repeated acts of reasoning before assent is granted.

> The conclusions which it draws from considering one circle are the same which it would form upon surveying all the circles in the universe (EU43).

But it would be unreasonable to conclude "merely because one event, in one instance, precedes another, that therefore the one is the cause, the other the effect" (EU42). Here, repeated acts of observing conjunctions are required in order to infer one from the other.

Hume makes the point that space and time relations along with identity are apprehended by perception, "by a mere passive admission of the impressions thro' the organs of sensation" (T73). No reasoning whatsoever is involved. Knowledge of these relations, then, cannot properly be described as arising from demonstrative reasoning a priori or causal reasoning a posteriori. Although these relations are changeable while their ideas remain unchanged, the perception involved is epistemologically infallible.

> The only existences, of which we are certain, are perceptions, which being immediately present to us by consciousness, command our strongest assent, and are the first foundation of all our conclusions (T212).

Perception is an aspect of awareness which yields its own type of certainty.

Commentators are hasty to attribute a clear-cut analytic/synthetic distinction to relations of ideas and matters of fact.[6] To be convinced that the angles of a triangle equal 180° one appeals only to the meanings of the terms involved. "Hume's contention is that no a priori propositions are synthetic, all a priori propositions are analytic, all synthetic propositions empirical."[7] I think it can fairly be granted that Hume thought all mathematical propositions are known analytically. The denial of a mathematical proposition is unintelligible, "inconceivable" and therefore implies a contradiction (EU164), "nor is it possible for the imagination to conceive anything contrary to a demonstration." We are bound, as Hume puts it, "determin'd" (T95) to conceive of mathematical propositions with necessity. To conceive of their denial is impossible. Negations of fact, however, are conceivable and hence not contradictory. "'Tis in vain to search for a contradiction in anything that is distinctly conceived by the mind" (T43). All demonstrative truths, therefore, are analytic only insofar as they rest on the notions of contradiction and conceivability. But it is not immediately obvious that Hume took mathematical propositions to be entirely analytic, where judgments are made solely on the basis of comparing the meanings of terms, and which do not require an inspection of the facts. As we shall see, Hume thought that mathematical judgments are descriptive of matters of fact and existence.

Hume offers as an example of an analytic proposition, "every effect necessarily pre-supposes a cause," since the idea of cause is "implied in" the idea of effect, "effect being a relative term, of which cause is the correlative." The same can be said of "every husband must have a wife." Statements of this sort are uninformative, undescriptive. They do not empirically unfold facts. As the former cannot establish that "every being must be preceded by a cause," so the latter cannot show that "every man must be marry'd" (T82). Hume would like to contrast such verbal definitions with, for example, the Pythagorean theorem which cannot be known, however clearly the terms are defined, "without a train of reasoning and enquiry." But to be convinced of the proposition "where there is no property, there can be no injustice, it is only necessary to define the terms, and explain justice to be a violation of property" (EU163).[8]

Hume thinks that mathematical judgments which are known only on the basis of definition are useless for describing physical space (T42,637). The "train of reasoning and enquiry" Hume has in mind for the judgment of geometric equality involves repeated acts of comparing objects by increasingly accurate methods of measurement. The discovery of equality will turn out to be nothing more than an awareness of a psychological propensity which is the outcome of repeated acts of comparison (T43).

> Since equality is a relation, it is not strictly speaking, a property in the figures themselves, but arises merely from the comparison, which the mind makes betwixt them (T46).

We shall see that the propensity which "arises merely from the comparison" extrapolates beyond the range of measurement and observation. The imagination, writes Hume, "is apt to continue, even when its object fails it" (T198). A perfect standard of equality is imagined which goes beyond what instruments and observation are able to achieve (T48–49).

Throughout the *Treatise*, Hume describes this propensity as a basic drive in human nature to bring order and regularity into experience beyond the order and regularity which is actually observed (T148,197,504). The same propensity, what I shall later call "Imaginative Supplementation," is responsible for generating one type of general rule which requires correction by another type of general rule (T150). "We may correct this propensity," Hume writes, "by reflection and general rules," though very often we do not and sometimes Hume goes so far as to claim that it ought not be corrected (T270). There is, as we shall see, an ongoing "opposition" (T149) of general rules down through the closing passages of the *Treatise*. For the present, let us see how this propensity of imagination contributes to the perfect standard of equality. Commentators that ascribe the view to Hume that knowledge of relations is analytic, as resting solely on the comparison of meanings, have failed to appreciate a certain propensity of imagination, the discovery of which is vital for the generation of mathematical, factual and value judgments.

THE STANDARD OF EQUALITY

Hume is notorious for presenting ideas in an offhand manner. He is rarely emphatic about what he thinks is important, and when he does stress the importance of what is to come, he seldom follows his introduction with a complete discussion of the matter, once and for all. Hume's ideas become clarified by accumulation, by noticing how he applies an idea to different subjects in different contexts.

I am taking some time to discuss Hume's views on the relation of mathematical equality. In so doing, my concern is not so much with Hume's account of mathematics or any empiricist account of mathematics.[1] I wish only to introduce a psychological propensity which shows itself early in the *Treatise*. By the "Conclusion" of Book I, Hume will seriously consider rejecting this propensity as a "trivial property of the fancy... destructive of all the most establish'd principles of reasonings" (T268). What I shall soon call "Imaginative Supplementation" is a source of false belief and unreasonableness which Hume prescribes should be controlled if the "authentic" (T150) operations of understanding are to be preserved. With respect to both belief and moral evaluation he urges that initial judgments ought to be corrected (T182,582). We will need to control this tendency of imagination to extend a general rule formed from one set of regularities to instances which are resembling yet different in "efficacious circumstances" (T150). Supplemental activities will require correction if "unphilosophical" beliefs are to be restored to a "reasonable foundation of belief" (T143).[2]

In the present discussion, Hume thinks the way we form the idea of perfect equality is "incomprehensible." Though he will not here speak of correcting the *residual* activity of imagination, the subject of correcting initial judgments is first introduced (T49). Hume's introductory remarks on the process of correction will be seen to re-emerge in the theory of belief and the moral theory. Earlier I mentioned that the degrees of sympathetic pains and pleasures vary according to the spatio-temporal relations holding between observer and agent. Variations in the intensity of the immediate sympathetic judgment are regarded as irrelevant for the appraisal of character. Initial moral judgments stand in need of correction no less than initial judgments of equality (T47). Judgments of sense and judgments of value, passional and moral judgments, judgments of fact as well as mathematical judgments stand in need of correction if genuine judgments are to emerge. By a "reflex act of the mind" the appearance of infallibility becomes corrected (T582).

Although mathematical propositions are known by a priori verification, the concepts of mathematics are grounded empirically. Hume argues against the rationalist view that mathematical concepts are "mere ideas in the mind... some spiritual and refin'd perceptions" apprehended by pure intellect (T42,72). The recognition of mathematical concepts is not explained by means of a mental intuition which "springs from the light of reason alone."[3] Mathematical ideas are reducible to impressions of sensation together with the workings of imagination (EU60,158).

For the most part, proportions in quantity and number are not discovered immediately by intuition but by a chain of demonstrative reasoning. The only objects of demonstrative certainty Hume finally admits at the close of the first *Enquiry* are quantity and number. When Hume speaks of proportions in quantity and number he has in mind the relations "superiority or inferiority betwixt any numbers or figures... equal to, or greater, or less" (T45,70). In the *Treatise*, algebra and arithmetic are the only sciences which yield exactitude and certainty, geometry falling short for want of a precise standard of equality. In cases of "very short numbers or very limited parts of extension," equality is immediately comprehended by intuition. In all other cases, we must proceed in a more "artificial manner" (70). What this "artificial manner" involves is by no means clear. What Hume finally decides upon is the manner in which geometric equality is established.

To employ the artificial manner is to establish a standard of equality. Hume does, in fact, establish the precise standard by which we judge numerical equality. The standard is expressed by way of definition. "When two numbers are so combin'd, as that the one has always an unite answering to every unite of the other, we pronounce them equal" (T71). Later in the *Appendix* Hume expresses dissatisfaction with the notion that numerical equality can be established simply on the basis of definition. Agreeing with philosophers who place the idea of equality on the ground of experience, Hume writes:

'Tis sufficient to present two objects, that are equal, in order to give us a just notion of this proportion. All definitions, say they, are fruitless, without the perception of such objects; and where we perceive such objects, we no longer stand in need of any definition. To this reasoning I entirely agree; and assert, that the only useful notion of equality, or inequality, is deriv'd from the whole united appearance, and the comparison of particular objects (T637).

Hume also considers definitions of geometric equality in terms of a one-to-one correspondence of units of extension obvious though useless.

Lines or surfaces are equal, when the numbers of points in each are equal; and that as the proportion of the numbers varies, the proportion of the lines and surfaces is also vary'd (T45).

According to the definition, by comparing the number of points which compose two lines, we judge the lines to be equal if the number of points are equal. The terms of one equality relation are equal to the terms of another equality relation. The equality holding between the points equals the equality holding between the lines. Hume grants that this standard is "just, as well as obvious." The equality of the lines, he would say, is "imply'd in" the idea of the number of points (T82). But the standard itself is incapable of describing physical space.

For as the points, which enter into the composition of any line or surface, whether perceiv'd by the sight or touch, are so minute and so confounded with each other, that 'tis utterly impossible for the mind to compute their number, such a computation will never afford us a standard, by which we may judge of proportions (T45).

We are left, therefore, with only one notion of geometrical equality which, though never attaining a perfect exactness, rests on the "least deceitful appearances" (T72).

When Hume speaks of settling the standard of equality by an "artificial manner," he has in mind empirical methods of measurement. Geometry is an art, "the art by which we fix the proportions of figures" (T70). Hume indicates that the way the standard of equality comes to be established rests on the same principle, the same psychological propensity, which fixes the standard of music and painting (T47). Later we will be told that our moral and aesthetic sense belong to the "calm" passions (T276). As I see it, then, there is textual evidence early in the *Treatise* which supports the view that the standard for judging action rests on the very same principle.[4]

By intuition we are immediately able to determine with certainty that two or more objects are equal, greater or less than each other. From the "whole united appearance and comparison of particular objects" we make the infallible judgment that a yard is greater than a foot. Although initial judgments are perceptually infallible, they are not immune from reassessment. Judgments of sense are subject to correction by a "review and reflexion" (47). The initial intuitive judgment of equality is infallible, Hume states, provided we do not compare the "minute parts" which compose the terms of the relation. As it turns out, the minute parts are the entities which constitute units of number and units of extension.[5]

Hume thinks he has found a medium between the doctrines of the infinite divisibility of matter and the non-existence of mathematical points by arguing for the existence of indivisible, colored and solid "atoms or corpuscles" (T38–40). Although the imagination cannot form mental images of such minima visibilia, it can form clear and distinct ideas of them.[6]

> When you tell me of the thousandth and ten thousandth part of a grain of sand, I have a distinct idea of these numbers and of their different proportions; but the images which I form in my mind to represent the things themselves, are nothing different from each other, nor inferior to that image, by which I represent the grain of sand itself, which is suppos'd so vastly to exceed them (T27).

Here is an instance where an idea of imagination does not exactly represent a simple impression of sensation.[7] Hume's point is that certain sense impressions, though indivisible to the eye, fail to represent what is "really great and composed of a vast number of parts." By continual divisions, the imagination separates the indivisible sense image until a "minimum" is reached "which cannot be diminished without a total annihilation" (T28,38). Although the imagined minimum lies beyond the reach of sensation, loss of content from image to idea occurs only in point of quantity. For Hume is convinced that in order for the imagination to comprehend the idea, it must be conceived as colored and tangible.[8]

If the first intuitive judgment of equality were strictly infallible, it remains puzzling why sometimes it stands in need of correction. Yet we often find after reflection that objects are judged to be equal which were initially judged unequal and vice versa. Under what conditions, then, do our judgments remain fixed, and when do they become subject to further scrutiny? Hume often stresses, upon his system of indivisible points, that the only useful notion of equality is taken from the "general appearance" and "comparison of particular objects" (T47,637). This idea of equality should be regarded as one of the infallible rules of demonstrative science

Hume discusses in "Of scepticism with regard to reason" (T180). Though the rule is infallible, we recognize the "weakness" and "inconstancy" of the understanding that judges. By a "reflex act of the mind," the initial judgment, derived from the general appearance and comparison of objects, becomes the object of a second more accurate measure, which, in turn, is tested for its veracity.

Once convinced that the initial comparison of particular objects does not guarantee an infallible judgment, we begin to employ more accurate standards of comparison by the use of instruments of measurement. The first appearance might roughly be corrected by congruence or juxtaposition. These methods may be further corrected by the use of measuring rods. Each new corrective judgment improves upon the preceding, successively increasing in accuracy as the instrument becomes more and more sophisticated. But the sequence of judgments and corrections is interminable despite the delicacy of the instrument employed (T182).

We recall that the imagination may form the idea of a minimum point far more minute than those that appear to sense. Hume's point is that the removal or addition of one of these points cannot be discerned by sense or measurement. However finely grained, no art of measurement could represent the minimum formed by imagination. "We are not possessed of any instrument or art of measuring, which can secure us from all error and uncertainty" (T43). And with this realization the imagination provides for what is lacking, supplementing, as it were, the series of progressively accurate judgments by supposing a perfect standard of equality, insusceptible of any further correction.

> We therefore suppose some imaginary standard of equality, by which the appearances and measuring are exactly corrected, and the figures reduc'd entirely to that proportion (T48).

By thus completing the series, the imagination has advanced beyond the limit of what can be tested empirically. The perfect standard, Hume makes clear, is "a mere fiction of the mind." Yet this sort of imaginative supplementation, even in the absence of empirical evidence, is very natural. It is "usual," writes Hume, for the mind to proceed in this way "even after the reason has ceas'd which first determined it to begin" (T48). By "carrying on the same action of the mind," repeatedly judging and correcting, but at the same time realizing that the imagined minimum is not empirically accessible, we form the idea of a perfect standard (T49). The notion of perfect temporal equality rests on the same propensity of imagination to persist beyond the corrections of measurement. The musician forms the idea of a complete octave but is unable to do so by the most delicate tuning device.

The painter, likewise, imagines that colors are capable of an exact comparison and equality beyond the judgments of sense.

Clearly, the idealized standard of equality is useless for empirically verifying the equality that holds between the general appearance of objects. According to the "experimental method," we are incapable of telling when particular objects are equal. Our final appeal falls back on the fallible judgment of sense, subject to further corrections and refinements, but remaining fallible nonetheless. The postulation of any further correction beyond the judgment of sense is fictitious, "useless as well as incomprehensible" (T48,51). Hume is justified in expressing some concern with this peculiar tendency of imagination to persist beyond the observable. The fiction of equality, to be sure, is neither grounded empirically nor applicable to experience. Hume has recognized that his discovery of imaginative supplementation sits awkwardly with his empiricist commitments. For it seems clear that the imagination has taken on a regulative capacity by adjusting the imperfections inherent in measurement according to an idealized rule. It would now seem as if the mind encounters experience, according to Kant, "not as a pupil but as a judge."[9] H.H. Price suggests that perhaps Hume did not realize the importance of his discovery. The above quotation would have us believe that Hume, very early on, intends to dismiss the fictitious construct as absurd. Yet, quite the opposite emerges. Throughout the *Treatise*, Hume repeatedly employs this gesture of thought to account for many important doctrines. The propensity of the imagination to persist in "carrying on the same action of the mind ... in spite of sense and reason" (T147), is the begin-all of such fundamental concepts as unreasonableness, factual prejudice and moral bias. Having, then, introduced the principle of imaginative supplementation, we are now in a position to look more closely at this principle and to see how it is applied to a number of salient doctrines in Hume's philosophy.

## IMAGINATIVE SUPPLEMENTATION

The importance of what I am calling imaginative supplementation cannot be overstressed. Following Hume's illustration, Price has named this tendency of the imagination the "Inertia Principle."[1] Both terms will be freely employed whenever appropriate. Though Hume offers no nice name for this tendency, he describes the matter very well. Reminding the reader of his discussion on equality, Hume continues:

I have already observ'd, in examining the foundation of mathematics, that the imagination, when set into any train of thinking, is apt to continue, even when its object fails it, and like a galley put in motion by the oars, carries on its course without any new impulse (T198).

Earlier I stated that general rules will have a great influence on factual and moral judgments. We shall also see, in Hume's discussion of the passions, that general rules regulate the standard which ought to be observed if a "just value" is to be attributed to the object of a passion (T293). When Hume finally takes up the subject of rules, the inertia principle is already assumed in order to explain our tendency to form them beyond their proper range of application.

The origin of general rules is to be sought in the same principles which govern the causal judgment (T147). Simply stated, the causal judgment is founded on our experience of constant conjunction which generates the habit of expecting one member of a conjunction when the other is given in sensation or memory. It should come as no surprise, therefore, that if the origin of general rules, a kind of "unphilosophical probability" (T143), relies on the inertia principle, straightforward philosophical probability rests on inertia as well. It could be said that all of our ordinary causal habits would not stand were it not for imaginative supplementation. It is something even more basic than the causal inference, without which "human nature must immediately perish and go to ruin" (T225). Without thus presupposing the supplemental activities of imagination, we would not be aware of an order of nature, nor would we be aware of a world of objects.[2]

'Tis this principle, which makes us reason from causes and effects; and 'tis the same principle, which convinces us of the continu'd existence of external objects, when absent from the senses (T266).

The reliance on inertia for our everyday habits comes out most notably in the "coherence" of our perceptions.

Our belief in the continued and independent existence of material objects depends on the "coherence and constancy" (T195) of certain impressions. The belief, however, does not arise from these qualities of impressions by themselves, but from a concurrence with "the qualities of imagination," the all important one being the Inertia Principle (T194). Constancy involves an interrupted series of specifically identical or resembling perceptions (T258), whereas coherence depends on a regularity in the alteration of perceptions.

My bed and table, my books and papers, present themselves in the same uniform manner, and change not upon account of any interruption in my seeing or perceiving them ... Bodies often change their position and qualities, and after a little absense or interruption may become hardly knowable (T194–195).

Coherence is not introduced as a brand new quality of perception but as an exception to the series of constant perceptions. It is characterized by a series of perceptions whose members change in quality while maintaining a regularity which is something like ordinary causal reasoning. Thus, following Hume's illustration, when I return to my fireplace at $T_2$, I perceive smoldering grey ash, while at $T_1$ I perceived an orange blaze. But I recall instances of an uninterrupted series where the same change had occurred over the same period of time. I perceive $A$ at $T_1$, $E$ at $T_2$, though I have frequently observed *ABCDE* continuously. Since the series has repeatedly preserved its order, we regard it as "a kind of reasoning from causation," and confidently infer the remaining members of the series from the perception of any one member (T195). By filling in the broken series we imagine the existence of particulars which are not presently perceived. The whole process sounds very much like ordinary causal inference whereby from a customary transition of thought we infer existences "which we do not see or feel" (T101,74).

The regularity in the coherence of perceptions, Hume admits, is "a kind" of causal inference, but by no means the same as ordinary causal reasoning. This is because we observe constant conjunction in past instances but are unable to observe the conjunction without interruption "since the turning about of our head, or the shutting of our eyes is able to break it" (T197). While coherence may seem to be the same as causal inference, Hume is intent to show that "they are at bottom considerably different" (T191). If we try to regard them as the same, we involve ourselves in a contradiction, "nor is it possible for us to reason justly and regularly from causes and effects, and at the same time believe the continu'd existence of matter" (T266). Hume will argue that in order to preserve our causal rules, in order to retain the same "dependence and connexion" which we have experienced, it is necessary to suppose that objects have a continued existence when unperceived. This supposition is not the outgrowth of causal inference but something which guarantees the causal inference itself, without which causes and effects "lose, in a great measure, the regularity of their operation."

Hume makes the point by illustration. While seated in his upstairs room, he hears the creak of a moving door without looking at the door, and then observes a messenger approach him with a letter. These events, Hume goes on to say, are "contradictions to common experience, and may be regarded as objections to those maxims, which we form concerning the connexions of causes and effects" (T196). This particular creaking sound has always been conjoined with the visual impression of a door moving on its hinges. We accordingly form the rule that whenever the sound occurs, the visual impression occurs as well. But it often happens that of two impressions regularly conjoined in the past, only one will make its appearance to perception. In this instance, the sound of the creak is not accompanied by the sight of the door. My causal rule, then, would seem to be contradicted. The force of the rule, to be sure, is not immediately contradicted by one negative instance, but the instance is to be regarded as an objection to the rule. And since it often happens that only one impression will make its appearance to sense, the rule must ultimately come to be refuted (T197).[3] Similarly, the rule that unsupported bodies descend is weakened on this occasion. For it has always been observed that gravity prevents messengers from leaping to an upstairs room, which this messenger must have done in order to deliver Hume's letter.

The way our causal rules can be saved from refutation is by supposing that objects continue to exist and events continue to occur when unobserved. We cannot preserve our rules about creaking doors and descending bodies "unless the door, which I remember on t'other side of the chamber, be still in being ... unless the stairs I remember be not annihilated by my absence" (T196). This supposition, Hume says, is the only one which can "reconcile these contradictions" (T197). Only by thus presuming the continued existence of objects and events can we preserve the coherence of experience and reinforce the relation of cause and effect (T238). It should by now begin to emerge that the supposition of continued existence from coherence is not a simple case of causal reasoning. Although Hume is prepared to admit that it may resemble causal reasoning in that it arises from ordinary habit in an "oblique manner" (T197), he insists throughout that they are very different.

According to Hume, straightforward causal reasoning is nothing but the psychological compulsion to anticipate one idea when its usual companion makes its appearance in an impression. The belief has been inculcated by repeatedly observing conjunctions. But in the case of the messenger or the creaking door, Hume indicates, we find ourselves imagining a "greater regularity" (T197) than what we actually observe, and this cannot be explained simply by the way habits come to be formed. Let us take a closer look at Hume's argument.

Hume proceeds by stating the principle underlying causal inference; a causal habit is generated by observing the constant priority of one perception to another. Given this principle, Hume continues, it is impossible for a habit to "exceed" the degree of regularity found in our perceptions. I suppose Hume's meaning is that the degree of force in any habit, its degree of felt expectedness, cannot exceed the extent to which a regularity among our perceptions has been observed. We cannot expect an object to exist or an event to occur with a stronger force of expectation than what previous observation warrants. So, Hume concludes, any degree of regularity in our perceptions cannot secure the inference to a "greater degree of regularity in some objects, which are not perceived" (T197).

It would certainly seem as if Hume is undoing his work on belief and causal inference. For his argument boils down to the admission that the extent to which we have observed the priority of one perception to another perception cannot be the foundation for the inference from one perception to another unperceived perception. It is a contradiction to suppose that a habit can be formed by "what was never present to the mind."

When we are reminded that the term "perception" covers impressions and ideas, Hume can be taken as meaning the following. The inference to a perception, which is not present to sense as an impression but present to the mind as an idea, is an inference to a perception, to a lively idea or belief, which has not previously been experienced. It is true, however, that perceptions exactly resembling the allegedly inferred perception have been present to sense as impressions. It is necessary to assume here that Hume is describing the point in our experience at which the feeling of belief finally takes hold after repeatedly observing the members of a regularity as impressions. It must be admitted that the inference from one perception, given as an impression, to another perception, which was not earlier experienced as a lively idea or belief, is an inference from what is now presently sensed to "what was never present to the mind" and is not now present to sense. Clearly, then, the inference to a perception which was never had, and is not presently sensed, flies in the face of the conditions under which habits are formed, namely by repeatedly observing the priority of one perception given in sense, to another perception given in sense. Hume's point is that when we infer the continued existence of a perception which was never present to the mind, we do so in order to bestow a "greater regularity" to our perceptions than what we actually observe.[4] Since the degree of felt expectedness keeps pace with the extent to which we observe a regularity in our perceptions, Hume concludes:

> The extending of custom and reasoning beyond the perceptions can never be the direct and natural effect of the constant repetition and connexion but must arise from the cooperation of some other principles (T198).

With this conclusion, Hume is prepared to account for the mind's propensity to extend habit beyond what is given in perception by imaginative supplementation.

> Objects have a certain coherence even as they appear to our senses; but this coherence is much greater and more uniform, if we suppose the

objects to have a continued existence; and as the mind is once in the train of observing an uniformity among objects, it naturally continues, till it renders the uniformity as compleat as possible (T198).

We may try to make Hume's meaning clearer.[5] We do not observe the members of a coherent order to be perfectly constant. We do so occasionally but not always. We have repeatedly observed, without interruption, fire change from red blaze $A$ to grey ash $E$. We now observe $A$ when igniting the logs and upon our return observe $E$. But we might have been so constituted as to believe that $BCD$ did not occur. I have often observed $ABCDE$, but on this occasion I observe only $A$ and $E$. My causal rule about the alteration of fire will now have to be revised. Some fires begin ablaze, become annihilated by my absence, and are newly created as grey ash by my presence. According to this way of thinking, our causal rules must eventually come to be refuted with every turn of the head. But Hume's point is that we do not think this way at all. In the absence of what we usually observe between $A$ and $E$, we continue to believe that $BCD$ occurred though unperceived. The confidence we place in our causal rule is not in the least diminished. We persist in our inductive generalization and resist revision even in light of contrary evidence. And in this case:

$A$---$E$
*qrstu*

it is not while gazing fixedly through intervals *rst*, perceptions occurred other than those which usually occur. Very simply, $BCD$ did not occur once we turned away from A. It is a case where we have a cessation of positive evidence rather than an instance of negative evidence. The propensity to extend inductive generalizations manifests itself not only in cases where there has been a cessation of positive evidence, but even in cases where a negative instance occurs, as when $HIJ$ occupies what has always been occupied by $BCD$. In such cases, we might be inclined to plead hallucination[6] rather than call into question our most basic causal laws.

It was Hume's conviction that in human nature there is a tendency to make inductive generalizations, a psychological propensity to expect given due experience of regularities. But there is also another tendency at work which protects and preserves the causal inference from the disconnectedness of our ideas. The occurrence of the isolated squeak is interpreted as positive rather than negative evidence for the existence of the door. The inference from an auditory impression to an unperceived existent supports the causal belief that from the sound we can expect the movement of the door. When confronted with the squeak without the visual impression, a hypothetical being might simply believe he was mistaken in believing that these two events always go together.[7] But Hume's point is that in human nature there is a tendency not merely to generalize, but to extend generalizations as far as possible and to suppose that there is order in the world even when apparently disruptive evidence would threaten this order.

Imaginative supplementation shows itself in various ways and in various contexts. Price maintains that Hume says nothing at all about inertia in his discussion of constancy.[8] While it is true that the inertia principle receives its proper introduction in the discussion of coherence, it continues to exert its influence on the constancy of our perceptions.

In order to explain why constancy impels us to believe that objects have a continued and independent existence, Hume has recourse to an earlier established general rule.

> Wherever the actions of the mind in forming any two ideas are the same or resembling, we are very apt to confound these ideas, and take the one for the other (T61).

Resemblance, says Hume, is a "fertile source of error." We fall into the belief that one idea is another not only when they are associated by resemblance, but also when the acts of thought in conceiving them are similar (T203). The mental disposition when viewing a numerically identical object, characterized by "invariableness and uninterruptedness," is similar to the disposition which views a discontinuous series of resembling perceptions. The movement of thought along the associative links of invariable yet interrupted perceptions is like the disposition of mind when viewing an uninterrupted and invariable object (T204). Although it is very "natural," Hume concludes, to confuse the series with an uninterrupted perception and believe that the succession is numerically identical, the recognition of interruption in the series instructs us that each member is a resembling yet "distinct being." We find ourselves holding two opposite beliefs. We are involved in a "kind of contradiction" which produces a "sensible uneasiness" (T205). The kind of contradiction Hume has in mind is of the form *A* is *B* and *A* is as if *B*. But since it is "impossible to over-look" the lacunae within a discontinuous series, we recognize that *A* is not *B*. The problem is we cannot help but believe that *A* is *B*. Confronted with the contradiction, the mind is perplexed. It feels "uneasy" when placed in situations of contradiction. The mind's desire for relief causes the second propensity, a "propension" to unite the broken series by the "fiction" of continued existence (T208). Here again, we see the inertia of imagination at work. We suppose that between resembling perceptions there exists other unperceived resemblants which join the series into one continuous whole.

The propensity to unite the series is not satisfied until the union is as complete as possible (T237).

We have thus found two propensities which "induce us" to believe in the existence of material objects (T187). The first consists in an oversight in gaps between a series of resembling perceptions by confusing the series with one continuous existent. Despite the realization that interruption and identity are incompatible, we persist in justifying the identity by a second propensity of imagination to supplement the gaps among perceived resemblants with other unperceived resemblants (T217). The initial propensity is reinforced by a back-up propensity which both contribute to that "nature" Hume so often speaks of which makes us take for granted the existence of material objects. Reflecting on the contradiction has little influence on the urge to complete a series of closely united perceptions into one whole thing. The belief in the independent and continued existence of body, Hume thinks, has become so deeply entrenched that it is "impossible ever to eradicate it" (T214).

Elsewhere, in his attack on mind-body materialism, Hume appeals to imaginative supplementation to account for our belief that thought and matter are united by the relation of "conjunction in place" (T237). Setting down the principle that "an object may exist, and yet be no where," Hume writes that many perceptions such as sounds, smells and passions exist without place or position. Perceptions such as these are non-spatial, unextended, incapable of occupying a location, and yet it is believed that they inhere within a physical object, which is extended and located in a particular place (T236). How do we end up believing what is "absurd," that an unextended perception is extended? Hume accounts for the "illusion" by imaginative supplementation.

By a "propensity" of imagination, we project qualities which exist nowhere onto an extended object so as to form a single whole. By an "inclination" of imagination, certain unextended qualities are "determin'd" to come together with extended, tangible qualities (T238). Like the relation of necessary connection, this "bias" of imagination is explained by that propensity "to spread itself on external objects." The same propensity which unites sounds and smells with extended objects accounts for the supposition that necessity lies in the "objects we consider, not in our mind, that considers them" (T167).

The belief that the taste of an olive lies in the visible and tangible body, Hume grants, is a very natural illusion. As we might expect, a compulsion of imagination to strengthen any relation that already associates two or more ideas is responsible for the illusion (T237). Let us look at the relations which already hold between the qualities of an object. Hume first notes that the qualities which make up our "complex ideas" of an object are "inseparable."[9] Secondly, causation holds between the extended object and the taste and smell. Whether we regard either as cause or effect, "they are always co-existent." They are also "co-temporary." The moment the extended body is applied to sense, the taste and smell are perceived. Given these relations the usual causal inference is drawn. Yet we do not stop at the inference to an extended object from an impression of taste or smell but "endeavor to give them a new relation, viz. that of a conjunction of place, that we may render the transition more easy and natural."[10] We pass from an impression of taste to an idea of an object but continue to strengthen the tie in order to complete the association. Like the "galley" which continues on its way "without any new impulse," we are "determin'd" to proceed beyond the incomplete union by merging the unextended taste within the extended body. Following the "galley" illustration, the inference from body to taste, further strengthened by temporal contiguity, may be seen as the "impulse" from which continued movement follows. As the oars are part of a causal nexus which result in the ship's movement, so the relations of causation and contiguity trigger the propensity to continue uniting until the union is as complete as possible.

Hume states that we are determined to persist in the belief even in light of the realization that a smell or taste cannot occupy a body without itself being extended. However reason and reflection show us the impossibility of the union, we cling to the belief that tastes and smells inhere in physical objects. Reflection shows us that it is impossible for a thing to be in a certain place and yet exist nowhere. But the sheer satisfaction in postulating the additional relation "draws us back to our former opinion." Here, again, we see the inertia of imagination determines our beliefs, and it persists in the determination, "even in the midst of our most profound reflections" (T214).

When Hume, in Book III, considers how property rules come to be established, he is certain that considerations of public utility play some role. But the "principal" cause of the rules, he goes on to say, is determined by imagination or "the more frivolous properties of our thought" (T504). Most of the general rules which determine property are founded on this psychological quirk of imagination we have been discussing. The first rule runs as follows:

> It must immediately occur, as the most natural expedient, that every one continue to enjoy what he is at present master of, and that property or constant possession be conjoined to the immediate possession (T503).

The formation of this rule is influenced by the inertia principle in a two-fold manner.

Hume first points out that we have a tendency to become attached to objects we have long enjoyed and to develop a sort of affection for them. This is just the nature of ordinary habit founded on the extent to which we have employed an object. My manual typewriter has served me well for years. So I form the habit of using it whenever I need to write. I spring to the idea of my old manual whenever the desire to write arises. But this is not all. We have a further tendency to cling to those objects we have grown used to, even in light of others which we believe to be superior, but which we have not experienced. The mind feels reluctance in moving toward what is new and unusual. Thus I persist in using my old manual even when presented with a shiny new electric, though I know full well that it will out-perform my manual. In view of evidence which devalues my typewriter in point of performance, I adhere to my machine, as if to preserve and protect my old habit.

In our discussion of general rules, we shall see that this phenomenon is accounted for by the differing influence which habit exerts on the imagination and the judgment (T148). For the present, we note that the propensity of imagination to persist beyond the conditions which first generated a habit is one reason why we agree that "every one continue to enjoy what he is at present possess'd of" (T504).

The same propensity which had us attribute "conjunction in place" to thought and matter serves to explain the second way inertia determines the first rule of property. We see again that when two ideas are already associated by imagination, "the mind is apt to ascribe to them any additional relation, in order to complete the union."

Since, therefore, we can feign a new relation, and even an absurd one, in order to compleat any union, 'twill easily be imagined, that if there be any relations, which depend on the mind, 'twill readily conjoin them to any preceding relation, and unite, by a new bond, such objects as have already an union in the fancy (T504).

And this propensity explains why we add the relation of constant possession or property to present possession. The mind, says Hume, is "determin'd to join" the new relation simply because the relation of present possession already holds. Hume is concerned to show that the imagination is endowed with a latent propensity to join objects which is triggered by objects already joined. The point is made by appeal to common experience.

We never fail, in our arrangement of bodies, to place those which are resembling in contiguity to each other ... because we feel a satisfaction in joining the relation of contiguity to that of resemblance (T505).

The remaining four rules of property are established primarily by what Hume calls this "trivial property" of imagination.

While imaginative supplementation tends to preserve and protect causal reasoning, it also extends causal inferences formed from one set of regularities to resembling regularities but different in causal features. We shall soon see that the inertia of imagination is a source of false and unreasonable belief. Hume will prescribe that we "ought to regulate" inertia if we want to protect the "authentic" operations of understanding and "check" its "destructive" influence (T150). Imaginative supplementation, then, at once preserves and destroys. Hume's recognition of this fact created for him a conflict of reason and imagination, an "opposition" which he found very difficult to resolve (T149).

We have discussed the principle of inertia at some length. When we take up the subject of general rules, we will again see inertia at work when "custom goes beyond those instances from which it is deriv'd" (T148). I stress throughout that a proper understanding of the inertia principle and general rules is essential if we are to come to grips with the moral theory, the theory of belief and other important features of Hume's philosophy.

CHAPTER TWO

# General Rules

In Book II, "Of The Passions," Hume attributes to general rules "a mighty influence on the actions and understanding" (T374). Somewhat later, during his remarks about conscience, Hume adds, "men are mightily addicted to general rules" (T551). The subject is early introduced in the section "Of unphilosophical probability"[1] but continues to play an increasingly prominent role in fixing "the just value" of factual, passional and moral judgment (T293). It is within the context of rules that Hume's more positive view of the place of reason in moral judgment will be found.

Given Hume's ease and grace of style, it is understandable that subtle turns of thought flow past the reader. But when we come across such strong assertions, we can be confident that something important is in the making. It is somewhat surprising, therefore, to find that the subject of rules has gone virtually unrecognized.[2] This is due, in part, to its unfortunate placement just prior to the long awaited discussion of necessity. Hume asks us to bear along with his search for the impression which gives rise to the idea of necessity. Having been through "all the neighboring fields" for most of Part III, Book I, the attention is easily diverted to the soon-to-be fulfilled promise. Yet Hume's work on "unphilosophical" probability is no casual prelude to the grand showing of necessity. General rules provide normative standards for the interpretation of immediate experience and for natural, "uncultivated" moral evaluations (T489).[3] The prominence of general rules in Hume's thought is evidenced by their repeated application to the fields of ethics, aesthetics,[4] psychology and epistemology.

Hume discusses two sorts of general rules which must be carefully distinguished. The first sort of rule is generated by a propensity of imagination which, if left unchecked, often results in false belief. The second sort of rule functions to check the propensity to form the first sort of rule. The same pattern is displayed in all three Books of the *Treatise*, an imaginative propensity to form one type of rule which requires correction by another type of rule. General rules of the first type are characterized by an obstinate adherence to them, even in disregard of contrary evidence. "Human nature is very subject to errors of this kind." Prejudicial belief is one among such errors (T147).

> An Irishman cannot have wit, and a Frenchman cannot have solidity; for which reason, tho' the conversation of the former in any instance be visibly very agreeable, and of the latter very judicious, we have entertain'd such a prejudice against them, that they must be dunces or fops in spite of sense and reason (T146).

Hume would have us look into the reason why we hold such rules, and why we continue to uphold them even in light of opposing evidence.

The first step in explanation is by way of analogical reasoning. The idea inferred from a present impression varies in strength according to the resemblance which holds between the impression and a member of a past regularity. Given that $A$ and $B$ are usually conjoined, if an $A*$ is presented which does not exactly resemble $A$, the belief reposed in $B$ will diminish accordingly. "In proportion as the resemblance decays, the probability diminishes" (T147).

According to Hume, "unphilosophical probability" is derived from the same principles as philosophical probability, although philosophers have not regarded the former as a "reasonable foundation of belief" (T143). But so far, there seems to be nothing unreasonable about analogical inference. We believe that $B$ will occur or has occurred when presented with an $A$ and continue to believe that $B$ will occur when presented with the resembling instance $A*$. In both cases, the content of belief remains the same. In the latter case, the "force" of belief is reduced according to the extent to which $A*$ resembles $A$ (T628–629). Hume makes clear that the reduction in resemblance is not decisive evidence for the belief that $B$ will not exist. Rather, the loss of exact resemblance accordingly reduces the evidence for the belief that $B$ will exist. The vivacity of the first impression $A*$ cannot be fully discharged to $B$ when it does not exactly resemble the $A$'s that have been conjoined with $B$'s. According to variations in degree of resemblance, the inference to $B$ becomes more or less believed (T142). Why, then, is analogical inference not considered reasonable inference?

At this point in the exposition, Hume is not concerned with the inertial tendency of imagination to "extend the scope"[5] of judgments formed from one set of regularities to another set of resembling regularities. Strength of belief quite reasonably follows extent of resemblance. The persistent inference of imagination first begins to show itself when Hume discusses the way general rules stand in opposition to each other (T150).

For the present, we may note that imaginative supplementation extends the scope of a belief in cases where the strength of belief exceeds the extent to which a present impression resembles a member of a past uniformity. The strength of belief would here overreach the original store of vivacity from which it was derived. We believe that a *B* will occur with greater assurance than what the evidence warrants. The strength of anticipation, as Hume calls it, the "vivacity of conception," is now greater than the vivacity discharged from a present impression. Such overinflated belief is partially due to the imagination's propensity to strengthen the association of closely resembling ideas to exactly resembling ideas. The projection of "specific identity" (T258) serves to close the relational gap of imperfect resemblance. We may call beliefs such as these "overextended" or "unreasonable" beliefs. Supplemental propensities will require correction if unphilosophical inference is to be restored to a reasonable foundation of belief (T143).

An important turn in the discussion comes at the point where Hume observes that custom often produces conflict in causal reasoning.

> Tho' custom be the foundation of all our judgments, yet sometimes it has an effect on the imagination in opposition to the judgment, and produces a contrariety in our sentiments concerning the same object (T148).

The conflict arises from a "complication of circumstances"[6] within causes. Most causes consist of a combination of factors, some of which are essential for the production of an effect, while others are "conjoin'd by accident." When the contingent factors are frequently intermingled with the essential, they influence the imagination to the extent that, even in the absence of the truly causal factors, the inference is drawn to the usual effect as if they were present. The inferred idea, writes Hume, is a vivid idea, a believed idea, "superior to the mere fictions of the fancy" (T148). "Here is the first influence of general rules" (T150).

Hume provides us with an ingenius illustration. A man placed in an iron cage and suspended from a tower cannot help but fear his descent though he believes himself to be secure. According to straightforward experience, whenever we have received the impression of great depth, we have usually been supported. Now suspended from a high tower we should anticipate, from the appearance of the mountain tops, that we are protected from descent by the supporting cage. But there is another causal rule at work. Having often observed the descent of bodies, whenever we think of a suspended object we think of the place immediately below it, "as if our ideas acquir'd a kind of gravity from their objects" (T435). We believe, then, that all unsupported bodies tend to the place below them while all supported bodies remain at rest. On this occasion, we receive the complex impression of depth, support and solidity, the combination of factors within causes. Hume points out that the depth factor is the "superfluous" circumstance which is regularly conjoined with the factors of support and solidity, since the perception of depth occurs whenever we look about from lofty places, and it occurs as well whenever we observe the descent of bodies. The resembling factor, on this occasion, supports the belief that our fall is imminent despite the opposite inference to support from solidity, which, according to Hume, "ought" (T148) to make us feel very secure. Under the enlivening influence of a resembling yet accidental feature of a cause, the inference is drawn from elevated support to descent.

> The same custom goes beyond the instances from which it is deriv'd, and to which it perfectly corresponds; and influences his ideas of such objects as are in some respect resembling, but fall not precisely under the same rule (T148).

General rules of the first type result from the combined influence of custom and resemblance on the imagination. What is involved is a generalizing tendency of imagination, what we have called the inertia of imagination, to extend the scope of a causal rule generated under one set of circumstances to different but resembling circumstances. Having acquired the habit of expecting *B* from *A*, we continue to expect *B*, given the resembling instance *A\**. Having formed the belief that objects descend to the place below them, and presented with the perception of depth, the belief is extended under conditions of support which resemble those of descent in point of depth.

> The circumstances of depth and descent strike so strongly upon him, that their influence cannot be destroyed by the contrary circumstances of support and solidity (T148).

We likewise form the belief that Irishmen are witless on the basis of a number of conversations with dull Irishmen but continue to preserve our rule when confronted with an Irishman who is very witty. Now presented with the accent of the Irish impression, which impression is common to both rule and instance, the inference is drawn to a witless Irishman. The inference is kept within the scope of the rule simply because of the resemblance which holds between rule and instance. Similarly, the belief to descent falls within the scope of the rule on account of the resembling instance of depth, which holds between descent and support.[7]

Here we have a misapplication of a causal rule which was itself generated under conditions where the causal features of a cause were misidentified. Hume points out that the resemblance holding between instance and rule is one which holds between the non-causal features of a cause. The perception of depth should no more support the inference to descent than should the accent of the Irish support the inference to a witless Irishman. This might seem somewhat question begging, but the assumption that the causal from the contingent features of a cause have already been distinguished makes it possible for Hume to lay down the factual imperative that only the causal features of a cause ought to determine belief (T149).

To extend a causal rule formed under one set of conditions to another set of resembling conditions is a potential source of error. Although it remains open for us to offset the supplemental activities of imagination to extend causal rules beyond their proper application, Hume insists throughout that the initial response to infer from any and every enlivened idea cannot be suppressed by reflecting on and distinguishing the causal from the contingent features of causes. "'Tis still certain, that custom takes the start, and gives a biass to the imagination" (T148).

Let us try to get clear on the way custom may bias the imagination. According to Hume's general theory of causal belief, $X$ is the cause of $Y$ whenever the constant priority of $X$ to $Y$ has generated the habit of expecting $Y$ when presented with $X$. The illustrations which Hume offers as instances of unreasonable belief can be expressed in more general terms as follows. $ABC$ are necessary and sufficient conditions of $X$ for the production of $Y$, and $qrs$ are usually though contingently conjoined with $ABC$. If an object $Z$ is presented, whose necessary and sufficient conditions for the production of $P$ are $DEF$, but which resembles $X$ in points of $qrs$, the inference is drawn to $X$, and $Z$ is taken for $X$, on account of the resemblance which holds between $Z$ and $X$. The subsequent inference to $Y$ is then drawn, and belief is reposed in $Y$ as if presented with an $X$.

Several points need sorting out. We may begin by noticing that the belief that $Z$ is $X$ is explained by a general rule we have already discussed. "Whatever ideas place the mind in the same disposition or in similar ones, are very apt to be confounded" (T203). Two instances of similarity, we recall, contribute to the error. First, the similarity which holds between $Z$ and $X$ and secondly, the similarity holding between the dispositions when thinking of $Z$ and $X$. Both instances of similarity cause the belief that $Z$ is $X$ (T203). Believing, then, that $Z$ is $X$, the inference is drawn to $Y$, and it is believed that $Y$ will exist, though probably it will not since $X$ and not $Z$ is the cause of $Y$.

Following Hume's illustration, let $ABC$ of $X$ represent the conditions under which bodies descend, i.e., the removal of support, and allow $qrs$ of $X$ to represent the contingent circumstances which usually lie contiguous with $ABC$, most notably, the perception of depth. Let us also allow $DEF$ of $Z$ to represent the conditions under which objects resist gravitational force, i.e., support and solidity, while again *qrs* of Z lies contiguous with *DEF*. Since Z is related to X by the resembling instance *qrs*, and since *qrs* is usually contiguous with *ABC*, the inference is drawn to *ABC*, i.e., the removal of support which, in turn, supports the inference to Y, i.e., descent. The inference to P, i.e., support, which ought to provide ease and security, is in opposition with the two-fold enlivening influence of resemblance and contiguity, which influence is so striking that it cannot be destroyed by the opposite circumstances of support and solidity.

Notice that the inference from Z to X is an "unphilosophical" inference, an inference which results in an unreasonable belief, most probably false, which, in turn, supports the inference to another unreasonable belief, most probably false. The perception of depth has so often occurred with the observation of descending bodies that, when given the perception, the inference is drawn to the removal of support and subsequently to the place below, which thought is believed under the enlivening influence of resemblance and contiguity. A causal rule is now extended to an instance which does not fall exactly under the rule. A Z is now believed to be an X. Instances of X are embraced by the scope of Z. The scope of the belief, that from solidity we can expect support, is now extended to instances of the removal of support from which descent is inferred.

The belief that Z is X, that solidity is the removal of support, may become further enlivened by that tendency of imagination to supplement the relational gap of approximate resemblance by the postulation of "specific identity." Since Z already resembles X by virtue of its contingent features, we recall,

> the mind is apt to ascribe to them any additional relation in order to compleat the union; and this inclination is so strong, as often to make us run into errors (T504).

The propensity to further associate Z and X to the point of numerical identity is halted by the belief that an X is not a Z. Instances of Z are short lived under the scope of X. Upon the removal of support, it is at once established that the supportive surface was not secure. The conflict of solidity and shaky ground is immediately resolved.

Although Hume will have us understand that it is unreasonable to respond mechanically to every vivid perception, he is also becoming aware of the "contradiction" (T150) in his theory of general rules. It is unreasonable to make causal transitions on the basis of evidence which is non-causal. The transition from Z to X, from solidity to the removal of support, is not a causal inference but a transition of thought under the enlivening influence of resemblance, contiguity and constant conjunction, the very conditions necessary for the causal inference (T87). The point of resemblance is a contingent feature of two opposite causes. The influence of these relations causes us to think of the removal of support, which results in what Hume calls a "counterfeit belief" (T123).

We might not, however, have developed any beliefs about which features of a cause are causal and which features are not. If we have not, as yet, discriminated the features of a cause by reflection, the indiscriminate inference, we would say, is potentially false but not unreasonable. As we shall see, the high watermark of unreasonableness will be exemplified in cases where a causal inference is drawn on the basis of evidence *believed* to be noncausal.

Hume is often quoted as saying that "belief lies in some sentiment or feeling which depends not on the will" (T624, EU48). It is not in our power to believe what we please. But Hume would also like to distinguish the enlivened but "weak and imperfect" perception from the "solidity and force" of a genuine belief (T121,631). The "real" sentiment of belief is achieved by reflection and a great mental effort, which, Hume asserts, ought to be made if the "authentic" causal rules are not to be subverted by those which are "irregular" and "destructive of all the most establish'd principles of reasoning" (T150). The emphasis will shift from an instinctive or "mechanical"[8] response theory of belief to a theory of belief which involves the adoption of a "proper" (T123) point of view. It will emerge that the proper viewpoint is one from which genuine judgments are made, both of fact and value.

By now the reader has recognized what is required to offset erroneous belief. We must be able to sort out the causal from the contingent features of causes. Only by a "reflection on the nature of those circumstances" (T148), can the "efficacious causes" be distinguished from the "accidental circumstances." "This is a second influence of general rules, and implies the condemnation of the former" (T150). When both sorts of general rules come into play, they produce conflicting judgments about the same object (T148). We shall also consider Hume's claim that the second class of rules "implies the condemnation" of the first class. In what follows, the first type of rule is governed by what I call "The Supplemental Employment of Imagination." The second rule is governed by the "Regulative Employment of Understanding." For brevity I refer to them as "Rules of Type *I*" and "Rules of Type *U*." The general problem can be succinctly stated. Rules of Type *I* are "rashly formed." They give rise to "what we properly call prejudice" (T146). We have seen that instances of "unphilosophical" belief are inferred analogically. But the analogical inference is not inconsistent with Hume's general theory of belief.

Shou'd it be demanded why men form general rules, and allow them to influence their judgment, even contrary to present observation and experience, I shou'd reply, that in my opinion, it proceeds from those very principles, on which all judgments concerning causes and effects depend (T147).

Rules of Type *U* will function to discriminate the features of causes. We will see that the rule of correction is aimed at the principles of custom and vivacity which have served Hume so well throughout his discussion of philosophical probability.

Hume has defined belief as a lively idea related to a present impression (T96). The present impression or "foundation" of the inference is either an impression of sense or an idea of memory, the two being equivalent in point of vivacity (T8,97). A "general maxim" in the science of human nature is set forth.

When any impression becomes present to us, it not only transports the mind to such ideas as are related to it, but likewise communicates to them a share of its force and vivacity (T98).

From Hume's discussion it emerges that not all perceptions possess the requisite vivacity to procure belief. Not every perception has the characteristic which triggers the disposition to anticipate its possible connection with other perceptions. When the present perception is weak, the thought of its related idea is weak and is thus weakly believed. The extent to which we are aware of its possible connection with other ideas is reduced as the vivacity of the present impression wanes (T102). But it is also the case that not every impression is so vivid as to cause belief. Not every impression opens up the possibility for an inference to other ideas. Only those impressions which are constantly conjoined will, when either is given, "elevate and enliven the thought" (T98). So we form the habit of expecting $Y$ from impression $X$ given the constant priority of $X$ to $Y$. The present perception, then, be it a sense impression or an idea of memory, must be characterized by a degree of vividness which sets off and sustains the disposition to anticipate its possible connection with other ideas.

Now where exactly does analogical inference go wrong? Hume allows, given his earlier remarks on belief, that the vivacity of a present impression cannot be fully discharged to the related idea when it does not exactly resemble a member of a regularity.

As resemblance, when conjoin'd with causation, fortifies our reasonings; so the want of it in any very great degree is able almost entirely to destroy them (T113).

Any departure from exact resemblance will reduce the force of the disposition to infer. The present impression has less vivacity to impart to the related idea and so cannot fully trigger the disposition to anticipate possible connections. But the loss of exact resemblance, to be sure, does not cut off the inference altogether.

> An experiment loses its force, when transferr'd to instances, which are not exactly resembling; 'tho 'tis evident it may still retain as much as may be the foundation of probability, as long as there is any resemblance remaining (T142).

Hume has us understand that not all analogical inference is a potential source of error. An impression may be given which resembles a member of a past uniformity in some of its causal features. Those causal features present produce almost the same effect which would have been produced were they all present.

> A man, who has contracted a custom of eating fruit by the use of pears or peaches, will satisfy himself with melons, where he cannot find his favorite fruit (T147).

He does not believe they will please him as much as, or more than, peaches or pears. He does not think that the pleasure to come will match or exceed the pleasure he usually receives from peaches or pears.

Analogical inference is unreasonable and is a potential source of error when the inferred idea is thought with a degree of vivacity which equals or exceeds what would have been felt had the impression exactly resembled those which first generated the belief. As in the previous example, if this fellow were given a melon and believed that it would satisfy him as much as, or more than, peaches or pears, then his belief is unreasonable. The unreasonable inference arises from the belief that a given impression will not produce the effect that a similar impression would produce, but the inference is drawn as if presented with that impression. The inferred idea is believed while it is also believed that the given impression is not its cause. Such cases involve the inference to an idea from evidence believed to be insufficient for the inference. When the evidence is "considerable" or "remarkable," we recall, as was the perception of depth or the accent of the Irish, the inferred idea is forcefully believed. According to reductions in resemblance, the idea is believed with less force, and given further reductions, the idea comes to be disbelieved altogether. The point to be stressed is that the transition from belief to simple conception is explained in terms of reductions in resemblance and not from the belief that the given impression lacks causal features.

We will presently see that Rules of Type *U* function to distinguish the causal from the noncausal features of causes. However, they will be unable to offset entirely the imagination's propensity to extend causal rules taken from one set of circumstances to resembling but different sets of circumstances. Given the impression which resembles a member of a uniformity, "the custom operates before we have time for reflexion" (T104). The resembling impression secures the inference "by a natural transition, which precedes reflection, and which cannot be prevented by it" (T147). The combined effect of vivacity, resemblance and custom inevitably "gives a biass to the imagination" (T148). According to the general theory of belief, then, Hume is forced to condone the persistent inference of imagination despite the belief that resembling instances of causes in points of contingent features have no causal power. Let us now turn our attention to the Regulative Rules.

## The Regulative Rules of the Understanding

By Norman Kemp Smith's account, the fundamental idea in Hume's thought is the doctrine that feeling and not reason is the determining influence on human life. Under the influence of Francis Hutcheson's theory of the moral sense, Hume entered his "new Scene of Thought"[1] through the "gateway of morals."[2] The judgment of value is not an inference of reason but a feeling of sentiment. The central claim of the ethics, "Reason is, and ought only to be the slave of the passions" (T415), Kemp Smith writes, is then extended to the epistemology, "being there the maxim: 'Reason is and ought to be subordinate to our natural beliefs'."[3] The judgment of fact, then, like the judgment of value, is not the result of rational insight or an inference of reason, but is likewise a feeling or sentiment.

While Kemp Smith's interpretation is plausible, it tends to overemphasize the slavery of reason to passion and natural belief. The "combat" (T413) of reason and passion first gets under way in Book I, as being there a combat of imagination and judgment, natural belief and reason, or, as I have put it, a conflict of Rules of Type *I* and Rules of Type *U*. But it is not immediately obvious that Hume took a decisive stand as to which rule is master and which rule is slave. Various texts can be cited which support the view that we believe as we must, that the initial reaction to an enlivened perception is the determining characteristic of belief. Belief is "sensitive," not "cogitative" (T183). It is simply a mechanical response to sensation which cannot be destroyed by reason.

Nature, by an absolute and uncontroulable necessity, has determin'd us to judge as well as to breathe and feel (T183).

The "sentiment" or "feeling" of belief, then, would seem to reign over reason, while reason would remain subordinate to our more immediate, instinctive beliefs. "Nature will always maintain her rights and prevail in the end over any abstract reasoning" (EU41).

But Hume, in Book I, finds it very difficult to draw a distinction between reason and natural belief, between Rules of Type *I* and Rules of Type *U*. Both rest on the principles of constant conjunction, vivacity and habit (T147). At times he claims that our more natural beliefs, those, we recall, which give rise to prejudice, cannot be controlled by reason and reflection. But nowhere do we find Hume claim that this is how we *ought* to believe. Instead, Hume would have it that reason "ought to regulate" the immediate response to sensation if our judgments are to be "real and solid" (T149). Immediate reactions to sense stimuli "ought always" to be corrected (T181). Not every indiscriminate response to sensation counts as a "real" belief. Genuine belief consists in a "peculiar manner" of conception "deriv'd from the nature of the understanding," and is not always characterized by sheer vivacity of conception (T630). And in the moral field, not every response to pleasure or pain which arises from the assessment of character constitutes real virtue or vice, but only a "peculiar kind" of pleasure or pain (T472). A "controul," therefore, ought to be imposed on all initial judgments. And if we recall Hume's assertion that ought implies can (T518),[4] that we cannot lay under an obligation to do something we are incapable of doing, it would follow that there is room in Hume's theory for the view that belief can and ought to be regulated by reason and reflection, and that we do not always believe as we must by an "uncontroulable necessity." On this reading, then, it makes sense to speak of the enslavement of passion or natural belief to reason. By placing too much stress on the "slave" passage, Hume's more constructive view of the relation of reason to feeling is not given the attention it deserves.[5]

Robert Paul Wolff has convincingly argued that Hume was not so much concerned with the contents of the mind as with "what the mind does with its contents."[6] The mind is equipped with a number of innate propensities which are the "necessary and universal conditions of all our ideas of causes and objects." These propensities are contributed by the mind to experience and are not simply derived from the characteristics of perception. Impressions and ideas are stimuli which activate "the basic machinery of the mind."[7]

Hume is thus read as the forerunner of Kant's Copernican Revolution. Toward the end of his discussion, Wolff likens Hume's propensities of imagination to Kant's "Categories of the Understanding"[8] but omits any mention of general rules. Although Hume would not hear of categories and faculties (T224), he does speak of the "universal" and "authentic operations of the understanding" (T150–151), Rules of Type *U*, which function to impose a "check or controul" on immediate experience (T180). Price has noticed that Hume's distinction between *I* Rules and *U* Rules comes very near to Kant's distinction between the Empirical and Transcendental imagination.[9] But Wolff does not include either rule among his Humean "Table of Categories."

Wolff then raises an objection, shared also by others,[10] to the problem in Hume's theory of belief. Belief is nothing more than an increased force or vivacity by which an idea is thought. But there are many beliefs which cannot be explained simply in terms of vivacity of conception. "The trouble with Hume's theory is that it fails to explain why we do not believe vivid and affecting fiction, and yet do believe dull history books."[11] The same objection may be extended to the judgment of value.[12] It could equally be claimed that Hume is unable to explain why we do not praise the vicious qualities of those we love, or blame the virtuous qualities of those we hate, and yet do praise those we hate and blame those we love. We shall see that Hume recognizes the difficulty and proposes a solution by means of the Regulative Rules. Judgment involves a good deal more than the simple enlivening of an idea.

> A like reflexion on general rules keeps us from augmenting our belief upon every encrease of the force and vivacity of our ideas (T632).

Had Wolff included general rules among the "activit[ies] of the mind,"[13] he might have avoided the objection that judgments of fact and judgments of value are coordinate with variations in the force of vivacity.

We recall a similar difficulty regarding the idea/impression distinction. Hume formulates the difference as being at once a difference of kind and one that admits of degree. The opening passage of the *Treatise*, however, suggests that "force and liveliness" are the only differences Hume will admit. Further text supports Kemp Smith's claim that Hume's remarks on the subject are "obscure and bewildering."[14]

> Their only difference consists in their different degrees of force and vivacity (T103).

What makes it "impossible to interpret Hume"[15] is his admission of cases which blur the distinction. Impressions can be so faint as to be mistaken for ideas and ideas so vivid as to be mistaken for impressions. Were variations in vivacity what "constituted"[16] the difference, the mistaking of ideas for impressions and vice versa would not occur.[17]

How would this admission land the theory of belief into bewilderment and obscurity? All dull impressions would be thought without any act of assent or belief, while all lively ideas would be believed or disbelieved. So far so good. Hume insists throughout, "'Tis on the degrees of force and vivacity that belief depends" (T143). But Kemp Smith's account places undue stress on the role of vivacity in Hume's theory. Clearly, the principle of vivacity is centrally located within Hume's system and nowhere does Hume relinquish the principle. But it is equally clear that the theory of belief is not explicable only in terms of the vivacity of ideas.

The objection is ultimately aimed at Hume's account of memory and imagination. Again, Kemp Smith interprets Hume as meaning that memory and imagination are distinguished "exclusively"[18] by force and liveliness. Just as an idea that is not clearly remembered may be mistaken for an idea of imagination, so an idea of imagination may become so vivid as to be taken for an idea of memory (T86). Force and vivacity are described as a "sensible property which varies only in degree, and which will not allow of further analysis."[19] As expected, the conclusion is reached that one idea would not be taken for another were shifts in vivacity the only difference between memory and imagination.

While Hume is aware of the issues raised by Wolff and Kemp Smith, the following passages would do more to support rather than undermine their stance.

> The vivacity produc'd by the fancy is in many cases greater than that which arises from custom and experience ... The common degrees of these are easily distinguished; tho' it is not impossible but in particular instances they may very nearly approach to each other ... our ideas may approach to our impressions: As on the other hand it sometimes happens, that our impressions are so faint and low, that we cannot distinguish them from our ideas (T123,T2).

Given the characteristic of vivacity as *constituting* the difference between memory and imagination, there is no way to distinguish fact from fiction. The vivacity of an idea, though not received inferentially, but by frequent repetition, may become so enlivened as to be believed. On the other hand, an idea of memory may merge into an idea of imagination. After a long period of time, one wonders whether an event occurred or whether it is the product of imagination. But Hume would like to qualify his remarks. A difference in vivacity is "a sensible difference" (T9) between memory and imagination, as being a matter of "immediate" (T86) experience. The sensible difference in force and vivacity makes all the "original difference" (T119). Variations in sensation, then, what immediately distinguishes memory from imagination, constitutes a, but not the, difference.

Hume's sparse remarks are given a fuller treatment in the *Appendix*. The frequently repeated idea, what Hume calls a process of education, may acquire a degree of vivacity equal to or greater than beliefs arising from causal inference. An idea of indoctrination may become so enlivened as to be mistaken for an idea inferred from a member of the the the most uniform regularity (T117).

The "poetical system" is a mixture of fact and fiction (T121). The thought that Socrates was beheaded may acquire a good deal of force given the surrounding historical facts of a trial, sentencing and talk of immortality while imprisoned. Hume recognizes that the intense but disconnected idea, those inculcated by prevailing opinion, together with the "raptures of poetry," are not always attended with belief and says that the "least reflection dissipates the illusions ... and places the objects in their proper light" (T123). Hume thus admits of a "proper light" distinct from the "sensible effect" of vivacity. "The mind can easily distinguish betwixt the one and the other" (T630). He says that the causal inference may often be quite dull, but claims that it is still more "forcible and real" than the heightened ideas of poetry or repetition. The judgment of belief, we are now told, is not coordinate with the immediacy of sensation. "The force of our mental actions in this case, no more than in any other, is not to be measured by the apparent agitation of the mind" (T631). The immediate response to an enlivened idea, Hume claims, feels very different from the "sentiment" which characterizes genuine judgment (T632).[20] Hume can go no further. The feeling of belief, like the feelings which characterize all the passions, can only be described, not defined (T277,EU48). The description has come to an end. "I confess, that 'tis impossible to explain perfectly this feeling or manner of conception ... its true and proper name is belief" (T6298). So far in the exposition, it is Hume's intention to distinguish the genuine judgment from the immediate propensity to infer given any enlivened perception. The distinction is crucial for an understanding of Hume's later analysis of the sympathy mechanism. The judgment of value, likewise, will remain "steady" notwithstanding variations in the intensity of the sympathetic response (T581). Hume is now concerned to further distinguish mere "vigour of conception" from the "serious conviction." "In the meantime I cannot forbear observing, that the great difference in their feeling proceeds in some measure from reflexion and general rules" (T631). The rules presently under consideration are the Regulative Rules of the Understanding.

We have already accounted for the generalizing propensity of imagination under the influence of vivacity, resemblance and habit. We have learned that it is not always unreasonable to argue from analogy. We believe that an event will occur when given the appropriate impression and continue to believe that the same event will occur, though not with full force, when given a resembling instance of that impression. The force of belief reasonably follows the extent of resemblance. But we recall that some analogical inference does result in false as well as unreasonable belief. We have seen that imaginative supplementation extends the scope of a belief on occasions where the force of belief exceeds the degree to which a present impression resembles a member of a past regularity. We believe that an event will occur with a greater force of expectation than what the present impression warrants. Instances were erroneously kept within the scope of a causal rule simply because of the resemblance that held between the instance presently given and instances which formed the rule. We found that the resemblance which held between instance and rule held between the non-causal features of the cause. And since belief arose only from causation, Hume laid down the imperative that only the causal features of a cause ought to determine belief. The supplemental activities of imagination will require correction if unphilosophical beliefs are to be restored to a reasonable foundation of belief (T143).

Kemp Smith has noted that the following passage was "calculated to bewilder"[21] the reader.

> The belief or assent, which always attends the memory and senses, is nothing but the vivacity of those perceptions they present; and that this alone distinguishes them from the imagination. To believe is in this case to feel an immediate impression of the senses, or a repetition of that impression in the memory. 'Tis merely the force and liveliness of the perception, which constitutes the first act of judgment, and lays the foundation of that reasoning, which we build upon it, when we trace the relation of cause and effect (T86).

So far from intentionally obscuring the passage, Hume offers an explicit statement which further drives the wedge between the primacy of sensation and the legitimacy of judgment. The initial response to an enlivened perception determines the "first act of judgment." The first judgment "lays the foundation" for causal reasoning, but does not constitute its entire structure. Hume later repeats the claim.

> I suppose, there is some question propos'd to me, and that after revolving over the impressions of my memory and senses, and carrying my

thoughts from them to such objects, as are commonly conjoin'd with them, I feel a stronger and more forcible conception on the one side than the other. This strong conception forms my first decision (T184).

The first judgment, although determined by vivacity, does not determine the final judgment. We will see that Hume is far from clear in determining whether the final word is spoken by imagination or understanding, by Rules of Type *I* or Rules of Type *U*. For the present we are told that the initial judgment is not the final judgment. The following prescriptive principle is now set forth.

> In every judgment, which we can form concerning probability, as well as concerning knowledge, we ought always to correct the first judgment, deriv'd from the nature of the object, by another judgment, derived from the nature of the understanding (T182).

Realizing that our beliefs sometimes turn out false, we impose a "check or controul" on our first judgment. "Here then arises a new species of probability to correct and regulate the first, and fix its just standard and proportion" (T182). The general rules which regulate the initial heightened response *should* regulate causal reasoning. These rules are prescriptive, evaluative and normative for the interpretation of immediate experience and are not mere propensities triggered by sensation. "These rules are form'd on the nature of our understanding, and on our experience of its operations in the judgments we form concerning objects" (T149). By thus imposing a control on initial causal inferences, a standard is formed which corrects and thereby restores the propensities of imagination to "reasonable foundations of belief" (T143).

Clearly for Hume, the Regulative Rules, while fixing the standard of belief, can have none other but an empirical origin. The "Logic" which governs the rules of causal inference are founded on our experience of causal reasoning (T175). By reflecting on causal reasoning itself, those features of causes which are causal are distinguished from those which are not. The process is one of straightforward experiment and observation. "In order to arrive at the decisive point, we must carefully separate whatever is superfluous, and enquire by new experiments, if every particular circumstance of the first experiment was essential to it" (T175). The general rule for causal inference is itself an inductive generalization. "When we find that an effect can be produc'd without the concurrence of any particular circumstance, we conclude that that circumstance makes not a part of the efficacious cause, however frequently conjoin'd with it" (T149). When Hume claims that the second sort of rule "implies the condemnation" of the first, the implication is clearly not one of logic. Hume never calls into question his thesis that beliefs cannot be demonstrated a priori. Although Hume sometimes calls the rules of causal inference "rules of logic" (T175), they ultimately rest on the "natural principles of understanding." By "natural principles," Hume has in mind straightforward observation and experiment, "experimental philosophy," which he contrasts with purely logical rules (T175). Sometimes Hume entirely collapses the distinction between understanding and imagination. The understanding is simply "the general and more establish'd properties of the imagination" (T267), as opposed to those principles of imagination that are "changeable, weak and irregular" (T225). "Nor is there any difference betwixt that judgment, which is deriv'd from a constant and uniform connexion of causes and effects, and that which depends upon an interrupted and uncertain" (T154). Hume is clearly intent on distinguishing reasonable from unreasonable belief on empirical grounds (T143).[22]

Both *I* and *U* Rules, then, stem from the same principles which underlie all causal inference, namely, habit and experience (T147). But it was habit and experience which first drove the imagination to unwelcome propensities. It would now follow that the Regulative Rules are subject to the same propensities which they are supposed to control. "These new experiments are liable to a discussion of the same kind" (T175). We recall that the belief that a certain feature of a cause is contingent was supposed to reduce the force of the earlier belief that it was causal. But the initial reaction to infer from an enlivened idea made us believe "in spite of the opposite conclusion from general rules." It is not immediately obvious, therefore, why Kemp Smith feels confident in asserting that on Hume's final view "custom is far from being king."[23] Hume will come to admit that the initial judgment, the original and immediate compulsion to infer from a vivid perception, cannot be destroyed by "mere ideas and reflection" (T184). It would seem that the Regulative Rules are not "clearly"[24] in possession of all that sovereign power which kings usually bear to their subjects.

The discussion will terminate at a point of complete scepticism. Reason is uncontrollably led into unreasonable belief under the influence of the principles of custom and resemblance and is then "sav'd by a new direction" of the same principles. The sceptic notes the contradiction in our reason.

> The following of general rules is a very unphilosophical species of probability; and yet 'tis only by following them that we can correct this, and all other unphilosophical probabilities (T150).

To rely on a propensity of imagination which extends our causal rules beyond the instances which first established them is unreasonable and is a potential source of error. So we should not rely on general rules of Type *I*. But this conclusion from a Rule of Type *U* may be yet another instance of yielding to this propensity. The corrective judgment remains prone to the same propensity which it ought to correct. So we are driven to reject general rules by the same propensity which compels us to accept them.[25]

According to Kemp Smith's reading, on Hume's final analysis "custom is far from being king," while Passmore is convinced that "psychology triumphs."[26] At this point, we need to examine the way both sorts of rules behave when they come into contact. We need a clear account of the notions of "correction" and subsequent "opposition" before Hume's view can be determined.

## THE CONFLICT OF GENERAL RULES

According to his usual procedure, we can expect that Hume will offer a constructive reply to his argument from skepticism. Hume was at least clear in expressing his intention to distinguish an "irregular" kind of reasoning, a "capricious and uncertain" reasoning, from the "constant" and "authentic" operations of understanding (T149). Commentators are in general agreement that Hume did not succeed in drawing the distinction which he thought so urgent to draw.[1] This is in part due to their having downplayed his positive response to the skepticism concerning inductive reason. We must now determine for ourselves if, and by what means, Hume satisfied his intention.

The analogical inference rests on a conglomeration of features among causes, some of which are required to produce the effect while others are "conjoined by accident" (T148). In its unphilosophical moments, a causal inference is drawn on the basis of evidence *believed* to be noncausal. Rules of Type *I* are characterized by a persistent adherence to them. A causal rule is established on the basis of observed regularities and is then applied to instances which do not fall under the rule. An inference is drawn as if this instance exactly corresponded to the instances which first gave rise to the rule. No doubt, imaginative supplementation is responsible for the belief that this instance resembles past instances to a greater extent than it does. According to Hume, habits have a way of preserving themselves under conditions which have changed. Once habits take hold, they are not easily driven away. The "galley" continues on its course "without any new impulse" (T198) and even against an opposite impulse, under conditions which have radically altered. "A person, that has lost a leg or an arm by amputation, endeavors for a long time afterwards to serve himself with them" (T117). Beliefs such as this are now to be placed in the service of understanding which will function to regulate the proper scope of our beliefs (T293). What stands in need of correction is the tendency to infer causes or effects under the enlivening influence of resemblance, contiguity and constant conjunction. Although Hume allows that the relations of resemblance and contiguity may enliven ideas, they can do so only when the resembling or contiguous object is also a cause. Belief in matters of fact arises only from the causal relation (T107). The transition of thought from an impression to an idea of an object that simply resembles or lies in close proximity to the impression is "arbitrary" unless it is believed that the resembling or contiguous object exists. "And indeed such a fiction is founded on so little reason, that nothing but pure caprice can determine the mind to form it" (T109). Hume would have us reject the influence of caprice as "destructive of all the most establish'd principles of reasoning" (T150). The general rule is set forth that no reliance is to be placed on "those momentary glimpses of light" that resemblance and contiguity occasion (T110).

The initial "agitation" of vivacity, the "momentary glimpse of light," are now sharply contrasted with a "proper" light, a "serious conviction." The Regulative Rules ought to control capricious judgments despite the fact that caprice cannot be silenced. The former "implies the condemnation" of the latter. Wise men are guided by the first, the vulgar by the second (T150). The moralist will soon face the same conflict which here confronts the scientist. If Hume sticks to his claim "that our reasonings concerning morals will corroborate whatever has been said concerning the understanding," the virtuous, alike, will be guided by genuine judgments of understanding, while the vicious will follow the capricious judgments of imagination.[2]

What started out as a theory of belief resting on the principle "all reasonings are nothing but the effects of custom; and custom has no influence, but by enlivening the imagination," ends up as a theory of what ought to be believed if our beliefs are to be reasonable, which rests on "almost the same foundation of custom and repetition" (T117). Judgment and imagination rest on "almost the same foundation … They are somewhat of the same kind" (T632). But *I* inferences "feel very different" from *U* inferences, and the difference in their feeling is not analyzable only in terms of vivacity.

> But however great soever the pitch may be, to which this vivacity rises … it never has the same feeling with that which arises in the mind when we reason, tho' even upon the lowest species of probability (T630).

The genuine feeling of belief is a "peculiar kind" of feeling, clearly explicable in terms of vivacity, but a vivacity characterized by reflective thinking.

The inference from understanding imposes a check on the inference from imagination. Thought is supposed to control sensation (T184). The understanding reasons causally about the reasoning involved in a causal inference, and by an act of reflection "the nature of our understanding, and our reasoning from the first probability become our objects" (T182). The perception from which the initial inference was drawn is now to be scrutinized. The "circumstances" of causes are empirically tested for causal features, and the features of causes are distinguished into causal and contingent features.

> We must carefully separate whatever is superfluous, and enquire by new experiments, if every particular circumstance of the first experiment was essential to it (T175).

Two habits are thus formed, one from the causal and one from the contingent features of a cause. We have learned that contiguity and constant conjunction hold between superfluous and essential features. It is believed that no causal relation holds between them and the causal features of a cause. Given the contingent perception, the inference is drawn to the belief that the effect is produced without the assistance of the contingent features (T149). The previous inference from contingencies was only an apparent inference, triggered by the vivacity which the relations of contiguity and constant conjunction occasion. But contiguity, like resemblance, cannot enliven an idea unless it is believed that the contiguous or resembling object exists.

> The influence of the picture supposes, that we believe our friend to have once existed. Contiguity to home can never excite our ideas of home, unless we believe that it really exists (EU52).

Having thus separated contingent from causal features, the inference is drawn to the effect from its "true and proper" cause (T629). Some parts of the perception are believed to be associated only by contiguity and regularity with other parts of the perception. The transitional reaction from the contingent part of a perception to its causal neighbor, and from there to the effect, is kept distinct from the inference to an "authentic" belief from the causal features of a cause. There is, Hume says, "a great difference in their feeling." "The vigour of conception ... is a circumstance merely accidental, of which every idea is equally susceptible; and that such fictions are connected with nothing that is real" (T631). By the employment of Regulative Rules, then, the unique feeling of belief does not vary in strength according to every increase or reduction in vivacity. Beliefs are rendered "stable," "reasonable," and restored to their "proper bounds."

> Where an opinion admits of no doubt, or opposite probability, we attribute to it a full conviction; though the want of resemblance, or contiguity, may render its force inferior to that of other opinions. 'Tis thus the understanding corrects the appearance of the senses (T632).

Hume's optimism soon takes a turn for the worse. Two arguments are advanced which threaten to overthrow the "laws" prescribed by the Regulative Rules. The first source of trouble is the mechanical response occasioned by resemblance, contiguity and regularity. The firmly established belief that two opposite causes resemble one another by their contingent features does not thereby cut off the transition from the perception of one set of contingencies to the thought of the opposite cause, and onward to its effect. Although it is believed that resemblance, constant conjunction and contiguity are the only principles of association at work, the transition is made to the opposite effect from the opposite cause. It is for this reason that we come to confuse two opposite causes and take a supporting surface for the removal of support and, thus, to the belief in our descent. The transition from one contingency to its resemblant, which in turn is contiguous with the opposite cause, has an "uncontroulable" influence on the imagination (T183).

> But as this frequent conjunction necessarily makes it have some effect on the imagination, in spite of the opposite conclusion from general rules, the opposition of these two principles produces a contrariety in our thoughts, and causes us to ascribe the one inference to our judgment, and the other to our imagination. The general rule is attributed to our judgment; as being more extensive and constant. The exception to the imagination; as being more capricious and uncertain (T149).

The truly wise scientist opts for regularity, and should so opt, if his most cherished laws are not to be usurped by the "irregular" inferences of imagination.[3] But the "mechanical tendency" to infer given every and any twitch of vivacity, writes Hume, does not "readily follow the determination of our judgment" (T583, EU54). The kind of probability Hume is concerned with, the inference from *I* Rules, easily tempts the unphilosophical – "all of us, at one time or another" – into unreasonable belief (T205). The wise philosopher, no less than the rest of mankind, always remains subject to the unphilosophical inference. "General rules create a species of probability, which sometimes influences the judgment, and always the imagination" (T585). Rules of Type *I* "always" influence the imagination. The perception which sets off the propensity to infer unphilosophically continues to exert its enlivening influence even when belief is withheld according to a Regulative Rule.[4]

According to the general theory, the strength of belief is coordinate with the vivacity of a present impression. For example, the belief inferred from a present impression loses in force as the impression becomes remote in time and is thus faintly remembered. But philosophers agree that it is unreasonable to establish a standard of belief according to the time at which beliefs are established, "because in that case an argument must have a different force today, than what it shall have a month hence" (T143). But whatever philosophers may say, "this circumstance has a considerable influence on the understanding, and secretly changes the authority of the same argument, according to the different times, in which it is propos'd to us" (T143). The Rules which are supposed to regulate the immediacy of sensation, then, are in constant danger of being overthrown by the insinuations of imagination.

Hume's first attack on the so-called "laws" of understanding is guided by a moderate scepticism. The opposition of imagination and judgment produces a "contrariety" between different and even opposite beliefs. "Sometimes the one, sometimes the other prevails" (T150). The belief of imagination may become so enlivened as to "secretly" overthrow the most reasonable judgment. In the second attack on the Regulative Rules, Hume unleashes a thoroughgoing scepticism.[5] He was prepared to call the habit formed from the essential features of a cause an "authentic" habit, one based on regularity in contrast to the irregular and capricious habit generated from contingencies. Now he proceeds to attack the authentic/capricious distinction by an argument from the "natural fallibility" of judgment (T183).

By reasoning causally about causal reasoning, we conclude that sometimes our beliefs turn out false. The immediate and unreflective tendency to infer, excited by a perception which has not yet been distinguished into causal and contingent features, determines the first belief. But we have seen that the initial response to unscrutinized perceptions often results in false belief. Therefore, we cannot rely uncritically on initial judgments.

> We must, therefore, in every reasoning form a new judgment ... deriv'd from the nature of the understanding ... as a check or controul on our first judgment ... deriv'd from the nature of the object (T180, 183).

We begin to sort out the causal from the contingent features of a cause, and infer the effect from one but not from the other. Any feeling of heightened vivacity from the contingent features is kept distinct from the genuine judgment. But it is also believed that the judgments of understanding, no less than the responses of sensation, sometimes turn out false. The second reflective judgment is then made, which is supposed to accomplish what the first reflection should have accomplished, namely, establish a "just standard" of belief.

> I suppose, that afterwards I examine my judgment itself, and observing from experience, that 'tis sometimes just and sometimes erroneous, I consider it as regulated by contrary principles or causes, of which some lead to truth, and some to error (T184).

The belief that our powers of discrimination are not infallible calls into question the reliability of the evidence for the second judgment which, it is now realized, only might have hit upon the truly causal features of a cause. It would again follow that we cannot rely uncritically on second judgments.

Generally, the belief in the fallibility of a judgment is the outcome of subsequent reflection. The belief that inferences from non-scrutinized causes are sometimes false arises only after the features of a cause have been scrutinized, and the belief that our scrutiny is not perfectly scrupulous follows from an inspection of our powers of discrimination. The conclusion of every new reflective judgment is evidence for the belief that prior judgments are inferred from unreliable evidence, "and so on in infinitum" (T182).

The reasonable man of science, the "wise men", in their attempt to ground belief by appealing to reflection, correction and general rules, must inevitably be reduced to utter scepticism.

> Let our first belief be never so strong, it must infallibly perish by passing through so many new examinations, of which each diminishes somewhat of its force and vigour ... and when I proceed still farther, to turn the scrutiny against every successive estimation I make of my faculties, all the rules of logic require a continual diminution, and at last a total extinction of belief and evidence (T183).

The argument from scepticism removes the claim to a genuine standard of belief which could function to correct the tendency to infer from any enlivened perception. Corrective judgments are no less immune from error than the judgments they are supposed to correct. Each reflective judgment cuts a share of vivacity from the preceding judgment, according to the conclusion that the reflective judgment itself rests on questionable evidence. The understanding, for all its claim to a regulative capacity, "entirely subverts itself, and leaves not the lowest degree of evidence in any proposition, either in philosophy or common life" (T267).[6]

All general rules, the rules of "logic" together with the rules of "prejudice," philosophical and ordinary rules alike, collapse into a "total suspense of judgment" (T184). According to Hume, the argument from scepticism is a proof for the eventual collapse of all belief. But Hume points out that although the sceptic does not commit any error in his arguments, no one is really convinced by them, not even the sceptic. Why is it, then, that we do not believe the "unavoidable" argument that establishes the groundlessness of belief?

Hume at once dismisses the philosophical refutation of scepticism.

> If the sceptical reasonings be strong, say they, 'tis a proof, that reason may have some force and authority: if weak, they can never be sufficient to invalidate all the conclusions of our understanding (T186).

Those who advance this argument have not fully appreciated the dynamics of the controversy. The sceptic holds the same weapon over the authority of reason as that which gives reason its authority over scepticism. Both remain equally prone to each other's attack (T187).

We recall that the first argument from scepticism resulted in the belief that the indiscriminate tendency to infer given any sense stimulus is a potential source of false belief. Therefore, we should not rely uncritically on immediate judgments. A conclusion of reason, however, supplied the sceptic with evidence in support of his claim when he inferred that some features of a cause are productive while others are there just for the ride. Hume's point is that the force of the sceptical argument can only be as strong as a conclusion of reason which, by the next reflection, will reduce the force of that conclusion. The sceptic can only be silenced when reason has entirely lost its authority, "till at last they both vanish away into nothing, by a regular and just diminution" (T187). The philosophical refutation of scepticism cannot be maintained. Reason and scepticism have correspondingly forceful and weak arguments "according to the successive dispositions of the mind" (T186). Both are destroyed simultaneously. "And as their forces were at first equal, they still continue so, as long as either of them subsists" (T187). The philosopher is unable to explain how it comes about that we retain any degree of belief at all. The only solution lies within the province of human nature.

The sceptic, in his attempt to reduce the reliability of judgments by an act of reflection, will be unable to withstand the continual loss of conviction with every argument he delivers. Hume is concerned to show that nature guards us from the excessive doubt which follows from incessant acts of reflection. We are kept from believing the argument from scepticism not by a philosophical argument, but by an insignificant characteristic of imagination which makes it difficult for us to enter into the sceptical reasonings, and so puts an end to our reflections very early on (T265). That the sceptic must enter into remote and complicated arguments in order to prove "the imbecility of reason" is just what keeps him from believing those arguments.

Hume settles the matter by appealing to the original source of trouble, the principle of vivacity, by which some ideas simply come to be more enlivened than others.

> After the first and second decision, as the action of the mind becomes forc'd and unnatural, and the ideas faint and obscure; tho' the principles of judgment and the ballancing of opposite causes be the same as at the very beginning; yet their influence on the imagination, and the vigour they add to, or diminish from the thought, is by no means equal (T185).

The arguments of the sceptic become less believable according to the mental effort required to enter into them. As we proceed to the estimation of causes, and to the judgments about our estimations, and so on, each successive conclusion becomes less vivid. The overstrained thought of the sceptic results in diminishing returns of belief.

Hume thus tells us that beliefs vary in strength according to the mental effort required to infer them. The crux of the argument lies with the claim that while the "principles of judgment" are the same in every reflective judgment, each belief becomes less vivid with every new reflection. The judgment that we sometimes fail to properly discriminate the features of a cause rests on the same principles of experience and habit as does the judgment that not all features of causes are causal features (T265). The judgment that $P$ is a causal feature of $A$ is weakened once it is learned that we sometimes fail to properly discriminate the features of a cause. But since the reflective judgment requires a greater effort of thought than the immediate judgment, the belief that $P$ is a causal feature of $A$ regains the vivacity it had lost. Less reliance is placed on inferences from unscrutinized causes according to the judgment that not all features of causes are causal. But the reliance we place on the indiscriminate conclusion is restored to its initial strength simply because the reflective judgment involved a greater effort of thought than the immediate judgment (T183).

The mechanical tendency to infer from immediate sensation, what first stood in need of correction, is just what protects reason from complete refutation. Our very unreasonableness keeps us from believing the arguments of the sceptic. Were it not for the fact that "belief is more properly an act of the sensitive, than of the cogitative part of our natures," the sceptical argument would destroy all reason and belief (T183).

In his refutation of scepticism, Hume is aware of the tension which results from his return to the spontaneous response theory of belief. It was just this theory which explained unreasonable inference, the inference from resembling instances of causes which differed from them in "efficacious circumstances" (T150). Rules of Type $U$ were then formulated in order to control our spontaneous responses. They were supposed to check the propensity to vary the strength of belief with every variation in vivacity. To believe $P$ rather than not $P$ was not, after all, equivalent to having a more vivid idea of $P$.[7] A man of wisdom "proportions his belief to the evidence" (EU110), not according to the "vigour" by which the evidence is thought. We hence come to believe as we ought rather than as we must.

But the view that "custom is far from being king,"[8] that reflective thinking reigns over the immediate claims of habitual response, cannot be long sustained. A strict adherence to Rules of Type $U$ involves a continuous series of reflective judgments, where each reflection takes a share of vivacity from both the preceding judgment and itself. The more distant and abstruse our reasoning becomes, the less we believe its conclusions (T185). More immediate judgments are simply more vivid than those mediated by other judgments. And this, Hume believes, has "fatal consequences."

> The understanding, when it acts alone, and according to its most general principles, entirely subverts itself, and leaves not the lowest degree of evidence in any proposition (T267).

So it would seem, after all, that the unreasonable inference circumvents total scepticism. The propensity to infer given a healthy dose of vivacity cannot be destroyed by reflections and remote ideas. Profound reasoning simply involves too great an effort of thought (T185,270).

> Without this quality, by which the mind enlivens some ideas, beyond others (which seemingly is so trivial, and so little founded on reason) we cou'd never assent to any argument, nor carry our view beyond those few objects, which are present to our senses (T265).

In the end, then, in order to preserve causal reasoning, the general rules of imagination have usurped the authority of the Regulative Rules.

But Hume is not in the least satisfied with the view that psychology triumphs over empirical reasoning.[9] Would it follow that a general rule should be established that forbids us to enter into complicated reasoning?

> By this means you cut off all science and philosophy ... Very refin'd reflections have little or no influence upon us; and yet we do not, and cannot establish it for a rule, that they ought not to have any influence (T268).

Hume finds himself involved in a dilemma. Should we accept the Regulative Rules or the "illusions" of imagination?

> If we embrace this principle, and condemn all refin'd reasoning, we run into the most manifest absurdities. If we reject it in favour of these reasonings, we subvert entirely the human understanding. We have, therefore, no choice left but betwixt a false reason and none at all (T268).

The solution to the problem of the justification of belief vanishes as unanswerable. At times Hume claims that we are determined by the propensities of imagination to believe as we must, and establishes the rule that "where reason is lively, and mixes itself with some propensity, it ought to be assented to." But Hume would also remind us that the inclination to reflect on our causal rules is no less a natural propensity than the inclination to extend them beyond their range of application (T274).

Hume is motivated by curiosity, or the passion for truth, and cannot help but enter into remote reflections which the Regulative Rules require. While reflective thinking is characterized by increasingly less vivid beliefs according to the extent of the reflection and the effort of thought involved, the mental exertion needed to infer a belief, mediated by a long chain of other beliefs, Hume later writes, is "the principle source of that satisfaction we receive from the sciences" (T449). Exercising the understanding is what gives pleasure to the most painstaking reflections (T449).

Hume is thus unable to "defend his reason by reason" (T187). He makes no claim to a justification of the Regulative Rules on any reasonable grounds. Whether one is guided by *I* Rules or *U* Rules depends on "the disposition and the character of the person … The vulgar are commonly guided by the first, and wise men by the second" (T150). But who, after all, are the wise? Hume can only "make bold" to recommend the philosophical rules, Rules of Type *U*, over the unphilosophical Rules of Type *I*. This is the "proper" choice and one which we "ought to prefer" (T271).

We recall that on Kemp Smith's reading, reflective thinking reigns over the immediate claims of custom, while Passmore concluded that psychology prevails over causal reasoning. We have seen that a good deal of text can be cited in support of both positions. But to come down exclusively on either side is to ignore Hume's intention at the close of Book I to establish the ongoing dialectic of reason and passion. Hume does not decide, once and for all, which rule ought to be followed. He will not later come prepared to readdress the issue with a knock-down argument in favor of one sort of general rule over the other. Very simply, "sometimes the one, sometimes the other prevails … according to the general character or present disposition of the person" (T150,418,585). Cures, but no solutions, will be found along the way, in particular instances and at particular turns, in man's social development (T269,273). We have already seen that some of the rules of property are established by the "frivolous properties" of imagination. Other rules will be similarly established, while others still will come about in a more judicious manner. We will need to examine, therefore, the circumstances under which one sort of general rule takes precedence over the other in determining passion, action and morals.

PART TWO

# Hume's Analysis of Sympathy

No account of Hume's theory of the passions or his moral theory can be adequate without paying close attention to his doctrine of sympathy. Within the "science of Man," Hume considers sympathy to be the most potent propensity (T316). From the outset of Book II to the conclusion of Book III, sympathy plays a fundamental role in the generation of the passions and the moral sentiment. "Sympathy" does not simply mean pity or compassion, as modern usage of the term might suggest, and is not confined to circumstances which involve suffering.[1] It is rather to be thought of as a tendency to share what one believes to be the feelings of others, whatever those feelings happen to be (T358).

The theory of the double association of impressions and ideas lies at the heart of Book II. From a twofold association whereby "ideas are associated by resemblance, contiguity, and causation, and impressions only by resemblance," the "indirect" passions arise: pride and humility, love and hatred (T283). But Hume soon insists that while the double relation is necessary, it is not sufficient to produce the indirect passions (T287,292). The pleasure we receive from our fine possessions cannot be a lasting pleasure unless "seconded" by the opinions of others (T316,349). The rich, for example, in addition to the initial pleasure of pride they receive from their possessions, receive also a "secondary satisfaction" by sympathizing with people who sympathize with them. The spectator's love or esteem for the rich is likewise explained by an initial sympathy with the pleasure of the possessor and, by a "second reflexion," a sympathy with the possessor's sympathetic pleasure (T365). Hume makes the point that this secondary satisfaction is really of primary importance for the arousal of the indirect passions. He now claims that sympathy, the "communication of senti-

66

ments," is a necessary condition for the production of all the passions (T363). The point is forcefully made.

> A perfect solitude is, perhaps, the greatest punishment we can suffer. Every pleasure languishes when enjoy'd a-part from company, and every pain becomes more cruel and intolerable. Whatever other passions we may be actuated by; pride, ambition, avarice, curiosity, revenge or lust; the soul or animating principle of them all is sympathy; nor wou'd they have any force, were we to abstract entirely from the thoughts and sentiments of others (T363).

Hume's account of moral evaluation also stresses the doctrine of sympathy. When it operates by itself, sympathy has enough force to produce "the strongest sentiments of approbation" (T618). The remark is soon qualified. Hume allows that sympathy is the "chief source" of moral distinctions, the source from which the artificial and natural virtues derive their merit (T578). Hume's meaning is that sympathy is the governing factor in moral evaluation, but that when it functions by itself it is unable to provide impartial moral judgments, nor can it bring about a wide range of moral agreement (T591).

We recall that the initial sympathetic judgment is governed by propensities which are triggered under conditions thought to have no moral relevance. We sympathize more with persons close to us in space or time than with those placed at a distance simply because of a tendency to pass easily from distant to near objects but with difficulty from objects close at hand to those remotely placed (T342). Our sympathy is more intense when directed towards persons related to us, especially by blood,[2] than with strangers, and more with persons who further our interest than with those from whom we expect nothing. Nevertheless, the same qualities of character are given the same judgment regardless of their tendency to our benefit and irrespective of their spatio-temporal location. It is due to the discrepancy between the immediate sympathetic judgment made from a changeable point of view and the corrected sympathetic judgment made from a stable point of view, that Hume takes sympathy to be the primary principle of morality, not the only principle. He states that sympathy is a "powerful" factor in moral evaluation but recognizes that it is insufficient to reconcile contradictory judgments among persons who are differently situated with respect to the object of evaluation (T581,602). We will see that sympathy, in conjunction with general rules, meets the conditions for the judgment of an impartial spectator (T581,563).

In Book II, general rules continue to play a prominent role in fixing the value of the passions (T294). In Book III, they "guide us" in the development of the artifices, correct partial viewpoints by reflection, and establish a standard by which we approve or disapprove of character traits. (T603). Early in Book II the reader is told that he will hear a good deal more about general rules (T293).

Thomas Hearn's account of general rules[3] attributes to the regulative rules, the reasonable rules of understanding, unchallenged precedence over the inauthentic rules of imagination – the rules which tend to unify experience beyond the given (T198), embrace instances not falling under them (T148), postulate fictitious particulars (T205) and relations (T237) and generally strengthen unions wherever they are found. The supplemental activities of imagination are really the expressions of a more general principle. "The mind moves in whatever direction will bring it most ease."[4] This is in keeping with Hume's claim that we are guarded from scepticism by an insignificant operation of imagination which makes it difficult to believe inferences arrived at by a strong mental effort. Hume is aware that we do not always judge as we ought though we sometimes speak as if we did (T582). It is not surprising, therefore, that in the development of the artifices and in the correction of immediate sympathy, imagination and understanding often conflict, and it is not unusual to find that a good deal of moral output is fed by unreasonable input.

What makes Hume's moral theory interesting is that we cannot conclude from the concession that "our passions do not readily follow the determination of our judgment" that the unreasonable rules of imagination do not have a vital role to play in the development of the artifices and impartial moral judgment. It is only because of a tendency to extend causal rules that chastity is morally required of women even after the age of child-bearing. Hume would say that the obligation to fidelity is unreasonably extended to "their extremest old age and infirmity" (T573). Character traits continue to be judged virtuous or vicious "even tho' some external circumstances be wanting to render [them] altogether effectual" (T584). It is only because of a tendency to *persist* in making the transition from a cause to its effect, in light of the belief that the cause is incomplete, that "virtue in rags is still virtue" (T584). In order to keep sight of the ongoing conflict of reason and passion, it is important to recognize that a good deal of moral development results from the unreasonable side of human nature.

Hume's overall theory of moral judgment involves a number of interlocking theories. The theory of belief, the indirect passions and the theory of sympathy are centrally located within Hume's moral system. Although Hume presents each theory completely and independently of the others, by the time we arrive at his treatment of moral judgment in Book III, all are presupposed and all come together to form one unified theory of moral evaluation. If we want to appreciate what it means for Hume's impartial spectator to adopt the moral point of view, it is important to recognize the function of belief in sympathy and the function of sympathy for the arousal of the indirect passions.

In clarifying Hume's ideas about moral judgment, the theory of belief and general rules must be retained. The principles of association which enter into the theory of sympathy confirm the theory of belief (T319). Hume's comments near the end of Book III about "steady and general points of view," achieved by reflection and "general rules of morality," send the reader to Book I where the theory of belief and general rules is given its full introduction. To omit from the account Hume's work on belief and causal inference would be to ignore Hume's intention to show that general rules determine whether the sympathetic judgment turns out to be partial or impartial (T583). The influence of general rules on the judgment of fact in Book I is extended to the judgment of merit in Book III. The same tendencies of imagination which were responsible for prejudice in our beliefs are again responsible for partiality in our moral evaluations (T149,488). Both should be corrected, Hume tells us in Book III, by "that reason, which is able to oppose our passion," that is, by general rules of understanding (T583).

Book II presents the theory of the "double relation of impressions and ideas," a process of association which explains the four indirect passions (T283). Pride, love, humility and hatred are the "unavoidable attendants" of the moral sentiment (T296). In Hume's explanation of the indirect passions sympathy plays a vital role, and in his explanation of the pleasure and pain which constitute approval and disapproval, there is an analogous reliance on sympathy. The indirect passions and the evaluation of character are repeatedly bracketed together in Hume's thought (T292,575,602). But it is not until the closing sections of Book III that Hume tells us that the unique impression of approval and disapproval is just a "calm" indirect passion (T614). We learn that the approving and disapproving sort of sentiment are impartial variants of the otherwise partial indirect passions. The difference in feeling between love and hatred and the evaluation of character is learned from reflection and general rules (T631).

Finally, in the "Conclusion" of Book III, Hume tells us that "sympathy is the chief source of moral distinctions." All the virtues derive their merit from sympathy. We would be indifferent to the pains and pleasures of others were it not for the tendency in human nature to "receive [them] by communication" (T317). By means of sympathy, people become interested in the good of mankind. It allows them to depart from their own concerns and grants them the capacity to have some concern for others (T578). But while sympathy is the source of disinterestedness, it does not guarantee impartiality. Changes in the intensity of communicated pains and pleasures vary the intensity of loves and hatreds. And these variations rest on the principles of association and the different "manner"[s] by which we conceive another's pains and pleasures. All these variations require stability if we are to "agree" on our evaluations. Here general rules will come into play. "We seek some other standard of merit and demerit, which may not admit of so great variation." The theory of belief and general rules in Book I, and the theories of the indirect passions and sympathy in Books II and III come together to form one coherent system of moral evaluation.

In the chapters to come, we will see that moral judgment involves a "peculiar manner" of conceiving the object of evaluation and a "peculiar kind" of pleasure or pain (T624,472). When the object of evaluation is not reasonably conceived, the unique pain or pleasure will not emerge. We will see that a reasonable conception only sometimes raises the pleasure or pain to that special kind which causes approval or disapproval. I argue that the "point of view" Hume discusses is one from which reasonable judgments are made according to the Regulative Rules of Understanding. Reflection will be required in order to stabilize changes in the intensity of the immediate sympathetic judgment. We will need to make allowance for the fact that nearness in space or time makes the heart grow fonder, and to ignore what our own set of interests and pleasures happen to be for the moment. Wherever qualities of character happen to be placed, or whoever has them or whenever they existed, is irrelevant to an impartial spectator.

But Hume's complete account of moral judgment will involve more than the simple view that general rules of understanding are determinative of impartial evaluation. We remind ourselves that reflective judgments are less vivid than initial ones. As a result they are less forcefully believed. Simple vivacity of conception will once again stake its claim against the genuine judgments of understanding. The conflict of general rules remains a conflict down through the closing pages of the *Treatise* (T587). Let us now turn our attention to the theory of sympathy in Hume's account of moral judgment.

# CHAPTER THREE

# Sympathy and Judgment

## THE SYMPATHY MECHANISM

In using the term "mechanism," I do not mean to imply that sympathy is exclusively an involuntary process over which we have no control.[1] While it is true that Hume's initial description of sympathy is explained in terms of a psychological mechanism – a propensity to infer a belief about the mental states of others from observing behavior which is typical of those of mental states, and an "instantaneous" conversion of this idea into an impression in accordance with the theory of relations and a vivid perception of self – the theory, as it stands, is incapable of coming to grips with the distinctly moral response which sympathy is supposed to occasion. To make allowance for the inherent limitations in the immediate sympathetic response, Hume leaves room in his theory for a stabilized and regulated sympathy, a sympathy which involves a "check or controul" (T180) on the first and frequently biased judgment, and which requires a "great effort of thought" in order to feel the particular pleasure or pain which characterizes the moral sentiment (T185,472). The sympathetic theory in its corrected moral form, therefore, as was the case with the theory of belief, is not properly described as a mechanical process which lies beyond our control.

The theory of sympathy is introduced in Book II, in the section entitled "Of the love of fame." Among the limitations Hume sets on pride, the third limitation requires that the "subject" cause of pride be "discernible and obvious" to others as well as to oneself (T292). For pride to be complete, it is necessary that we "share" the pleasure others reap from our own pleasure-giving possessions. In his attempt to provide an adequate account of how a passion like pride is generated, Hume calls upon sympathy and leaves little question as to the importance he attributes to the "communication of sentiments" (T363) between persons.

No quality of human nature is more remarkable both in itself and in its consequences, than that propensity we have to sympathize with others, and to receive by communication their inclinations and sentiments, however different from, or even contrary to our own (T316).

The essential points of Hume's explanation of sympathy in its simple, uncorrected form run as follows. The process of sympathizing has two stages, a cognitive and an affective stage. The first stage explains how we acquire the idea of another's passional state. The second stage involves the conversion of this idea into an impression, so that we come to feel the emotion we believe another is having. The first movement of sympathy is an inference to the existence of another's state of mind from "external signs" and "expressions" (T597), from the "countenance and conversation" given to us (T318). Unlike our own mental states, we do not have access to the mental states of others by direct inspection. We can only form beliefs about their causes or effects. "From these we infer the passion: and consequently these give rise to our sympathy" (T576). The idea of another's state of mind is conceived just as any other matter of fact is conceived (T319). From observing bodily gesture or modulation of voice, or from a simple report of a state of mind – the "effects" of passion – we are led to infer its cause and are thus informed, in idea, of the presence of a passion in another. We likewise infer a passion from its "causes," as when we come to have the idea of another's sorrow from his or her present misfortune (T576). Hume realizes that sympathy involves knowing and feeling. "A mere idea," even when a believed idea "wou'd never alone be able to affect us." It is necessary that a vivid idea be converted into its impression if the beliefs and passions of others are to become, "in some measure," our beliefs and passions (T319,593).

Stage two meets this provision wherein the idea of another's passion is transformed into an impression or the passion itself. One now experiences the emotion believed to belong to another. The process very much relies on the doctrine that ideas differ from impressions only in degree (T319).[2] So as to bring about the conversion, Hume freely appeals to the "idea, or rather impression" of self which is always present to the mind and is, by far, the most lively impression.[3] The impression of self is called upon in order to discharge its native vivacity, through the relations of resemblance, contiguity and causation, to the idea or belief of another's passion.

This idea is presently converted into an impression, and acquires such a degree of force and vivacity, as to become the very passion itself, and produce an equal emotion, as any original affection (317).

So in addition to the initial causal inference which satisfies the cognitive requirement of sympathizing, the relations of resemblance, contiguity and causation must hold between self and other if the affective requirement is to be satisfied, that is, "in order to feel the sympathy in its full perfection" (T320).

Hume clearly emphasizes the role played by the initial causal inference in the sympathy mechanism. "The relation of cause and effect alone may serve to strengthen and inliven an idea" (T32O).[4] Were it not for the causal inference, the conversion from idea to impression would never arise. Sympathy, writes Hume, "is exactly correspondent to the operations of our understanding" (T320). While it remains open for us to know the mental states of others without actually feeling them, we are closed off from feeling as others feel when we are ignorant of their mental states.[5]

Having briefly stated what it is, for Hume, to sympathize with our fellows, we will presently turn our attention to the role of believing in sympathizing. Hume has told us that belief involves a particular "manner" of conceiving ideas. He reduced the "manner" of belief to "force and vivacity," and then defined belief as a vivid idea associated with a present impression (T94–98). What we shall now consider is how the manner in which we conceive our ideas of the feelings and beliefs of others carries through to the manner in which we feel about those ideas. The way we come to experience the beliefs and passions of others is a direct result of the manner in which we conceive those beliefs and passions. It is important to recognize from the start that Hume's ideas about sympathy rely heavily upon his doctrine of belief. If we can accept this much, we will not be surprised to find that general rules will play a vital role in determining the reasonableness of our sympathy.

## SYMPATHY AND BELIEF

It is not until the closing sections of the *Treatise* that Hume squarely addresses and proposes a solution to the problem of how the theory of sympathy can overcome the natural bias inherent in the immediate sympathetic judgment. The factors which tend to disrupt the growth of a publicly shared and impartial morality are explicable in terms of Hume's associationist psychology. The first source of trouble lies in the way we acquire the beliefs and passions of others, namely, by straightforward causal inference. More often than not, inferences to another's state of mind are governed by propensities of imagination which, if left unchecked, result in judgments which are highly variable and from which little or no moral agreement can be expected (T581). Changes in the intensity of the immediate sympathetic response, the sort of changes Hume wishes to stabilize, are traceable to the inference from an impression to an idea. In what follows, I stress the importance of belief and the causal inference in the explanation of Hume's point of view theory of moral judgment. The theory of general rules will be seen to play the decisive role in the genesis and correction of judgments which are made from one's "peculiar point of view" (T581).

In Hume's initial statement of sympathy, ordinary causal inference grants us access to the beliefs and passions of others. It is important to recognize at the outset that the first, untutored sympathetic judgment is largely determined by the initial causal inference. The manner by which we conceive our ideas of the beliefs or passions of others will carry over to the way we feel about them, when, by the second stage, the idea is converted into an impression. The conversion involves a more heightened vivacity of an already enlivened idea or belief (T319).[1] Our beliefs about the feelings and beliefs of others might simply be false, or they might be governed by a propensity of imagination, or they might be corrected by the reasonable sort of general rule. But a belief does not become stronger, in that more evidence has been gathered for its support, simply by becoming more vivid. Nor does it become true, or unreasonable, or reasonable, by becoming more vivid. When we finally come to feel what we believe another is experiencing, the contents of our belief and feeling are exactly alike (T319). Furthermore, the manner in which we understand the content of our belief carries through to the manner in which we feel about that content. The causal inference in the first stage of sympathy is just an application of the general theory of belief. It follows that the pitfalls and remedies to which all our beliefs are subject are extended to our beliefs about the mental states of others.

From a person's behavior, words, or the way in which words are spoken, the inference is drawn to the state of mind associated with the expression.

> When any affection is infus'd by sympathy, it is at first known only by its effects, and by those external signs in the countenance and conversation, which convey an idea of it (T317).

At first sight, there would seem to be no difference between the inference to pain from grimaces and bodily contortions, and the inference to pain from the words of another who tells us he is in pain. In both cases, we receive the idea of another's pain (T317,576). Whether a person offers a report of anxiety in the course of conversation or shows "signs" of anxiety according to the tone of voice or gesture of body, in either case there is a causal relation between the report and the presence of a passion and the sign and the presence of a passion. It would seem that Hume is simply identifying[2] the "effects" of passion with the "signs" of passion. Yet he distinguishes voluntary from involuntary signs. We tend to believe involuntary signs to a greater extent than voluntary ones.[3] We might receive a detached report of pain, or hear the groans commonly associated with pain in the report, or simply hear the groans of pain. But, in all cases, the inference is drawn to the idea of pain, and this is the first step in sympathizing.

Should we accept the criticism that Hume denies the distinction between the causal relation and the relation between a sign and what it customarily signifies?[4] When observing a person trembling, we immediately infer that he is afraid in the same way that we infer that emotion from his report of fear. "Nothing is requir'd but the hearing of that word to produce the correspondent idea" (T93). According to the criticism, the *signs* of emotion are the words employed in the report, while the *effects* of emotion involve the expressive manner in which the report is delivered. Causal language and the language of signs are identified as a habitual transition of mind from one perception to another. Distinctions are needed which Hume cannot provide.

While it is not at once obvious what sort of distinctions the critic requires, it is clear that the objection fails to capture the richness of Hume's theory. Part of the trouble lies in the fact that discussions of Hume's views on sympathy commonly take their start from Book II, where the subject is given a full introduction. But the germs of the theory can be found in Book I within the context of the discussion on general rules. The first stage of sympathy is there clearly disclosed.

> Whether a person openly abuses me, or slyly intimates his contempt, in neither case do I immediately perceive his sentiment or opinion; and 'tis only by signs, that is, by its effects, I become sensible of it (T151).

According to the objection, it would appear that Hume is equivocating on the terms "signs" and "effects." Let us allow that Hume has *identified* the causal "transition,"[5] the transition from, say, the glow of pride, with the transition from the signs or words "I feel proud." Let us also allow that the manner of presentation is characteristic of causal language, while the verbal presentation itself, the nonemotive report, characterizes the language of signs. It would follow:

1. Of two different signs associated with the same emotion, the transition from one sign to its usual emotion exactly resembles the transition from the other sign to that emotion.
2. Of two different manners of presentation associated with the same

emotion, the transition from one mannerism to its usual emotion exactly resembles the transition from the other mannerism to that emotion.

3. Of a sign and a mannerism associated with the same emotion, the transition from the sign to its usual emotion exactly resembles the transition from the mannerisim to that emotion.

In all cases, Hume would allow that an *inference* is drawn to the idea of an emotion associated with various signs and mannerisms, but he would deny that the *transitions* from various signs and mannerisms to the idea of an emotion are alike.[6] A difference in the transitions from different signs or effects commonly associated with the same passion varies the manner in which ideas are thought.

Hume speaks of easy and difficult transitions of imagination and points out that while the relations of resemblance, contiguity and causation are logically symmetrical, the transitions from one idea to the other and back to the first are by no means psychologically symmetrical. In certain cases, the imagination "goes with facility, but returns with difficulty" (T356). Ideas are always more closely associated when the transitions from either one to the other are made with the same ease. But the transitions of imagination are governed by their own special propensities which greatly influence the way we think about ideas. In explaining why we do not love our sibling for the virtue we discover in ourselves, but feel proud of ourselves for the virtue we discover in our sibling, Hume points out that the transition from the idea of oneself to the idea of one's sibling is made with greater difficulty than the transition from one's sibling to oneself (T339). According to a general rule, the imagination makes the transition from dull to vivid ideas more easily than from vivid to dull ones, and more easily from remote to contiguous ideas than from contiguous to remote ideas (T342). Hume repeatedly states that the idea of self is the most vivid idea we can have (T317,339). We are always more conscious of our own beliefs and passions than the ideas we have of the beliefs and passions of others. We become immediately aware of our own feelings given the slightest relation we bear to other persons. Once a belief or passion is present to the mind, "it engages the attention, and keeps it from wandering to other objects ... while the relation of ideas, strictly speaking, continues the same."

> The passage is smooth and open from the consideration of any person related to us, to that of ourself, of whom we are every moment conscious. But when the affections are once directed to ourself, the fancy passes not with the same facility from that object to any other person, how closely so ever connected with us (T340).

Causal inferences and transitions of thought between resembling and contiguous objects are drawn in accordance with or in opposition to the natural propensities of imagination (T343). "In the one case the relation is aided by another principle: In the other case, 'tis oppos'd by it" (T339).

As it turns out, the critic identifies the *transition* with the *causal inference* and so collapses the distinction he claims Hume did not draw.[7] But had Hume drawn no such distinction, he would have been unable to account for the fact that the way we think about ideas varies according to the ease or difficulty with which transitions are made from various signs and mannerisms. The difference is to be explained in terms of general rules operating on two different levels.

> Everyone knows, there is an indirect manner of insinuating praise or blame, which is much less shocking than the open flattery or censure of any person (T150).

Hume first points out that whether another expresses his state of mind secretly or openly, we infer the same idea commonly associated with the expression. Given a more "conceal'd" manner of presentation, the idea we infer is no less understood than when our inference follows from an "open" presentation, though our manner of understanding the idea is not the same.

> One who lashes me with conceal'd strokes of satire, moves not my indignation to such a degree, as if he had flatly told me I was a fool and coxcomb; tho' I equally understand his meaning, as if he did (T150).

The open manner of presentation differs from the concealed intimation in that the former employs signs which are "general and universal," whereas the latter's signs are more "singular and uncommon." What follows is that the transition from signs more commonly employed is made more easily than the transition from "rare and particular" signs. Therefore, the ideas derived from common manners of presentation are thought with "greater force" than those derived from unusual presentations.

> The difference betwixt an idea produc'd by a general connexion, and that arising from a particular one is here compar'd to the difference betwixt an impression and an idea (T151).

The crux of the analysis lies with the claim that while both ideas are "equally assented to by the judgment," while both are "known with equal certainty," the idea inferred from the particular manner of presentation is less vivid and, consequently, less forcefully believed. Hume attributes this difference to general rules (T151).

When Hume claims that we "equally" assent to both ideas, his meaning cannot be construed in terms of belief, for he has just told us that one idea is conceived with "greater force" than the other. Nor can we take Hume's meaning literally when he asserts that ideas derived from indirect signs are "known with equal certainty" as those derived from direct manners of presentation. For our awareness of the mental states of others is not a claim to knowledge in the strict sense, arrived at demonstrably or apprehended immediately by intuition (T576). Throughout, Hume insists that we become cognizant of the states of others by reasoning from causes or effects. "From these we infer the passion" (T576).

Hume's meaning rests with his claim that the conceptual content of an idea is an inseparable aspect of its feeling quality. By a "distinction of reason," we recall (T25), content comes to be distinguished from sensation when we distinguish thought from feeling and admit them as inseparable but consider them apart (T24,493). We come to learn the difference between "the simple conception of the existence of an object, and the belief of it" (T94) and learn that the content of an idea is an exact representation of the content of its antecedent impression (T4,319). Therefore, the contents of ideas inferred from their unusual and usual manners of presentation are exactly resembling and are "equally" thought or understood, though the latter are believed as well.

What is noteworthy in the account is Hume's hidden assertion that it is unreasonable not to believe the insinuations we clearly understand, and that if we reflected for a moment, our ideas would be thought as they should be thought, with that "peculiar manner of conception" which characterizes the reasonable belief. However, this claim fits ill with the general thesis that we understand many ideas we do not believe, "that Caesar dy'd in his bed" and so forth, and to believe statements such as this would undoubtedly be unreasonable (T95). Hume points the way to the solution along the lines of general rules. How can the theory of rules explain that an indirect manner of presenting one's thoughts or feelings has a tendency to produce in a spectator a "less shocking" response than the response usually evoked given a more open and straightforward presentation?

The unreasonable inference was initially borne out of a basic drive to bring order into experience beyond given regularities. It was Hume's contention that unreflective beliefs are often sustained in light of other beliefs which detract from the original evidence. The initial response to make causal connections triggered by sheer vivacity of conception suffices for belief and, more often than not, holds its own against the reasonable, reflective judgment. Given an object that resembles a cause in noncausal features, the imagination springs to the idea of the effect usually conjoined with the cause. The mind is unwittingly led to the idea of the cause by the transitions prompted by resemblance and contiguity and so goes on to the idea of its usual associate. Of course, the believer only becomes aware of this sequence of moves after he has disentangled the causal from the noncausal features of a cause. That the initial belief persists in the face of reason is evidenced by the conflict that ensues between imagination and understanding. Hume remains hesitant throughout in deciding whether imagination or understanding ought to reign as the final court of appeal (T268).

How does the above account square with the differing influence overt and covert manners of presentation have on a spectator? The first and most obvious similarity is the difference Hume notes between "general" and "uncommon" signs, and "general" operations of understanding versus "irregular" operations of imagination. The former, in both cases, are more "constant," the latter, more "capricious and uncertain" (T149). A second similarity may be drawn from the claim that the signs employed in a hidden insinuation are "numerous, and decide little or nothing when alone and unaccompany'd with many minute circumstances." They are, nonetheless, sufficient for a spectator to understand the meaning of the insinuation, for otherwise, how is it that one "understand[s] ... as if" presented with the most open and avowed report? The various signs by which we understand the meaning of an insinuation may be likened to that "complication of circumstances" Hume speaks of which comprises the causal and noncausal features of a cause (T148). We recall that some of these are usually, though noncausally, conjoined with the causal features. Let us then say that the "superfluous" features characterize the words or mannerisms of a presentation that, when given by themselves, are not customarily associated with the belief or passion the speaker nevertheless conveys. With what, then, are the noncausal signs or mannerisms usually associated?

In the first account of rules, Hume allowed that the noncausal features, even when given in the absence of the causal features of a cause, still called to imagination a vivid idea of the effect associated with the cause (T148). The noncausal feature was there held to be in common with two opposite causes. The perception of depth occurred in observations of descending and supported bodies. Given the perception, whenever we were suspended from a tower in an iron cage, imagination inferred descent and understanding inferred support. What followed was the opposition of the fear of descent and the belief of support.

This is just how the noncausal constituents of signs or mannerisms function. The speaker commonly has the intention, by employing noncausal signs or mannerisms, to convey the opposite belief or passion from the one he actually has. We have often heard, "You're a very nice person. You have many shining qualities, but...", or the report of pain on a smiling face, or the still voice of intense anger. The perception of depth, however, is a noncausal feature of two opposite causes since the perception is neither the cause of support nor descent, while the noncausal constituents of an expression are *causally* associated with a different and sometimes opposite belief or passion from the one expressed by the causal constituents. What is "uncommon" is the conjunction of signs or mannerisms with certain states of mind that are commonly associated with different or opposite states of mind. Actually, the noncausal members of a manner of presentation can only be construed as noncausal when placed within the context of signs or mannerisms which are intended to convey an *authentic* idea or passion. For the same signs and mannerisms which are noncausal in one context are causal in another. From the context of signs which are in common usage, the quiet tone is noncausal with respect to rage but causal within the context of affection. The presence of noncausal signs within an expression makes the idea of the speaker's genuine passion or belief less vivid, and hence less believed, than the idea inferred from causal signs when presented by themselves. The more easily ideas are understood, the more forcefully they are believed.

> Any reasoning is always the more convincing, the more single and united it is to the eye, and the less exercise it gives to the imagination to collect all its parts, and run from them to the correlative idea, which forms the conclusion (T153).

The "parts" here comprise not one but two frequently opposing beliefs. The added effort of thought involved in discriminating the causal from the noncausal features of a presentation reduces the belief from the speaker's causal signs.

It was Hume's view that the effort of thought expended on ascertaining evidence always reduces the force of the evidence. Although inferences drawn from "particular" signs should be regulated by general rules of understanding founded on common usage, a presentation containing uncommon signs inevitably reduces the belief of another's genuine belief or passion. Hume thought that the tendency to settle one's beliefs according to the ease with which they are acquired is at once unreasonable yet inescapable and so felt quite confident in accounting for the "rules of good-breeding" according to that tendency.

> For if an idea were not more feeble, when only intimated, it wou'd never be esteemed a mark of greater respect to proceed in this method than in the other (T151).

We tend to condemn people who employ language that is openly offensive but are more willing to pardon those who, though they communicate the same idea, do so in a more implicit manner (T151).

In the section "Of greatness of mind," Hume explains why an excessive show of pride is always considered a vice and why we have a duty to avoid all signs and mannerisms which are overtly expressive of that passion (T597). For Hume, to conceal one's pride, even when justified, to resist all expressions of pride by direct manners of presentation, to "prefer others to ourselves" and to show them humility and deference ranks as the penultimate "natural" virtue, giving way only to benevolence and humanity (T605). Hume has us understand that the virtue of "conceal'd" pride relies on the unreasonable response of a spectator.[8] For were it not for the fact that an implicit manner of presenting pride reduces the force of the belief that another is proud, concealing one's pride by employing noncausal expressions would never have become a duty. If our inferences were invariably governed by the reasonable rules of understanding, it would make no difference to a spectator how or in what manner pride was presented. Any presentation, covert or overt, would always be judged vicious. It would, therefore, be pointless for Hume to found a duty to refrain from overt expressions of pride if neither overt nor covert expressions made any difference in the way we think about ideas. In explaining the virtue of proper pride, Hume relied on his conviction about human nature, that "so little are men govern'd by reason" (T372).

We have been discussing the influence of belief, causal inference and various transitions of thought on the sympathy of a spectator. We occupied ourselves with Hume's general theory of belief in order to become acquainted with some of the limitations of sympathy, limitations Hume thought stood in need of correction for the emergence of an impartial system of moral sentiments (T581). Some of the factors which threatened the stability Hume sought were found to rest on the principles of association and the various *manners* by which ideas were thought. Certain propensities of imagination which governed mental transitions determined the character of our sympathy. We saw that the inference from causes, effects or "signs" of a passion to the existence of the passion was, for Hume, a straightforward causal inference. The function of belief in the process of sympathizing was an application of the general theory of belief. So we were not surprised to find that the theory of general rules was applied to our beliefs about the mental states of others, and we saw that they had, as usual, their "mighty influence" on the way we sympathized with those states.

Hume thought it was unreasonable not to believe the insinuations we understand and prescribed that we should regulate inferences drawn from unusual manners of presentation by general rules of common usage.

Nevertheless, whenever a speaker employed expressions that sent the hearer to the conception of a different state of mind from the speaker's "authentic" state of mind, they reduced the force of the belief that the authentic state of mind exists in the speaker. This was, Hume thought, "as it must be" (T265). He was confident that human nature would respond unreasonably, despite reflections, corrections, and general rules of understanding (T585).

SYMPATHY AND COMPARISON

We shall now consider a tendency in human nature, "an original quality of the soul" (T372), which Hume says is "directly contrary" (T593) to the generalized sympathy needed to judge persons impartially. We shall consider Hume's principle of comparison (T593).

In Part III of Book III, Hume describes the way unreflective sympathy gets corrected by "general rules of morality" (T583). In the final chapter of this work, we shall see how we correct immediate sympathy by adopting a "general" (T581) point of view. But whatever the corrective method involves, Hume always retains sympathy as a vital component in the generation of impartial moral judgment. He insists throughout that the moral sentiment depends on the principle of sympathy (T590). And by now we know that sympathy requires that we receive pleasure from the pleasure of others and pain from their pain. But comparison has an opposite effect to that of sympathy. It "makes us" receive pain from the pleasure of others and pleasure from their pain (T594). Comparison gives us "joy in the sufferings and miseries of others, without any offense or injury on their part" (T372). The comparative judgment, then, has a considerable influence on the way impartial moral judgment may go awry. It is, thus, a tendency of human nature which requires correction if impartial moral judgment is to obtain. In what follows, we will see that the difference between sympathy and comparison boils down to the *manner* in which we conceive our ideas of the pain and pleasure of others. Again, ordinary causal inference, transitions of thought and the influence of general rules will determine whether we respond sympathetically or comparatively to the pains and pleasures of others.

Why is it that we should feel the *pain* of humility and sometimes even hatred and envy when, from the first stage of sympathy, we are informed of another's *pleasant* state of pride? Much of the analysis relies on the principle of comparison,[1] or a "pity reverst," a tendency to judge the qualities of objects and persons, including ourselves, according to the judgments we make of other objects and persons (T375).

In all kinds of comparison an object makes us always receive from another, to which it is compar'd, a sensation contrary to what arises from itself in its direct and immediate survey. The direct survey of another's pleasure naturally gives us pleasure; and therefore produces pain, when compar'd with our own. His pain, considered in itself, is painful; but augments the idea of our own happiness, and gives us pleasure (T594).

Whether we respond sympathetically or comparatively to another's pain or pleasure is determined by the initial causal inference. More specifically, whether we receive pleasure or pain from another's pleasant or painful state depends upon how, or the manner in which, we conceive his or her pleasure or pain.[2] All depends upon the vividness of our idea of another's pleasure or pain.

If the idea be too feint, it has no influence by comparison; and on the other hand, if it be too strong, it operates on us entirely by sympathy, which is the contrary to comparison (T595).

The principle of comparison is first introduced to account for the passions of malice and envy. Hume at once makes the claim that the tendency to judge persons and objects according to the relations they bear to other persons and objects is an unreasonable aspect of human nature.[3]

So little are men govern'd by reason in their sentiments and opinions, that they always judge more of objects by comparison than from their intrinsic worth and value (T372).

The phenomenon of comparison is displayed in everyday experience of immediate sensation. The same water feels warm when our body is cool and feels cool when we are warm. A slight pain following intense pain reduces to no pain and at times becomes a pleasure, whereas intense pain following slight pain becomes "doubly grievous and uneasy" (T372). Hume's present concern, however, is not with the influence of comparison on impressions of sensation. Any elaborate analysis of immediate sensation falls outside the field of moral science and is more properly the work of the anatomist or natural scientist (T8). Hume is more interested in giving an account of our ideas of objects and, specifically, why a large object makes a small one appear smaller, while a large object appears larger when compared with a small one. Hume makes sure to note that the comparison will not occur unless the objects are related by proximity and similarity. Either relation by itself is insufficient to trigger a comparative judgment. Our perception of a mountain would not be altered when seen together with a horse, nor would a mediocre author be likely to envy a great poet. But when a horse and a pony are seen together, the pony appears smaller and the horse larger than when each is seen by itself, and a great poet is apt to note envy in writers that closely approach him in greatness.[4] Why is it then, that when a large and small object of the same kind are presented in proximity, the large object appears larger and the small one smaller than when each is viewed separately?

The explanation proceeds along the lines of two principles. First, the principle is set forth that all perceptions of objects, all impressions and ideas of objects, are accompanied by an emotion which is distinguished from the content of a perception by a distinction of reason (T373). By means of the distinction, we separate and attend to the emotional aspect of an impression or idea. The emotion Hume has in mind is "admiration," a kind of awe, and to illustrate he points out that we always feel "a sensible emotion" whenever we view a vast expanse like an ocean, or a great number of objects like a crowd, and this emotion contributes to the pleasure of admiration (T374). Since the intensity of the emotion increases or decreases according to the number of parts that compose an extension or a collection of objects, Hume concludes that the emotion is a compound effect which arises from each part of the cause (T174).[5] "Every part, then, of extension, and every unite of number has a separate emotion attending it, when conceived by the mind" (T373).

The second principle Hume puts forth is the "adherence" to general rules, rules formed as a result of a tendency to extend causal generalizations formed from one set of regularities to resembling but different regularities. Transitions of thought are made unreflectively to a false belief and continue to be made unreasonably even after reflection, from objects that merely resemble and lie in close proximity to causes. Ideas are thought in as vivid a manner as if they were inferred from a genuine cause, that is, from an authentic rule of understanding.

> When an object is found by experience to be always accompany'd with another; whenever the first object appears, tho' chang'd in very material circumstances; we naturally fly to the conception of the second, and form an idea of it in as lively and strong a manner, as if we had infer'd its existence by the justest and most authentic conclusion of our understanding (T374).

From the above two principles, Hume argues that since the perception of any object occurs with an emotion which increases with every part of extension, a great object seen immediately after a small one makes a great emotion follow a small emotion. But a great emotion following a small emotion continues to increase beyond its usual sensation. It becomes "still greater, and rises beyond its ordinary proportion." The emotion swells beyond the pitch it usually has when the object is seen by itself, and is not compared with a small object.

At this point, it might seem as if Hume is employing the principle he wants to explain. What needs explanation is the residual increase of emotion whenever a great object is viewed after a small one. In the present discussion, Hume says nothing about the inertia of the passions. But in a later section, Hume describes ideas as being like wind instruments where a cessation of sound follows abruptly from a release of the mouthpiece. But the passions are more like string instruments and continue to emit sound after each pluck of the string. Transitions of thought from one idea to another are "quick and agile," but the transition between passions is "slow and restive" (T441). The perceptions of the small and great *object* are unaffected by the transition and remain discrete while the small *emotion* does not stay put but lags behind in the transition of perceptions and becomes "mixt and confounded" with the great emotion. Elsewhere, Hume writes that "the predominant passion swallows up the inferior, and converts it into itself" (T420).

Having distinguished the emotion which occurs with every perception of an object, and having accounted for its increase beyond its usual sensation, Hume is prepared to show how we confuse an exaggerated emotion with the impression of a large object. Since a determinate degree of emotion customarily occurs with a particular dimension, when the emotion increases, it is imagined that the object has also increased. The enlarged emotion habitually calls to mind its usual cause, an object of a particular dimension. The vivid idea of an object of this dimension is *transferred* to the immediate impression of an object of a lesser dimension.[6] The large object is thus believed to be larger than the object immediately given to sense. The inference from an enlarged emotion to the idea of an object which is not present to sense distorts the impression of an object which is present to sense. While it remains open for us to check the transition from a bloated emotion to a vivid idea of an object, the habit of calling to mind an object proportionate to the emotion makes us judge that the object given to sense is larger than it appears. "Nor do we consider, that comparison may change the emotion without changing any thing in the object" (T374). The reflection that a great emotion following a small emotion becomes still greater does not cut off the transition from the emotion to the thought of its usual attendant. The judgment, here, inevitably perverts the impression given to sense. The most to be hoped for is a conflict between the senses and the judgment (T149). Hume insists, however, that the comparative judgment is unreasonable, and a potential source of false belief, and ought to be corrected if our judgments are to to be made from an impartial point of view (T374,582).[7]

The analysis of comparison and its influence on our judgments of objects is extended to our judgments of ourselves and others. We tend to estimate our circumstances according to the judgments we make of the circumstances of others. In comparison, a spectator receives an opposite sensation from what he feels when sympathizing with another's pain or pleasure. From the comparative point of view, the belief that another is pleased is painful to us. It "makes us" receive less pleasure from our good circumstances than what we would ordinarily feel had we not considered the good circumstances of others. And if we are already miserable, we will only fall more deeply into our plight, and the pain of humility will be further heightened.

From the sympathetic point of view, the belief that another is pleased is pleasing to us. Sympathizing with the pleasure of pride others receive from their pleasure-giving items tends to produce love. Similarly, the belief that another is pained is painful to us by sympathy and, on some occasions, produces hatred, on others, pity and compassion.[8] But when we consider our own circumstances, the belief that another is suffering seems to reduce our pain, and if we are already well off, may increase our pleasant sensation of pride.

Hume's present concern is to discover the conditions under which sympathy or comparison takes precedence in our judgments of others. All the differences will be seen to emerge from the different *manners* in which we conceive our ideas of the pleasures and pains of others. In short, sympathy and comparison will be distinguished according to the principle of vivacity. It is the first stage of sympathy, then, the ordinary causal inference, that will determine whether we receive pain or pleasure from the pains and pleasures of others.[9]

Hume asks us to imagine that we are resting by the sea and that we would like to take some pleasure in the thought of our safety. Initially, we might *think* of the unpleasant circumstances of those who are on a ship during a storm and how painful it must be to be thrown by the waves, fearing that the ship will capsize at any moment. But in order to *feel* the pleasure of safety, to become "sensible" of it, we would try to make our idea of their pain and misfortune as vivid as possible. We would try, perhaps by frequent acts of repetition, to believe that such a misfortune was presently occurring (T116,423). But the effort of thought expended on repeatedly conceiving their calamity would disturb the "flowing of the passions and sentiments ... on which the belief depends" (Tl85). The comparison would not be as effective as it would be were we really standing on the shore, watching a ship, "at a distance," tossed in a storm and in danger of capsizing. Our idea of their difficult situation would become more vivid and would thus increase the pleasure of our safety. It would seem that the pleasure we receive from our safety increases as the vividness of our idea of their pain increases. But it is important to recognize that we are not actually seeing the ship submerged under the waves, nor do we really believe that the ship will go down. Our idea of their desperate situation is made more vivid by a present impression of a ship in the midst of a storm. We certainly believe that their situation is threatening but not imminent in the sense that we believe in their inevitable destruction. Since it is believed that the crew usually pulls out of such difficult circumstances, the understanding, Hume would say, infers their safety while the imagination (prompted by a perception which occurs whenever we have observed such disasters) infers the sinking of the ship. Hence the "opposition" that ensues in our ideas of their safety and their destruction.

Notice, however, that in order for us to reap pleasure from their pain, in order to strike the comparison, the way we conceive our idea of their destruction must only be "as if" the ship were to go down. If we really believed that the ship and crewmen were doomed, if our idea of their plight became too vivid, our response would be one of sympathy rather than comparison.

> Suppose the ship to be driven so near me, that I can perceive distinctly the horror, painted on the countenance of the seamen and passengers, hear their lamentable cries, see the dearest friends give their last adieu … No man has so savage a heart as to reap any pleasure from such a spectacle, or withstand the motions of the tenderest compassion and sympathy (T594).

Hume's general conclusion is that in order for comparison to take place, our idea of another's pleasure or pain must be in a "medium" range of vividness. If our idea is too weak, as when we merely imagine another's pleasant or painful circumstances, the pain or pleasure we receive from our circumstances will not in the least be augmented. If the vivacity of our idea of their circumstances is too strong, as when we believe that they really are pained or pleased, we will respond sympathetically and feel pain from their pain and pleasure from their pleasure. Sympathy requires a greater degree of vivacity in the idea of another's belief or passion than does comparison (T595).

Notice that the virtue of presenting pride in an implicit manner relies on the comparative response of a spectator. For were it not for the fact that we tend to compare our pleasures with the pleasures of others, the duty to express pride in a concealed manner of presentation would never have arisen. If we did not unreasonably persist in the belief that another's pride is well founded, while we reasonably believe that it is "ill-grounded," we would never strike the comparison and suffer the pain of humility from another's pleasure. Again, it is the unreasonable side of human nature which accounts for "greatness of mind," the virtue of deftly expressing pride, when we really do possess valuable qualities (T596).

It was Hume's view that there would be widespread indignation were everyone to express their pride in a manner which overrated the objects or qualities they believed themselves to have. In the same way that the "laws of nature" are established in order to redirect self interest, secure property and fulfill promises, the "rules of good-breeding" are established in order to prevent a continual conflict of each other's pride. Just as self interest is an aspect of human nature, so is the tendency to overvalue what we believe to be in possesion of and to express ourselves to others accordingly. Both need to be redirected, the former outwardly, the latter more inwardly. Self interest is restrained by a common interest expressed by a "convention" which ensures the security of each individual's possessions (T490). The tendency to publicly overrate one's objects and character traits is redirected to a private sense of pride by the "decorums of good-breeding," in order to prevent an inevitable and "shocking" comparison and "render conversation agreeable and inoffensive" (T597,600).

Hume extends his analysis of sympathy and comparison to account for the conditions under which we either sympathize with the proud and feel pleasure from their pleasure or compare our pleasure with theirs and feel pain from their pleasure. The beliefs of others are included among the objects of sympathy. Hume at once stresses the involuntariness which characterizes the initial sympathetic judgment.

> No sooner any person approaches me, then he diffuses on me all his opinions, and draws along my judgment in a greater or lesser degree (T592).

Whatever our system of beliefs happens to be, and regardless of whether we agree with the beliefs of others, we always "implicitly" sympathize with their beliefs. We do not respond indifferently to the beliefs of others, and at times it is difficult to continue believing our ideas when set in opposition to another's beliefs (T317,592). Hume is not saying that our sympathetically inherited beliefs usually involve a change in one or more of *our* beliefs. Rather, our idea of another's belief is usually in that range of vivacity which triggers a kind of disturbance or "commotion" between the belief which is "natural" to us and our sympathetic belief (T593). If we reflected on the circumstances which caused us to acquire another's belief and gathered some evidence which displayed an unreasonable acceptance on our part, we would retain our belief but would, nevertheless, continue to believe his or her belief as if it were "originally" our own. The principle of sympathy "is of so powerful and insinuating a nature" (T593).

Why is it that we cannot help but believe the beliefs of others which, upon reflection, we do not actually believe? It is not a case of simply believing that another is having a belief, but of our believing the same idea another believes. Again, an explanation is to be sought in the theory of general rules.

Rather than judge our beliefs according to the evidence by which they are established, we tend to judge them by comparing them with the beliefs of others. Since sympathy involves a conversion of an idea into an impression, if we simply imagined the presence of a belief in another, our idea of the content of that belief would be too weak to be sympathized with. Nor would it be strong enough to trigger a comparison between it and our own belief. An object that appears too small cannot make a large object appear larger than it does when viewed by itself. If my idea of another's pain has a very low degree of vividness, the vivid idea of my pain will not become less vivid, nor will I believe that my pleasure has increased. Too great a difference in the vivacity of our ideas prevents the transition from another's to ours and either cuts off the comparison altogether or greatly reduces it. "A common soldier bears no such envy to his general as to his sergeant or corporal" (T377). Likewise, when we only imagine another as having a certain belief, our idea is too weak to make the idea of our own contrary belief less vivid, nor would we come to disbelieve it altogether. However, if we are presented with an idea that we do not ordinarily believe, and it is presented in such a manner as to make us believe that the person is completely convinced by it, his very conviction causes us to believe his idea and the force of our idea becomes reduced. Our idea of his content becomes enlivened while our idea of the same content, as belonging to us, becomes weakened. The intense conviction expressed in the manner of presentation "takes hold of the imagination" and reduces the vivacity of our own idea, and we begin to believe that anyone who is so convinced by an idea must surely be correct. While it is true that we do not disbelieve our idea altogether, we cannot help but believe his idea to a certain extent, at least to a greater extent than the ideas of imagination (T595).

This situation displays the sort of "commotion" Hume has in mind. His analysis relies on general rules operating on two different levels. Hume thought it was a weakness of human nature to believe the reports of others too easily, and human testimony is even more easily believed when presented in a manner that exhibits deep conviction. The connection between the ideas reported to us with their facts, Hume writes, "commands our assent beyond what experience will justify" (T113). If we really do not believe a certain idea, and that idea is presented by someone convinced by it, the speaker's conviction reduces the force of our belief compared to its force when thought by itself. Although we continue to disbelieve *our* idea, nevertheless, we also believe the very same idea *he* believes. The idea we do not believe is unreasonably extended to the scope of an idea we do believe by the habit of believing people who are convinced of what they believe. Again, "custom takes the start, and gives a biass to the imagination" (T148,595). If we disbelieve that another is worthy of the pride he believes himself worthy of, his airy sort of presentation "diminishes us in our own eyes" in the same manner as if he really matched up to the qualities he attributes to himself. If we believe that he does possess those qualities, our response will be one of sympathy rather than comparison, and our emotional reaction will be one of love rather than humility (T601).

It would be misleading to suppose that we only sympathize when we believe that someone is actually holding a belief or experiencing an emotion. In the discussion of the relationship between sympathy and moral judgment, Hume allows for a special kind of sympathy which largely depends on the inertia of imagination and which continues to operate even when we do not believe that another is experiencing the passion with which we are sympathizing. It will not be necessary to believe that a passion exists in another for it to be communicated by sympathy. In fact, Hume tells us, our very disbelief is a condition for judging persons from a general point of view (T586).

The influence of comparison on the judgments of an impartial spectator will compete with the sort of generalized sympathy required for the impartial moral judgment. The comparative judgment will need to be restrained if character traits and the actions which display them are to be judged from a general point of view (T489). The sentiment of approval and disapproval varies according to a number of factors Hume regards as irrelevant from an impartial viewpoint. "But these variations we regard not in our general decisions." The variations which Hume speaks of are often reduced to variations in the vivacity with which ideas are thought. When our ideas of the pains and pleasures of others are thought in that range of vivacity which triggers a comparative response, we overlook the fact that we are pleased by another's pain or pained by their pleasure. The passions of malice and envy have no part to play in the evaluation of character.

CHAPTER FOUR

# Passion and Judgment

## THE INDIRECT PASSIONS

It was Kemp Smith's view that Hume's treatment of the indirect passions in Book II – pride and humility, love and hatred – have "little direct bearing" on the problems of knowledge addressed in Book I and play "no really distinctive part" in the moral theory of Book III.[1] I think the second of Kemp Smith's claims has been successfully answered by Ardal in his *Passion and Value*. The first claim has received far less attention. As I see it, one must acknowledge the role of belief in sympathy and the role of sympathy in the production of the indirect passions in order to appreciate what it means for an impartial spectator to adopt a general viewpoint and make a moral judgment. The theory of belief in Book I and the theories of sympathy and the indirect passions in Books II and III come together to form one unified theory of moral evaluation.

Since the publication of Ardal's work, commentators have grown to recognize how closely the indirect passions and moral evaluation are connected in Hume's thought.[2] The indirect passions are the "unavoidable attendants" of the moral sentiment (T296). Love and approval are regarded as "equivalent" with regard to qualities of mind, "virtue and the power of producing love or pride, vice and the power of producing humility and hatred" (T575). The indirect passions and moral evaluation are mediated[3] by sympathy. It is by sympathizing with the feelings of others, or with persons related to them, that we "approve of [their] character, and love [their] person" (T362,602).

For our purposes, a short passage at the end of the *Treatise* sketches what it means to adopt a general point of view. Hume is now identifying the judgment of merit and the indirect passions.

> The pain or pleasure, which arises from the general survey or view of any action or quality of the mind, constitutes its vice or virtue, and gives rise to our approbation or blame, which is nothing but a fainter and more imperceptible love or hatred (T614).

By "imperceptible," Hume has in mind a "calm," as opposed to a "violent," love or hatred. The difference between them is explained in terms of emotional intensity in the same way that vividness distinguishes impressions from ideas (T276).[4] It is important to keep in mind that the calm/violent distinction of the indirect passions is coordinate with the weak/lively distinction of impressions and ideas. Weak ideas produce little emotional intensity to the indirect passions. Vivid ideas make them more intense. If the transition from an impression to an idea does not take place, "its influence on the passions must also cease, as being dependent entirely on that transition" (T340). So the calmness or violence of an indirect passion depends, again, on the vivacity of ideas.

> Wherever our ideas of good or evil acquire a new vivacity, the passions become more violent; and keep pace with the imagination in all its variations (T424).

The feeling, sentiment, or attitude[5] of approval or disapproval is a "soft and gentle" (T470) indirect passion. Virtue and vice are the "most obvious causes" (T295) of the indirect passions, and the indirect passions are "the most considerable effect[s]" (T473) of virtue and vice. Near the end of the *Treatise*, Hume is decidedly clear on identifying the judgment of merit with the passions of pride and love. The moral sentiment is subject to the same causal explanation that is offered for the indirect passions.[6] As was the case with the long-awaited exposition of causal necessity, the reader has likewise been asked to wait through the entirety of Part II, Book III for an exposition of the sentiment of right and wrong (T498). I will, therefore, quote the opening passage in full.

> Moral distinctions depend entirely on certain peculiar sentiments of pain and pleasure, and that whatever mental quality in ourselves or others gives us a satisfaction, by the survey or reflection, is of course virtuous; as everything of this nature, that give uneasiness, is vicious. Now since every quality in ourselves or others, which gives pleasure, always causes pride or love, as every one, that produced uneasiness, excites humility or hatred: It follows, that these two particulars are to be consider'd as equivalent, with regard to our mental qualities, virtue and the power of producing love or pride, vice and the power of producing humility or hatred. In every case, therefore, we must judge of one by the other; and

may pronounce any quality of the mind virtuous, which causes love or pride; and any one vicious, which causes hatred or humility (T575).

Notice that it is by means of reflection that the particular sort of pain or pleasure arises. At the same time, the pain or pleasure constitutes the "essence" (T296) of virtue and vice. "The very feeling constitutes our praise or admiration." Although Hume denies there is an inference from a pleasant or painful impression to the idea of virtue or vice,[7] he insists that a "particular manner" of conceiving an object of appraisal is required before one's feelings count as impartial feelings. "But in feeling that it pleases after such a particular manner, we in effect feel that it is virtuous" (T471).

Moral consciousness is more a matter of feeling than judgment. Yet it is clear that in Hume's complete discussion of moral discernment, certain judgments, ordinary causal judgments, play a significant role in the emergence of "proper" moral feeling. In the second *Enquiry*, Hume allows reason the role of preparing the way for the special pain or pleasure which characterizes moral feeling. "It is often requisite to employ much reasoning, in order to feel the proper sentiment; and a false relish may frequently be corrected by argument and reflection" (2E173). It will be shown that Hume's theory of moral judgment involves adopting a reflective viewpoint from which an impartial spectator considers the moral scene according to general rules.

Hume is clear in maintaining that the unique pain or pleasure which characterizes moral feeling is the outcome of considering qualities of mind from a "steady and general" point of view, a "distant view or reflexion," which causes a pain or pleasure of a special kind (T472,583). The unique pleasant or painful sensation, in turn, "gives rise" to approval or disapproval, which is simply a less violent love or hatred, one felt with a low degree of emotional intensity (T614). While Hume insists that "the very feeling constitutes our praise or admiration," the feeling only becomes one of praise or blame, instead of resting with love or hatred, when it is regulated by reflection. When unreflective propensities of imagination have their way, when the view shifts from a general to a particular point of view, the feeling which emerges can no longer be described as one had by an impartial spectator. As Hume would have us see it, the relationship between judging and feeling is a causal relationship and so must involve belief, either of the natural or reflective sort, or both face to face.[8] Specifically, the relation Hume has in mind is "the double relation of impressions and ideas," the relation which explains the four indirect passions – where a transition from an impression to an idea brings with it a transition of impressions – and which serves equally in the explanation of moral evaluation. We will look more closely at Hume's double relation and its relation to sympathy and belief. First, a few remarks regarding Hume's overall position on moral judgment.

When Hume speaks of the principles which explain the approving and disapproving sort of feeling, one of them is clearly the principle of general rules. The imagination "makes us" (T472) have a feeling of one kind, the understanding prescribes what feeling we "ought" (T149) to have if we want to be impartial. Persons of judgment may safeguard themselves from the "illusions" of imagination by reflection (T631). The vividness of an idea together with its correspondent emotional pitch is no more the standard of moral judgment than was sheer vivacity of conception the standard of reasonable belief. Given that approval and disapproval are the passions of love and hatred, but felt with low intensity, it should begin to emerge that the conflict of general rules regarding belief is extended to the calm/violent dichotomy of the indirect passions. So far from resolving the opposition of general rules at the close of Book I, where a single association of ideas brought about a conflict of imagination and understanding, now in Book III, the same association of ideas "forwards" another association of impressions, certain pains and pleasures of varying degrees of intensity. That is, a "double relation" of impressions and ideas heralds in the dialogue of the calm versus the violent indirect passions, a dispute completely instigated by causal reasoning, belief and general rules.

The interpretation gains support if we recall that a reflective judgment is commonly less vivid than its preceding judgment and, as a consequence, less forcefully believed. We continue to believe ideas that are easiest to understand in light of evidence which would reduce their believability. And it is only because of this persistent unreasonableness that we are protected from the reasonable arguments of complete scepticism. Simple vivacity of conception is, more often than not, determinative of the final judgment. The principles of reflection and correction "are not altogether efficacious." However reason requires it, "'tis seldom we can bring ourselves to it; our passions do not readily follow the determinations of our judgment" (T583). When the judgment is unreasonable, the passion is violent and partial, when reasonable, calm and impartial. We are thus able to "give praise to what deserves it," provided we believe as we ought, though we might hate whom we praise (T472). The "combat" of reason and passion, "call'd so in an improper sense,"[9] is just a conflict of calm and violent indirect passions, where the "opposition" of general rules is responsible for the conflict between, say, hatred and praise.

It is important to keep in mind that the dialogue between calm and violent indirect passions cannot be construed as a dialogue of moral and

premoral[10] judgments. "Natural" and more "crude" evaluations are corrected by reflective moral judgments in the same way that reflective belief
corrects natural belief. Just as the latter are equally fact judgments, one
reasonable, the other unreasonable, so the former are equally moral judgments, one partial, the other impartial. In Hume's account of the development of judgment, from "uncultivated" judgments to critical and reflective
ones, he speaks no more of a pre-factual stage in the development of fact
judgments than he does of a pre-moral stage in the development of moral
judgments. There is no point at which we do not judge of facts, and there is
no point at which we do not judge of values. The former may be reasonable
or unreasonable, the latter, impartial or partial, but nowhere in the *Treatise*
is there talk of a period of development where neither was operative. Just
the contrary, even with the advent of reasonable and impartial judgments,
the initial tendency to unreasonableness and partiality continues to have its
say, so much so that Hume was at pains to decide which side of human
nature ought to determine judgment. Let us now look more closely at
Hume's "double relation" in order to explain, first, how the indirect
passions emerge and, secondly, how sympathy figures in the explanation of
the indirect passions.

The double relation of ideas and impressions contains the necessary
conditions for the passions of pride and humility, love and hatred (T336).
The former have oneself for their "object," the latter, another self. In
addition to the double relation, love and hatred require the mediation of
sympathy in order to get initially aroused, while pride and humility require
sympathy, but only to become more enhanced, complete and "constant." In
some way, both sets of passions are dependent on sympathy.

Hume notes that one's reputation is a matter of great importance.

> We commonly consider ourselves as we appear in the eyes of others, and
> sympathize with the advantageous sentiments they entertain with regard
> to us (T615).

Aside from the "original causes" of the indirect passions – mental and
physical qualities along with objects related to self or others – sympathy is
their "secondary cause" but no less productive.

> Even the other causes of pride; virtue, beauty and riches; have little influ-
> ence when not seconded by the opinions and sentiments of others (T316).

It is a limitation[11] of pride that one be able to sympathize with the pleasure
others receive from one's own pleasure. The cause of an indirect passion,
an *independent* source of pleasure or pain, should be recognized as such by
oneself and by others (T292). Without the intervention of sympathy, the

pleasure I receive from my *beautiful* garden, coupled with the pleasure in the thought that it is *my* beautiful garden, cannot be a pleasure of any great duration when not reinforced by the pleasure from sympathizing with persons who sympathize with me. The sympathetically acquired pleasure is just a "second reflexion" of the original sensation of pride, and yet the main reason why we desire to be wealthy is to be able to sympathize with our admirers. Pride is thus given "support," and its pleasure is "sustain'd," which would otherwise be short-lived when experienced in isolation from others. The feeling of pride, no less than love, cannot be maintained in a solitary condition (T353).

Our high regard for the rich is likewise a result of sympathy. While it is necessary that the "cause" of love acquires a double relation of ideas and impressions to the "object" of love, we only come to love the rich by sympathizing with the pleasure they receive from their possessions. They, in turn, sympathize with us, which keeps their pride going (T320).

> Now I assert, that where we esteem a person upon account of his riches, we must enter into this sentiment of the proprietor, and that without such a sympathy the ideas of the agreeable objects, which they give him the power to produce, would have but a feeble influence upon us (T360).

Sympathy, then, and the double relation are sufficient for the production of the indirect passions. And if they are responsible for passions like love and hatred, they are likewise responsible for the *calm* passions of approval and disapproval, adjusted, of course, by general rules. Together they form a complex of relations, associations, impressions, ideas, pains and pleasures which have been appropriately described as a "mare's nest."[12]

By the conclusion of Book III, Hume is convinced that sympathy is the "chief source of moral distinctions ... that is has force sufficient to give us the strongest sentiments of approbation, when it operates alone, without the concurrence of any other principle" (T618). We have already seen that sympathy does not assure an impartial morality without the intervention of reflective thinking. It does, however, when it functions by itself, without the aid of reflection, provide a partial, unregulated morality. Again, it must be stressed that the development of an impartial morality does not follow from a premoral condition. Hume has us understand that from the point of view of the "natural and usual course of the passions," so far from being guilty of an immorality by preferring our interest and the interest of our family and friends to the interest of strangers, we consider any "remarkable transgression of such a degree of partiality, either by too great an enlargement, or contraction of the affections, as vicious and immoral" (T488). When our concerns do not extend to people remotely related to us, our sympathy is "weaker and our praise or blame fainter and more doubtful," and this is exactly as it must be (T265,483,603).

A man naturally loves his children better than his nephews, his nephews better than his cousins, his cousins better than strangers, where everything else is equal. Hence arise our common measures of duty in preferring one to the other ... our sense of duty always follows the common and natural course of our passions.

One's natural and unreflective sense of morality, instead of correcting for the built-in partiality of initial judgments, "[does] rather conform [itself] to that partiality" (T489). In order to overcome the contradictions which follow from too rigid an adherence to the unreflective side of moral judgment, we adopt a point of view in which our judgments may agree with the judgments of others (T602). "Nature provides a remedy in the judgment and understanding, for what is irregular and incommodious in the affections" (T489). The dialogue which emerges is thus one between "natural" and "artificial" judgments. So the way we *ought* to judge, in accordance with general rules of understanding, is an artificial judgment, while the way we *must* judge, in accordance with the propensities of imagination, is more natural. In any case, the subsequent dialogue is always a *moral* dialogue, where each party comes with its own *moral* claims.

Part of Hume's conviction that sympathy is a necessary condition for impartial moral judgment stems from his reply to the first of two objections he raises against the moral potency of sympathy. Hume first notes that the degree of felt sympathy changes according to the relations which hold between appraiser and appraised. Judgments of approval and disapproval, however, are stable and are not the outcome of changing degrees of emotion. There is no coincidence of feeling between what is initially felt and what is felt upon reflection, between, say, a violent love and the calm pleasure of approval. So, independently of changes in the degree of felt sympathy, the same judgments are made about the same qualities of character wherever they are placed. The position of each person in relation to the object of evaluation is constantly changing. Strangers may soon become friends and friends may become enemies. Each person occupies a unique point of view, assessing their objects through a unique set of relations. The judgment of an impartial spectator, therefore, overlooks the fact that changes in the relations vary the intensity of the sympathy. "The sympathy varies without a variation of our esteem." The objection concludes, "our esteem, therefore, proceeds not from sympathy" (T581). When Hume speaks of the variableness of sympathy, he has in mind changes in the degree of love or hatred. For sympathy is not itself a passion but the transference of passions from one person to another. How, then, do we sympathize with the passions of love and hatred and, once sympathized with, what are the conditions which vary their intensity? Finally, what conditions stabilize the variation?

Hume insists that sympathy is the "animating" principle of all the passions. Were we unable to sympathize with others, or others with ourselves, the causes which ordinarily produce pride and love in a sympathetic community would have no effect (T363). Yet Hume also claims that nothing can produce any of the indirect passions without a double association of impressions and ideas. Let us then say that the double relation sets up the conditions for sympathy. The double relation is necessary to arouse the passions, sympathy is necessary to conserve and sustain them. Both are sufficient for the production and maintenance of pride and humility, love and hatred. And both, together with general rules, suffice to explain the passions of approval and disapproval. What, then, are the conditions for the sympathetic point of view? What role does the double relation play? What role do general rules play?

## PRIDE AND HUMILITY

We will now consider more closely Hume's theory of the double relation of ideas and impressions. We will need to get clear on this theory before we can appreciate the way sympathy and the double relation work together for the production of love and hatred. These passions, we recall, are "uncultivated" and "violent" variants of the "calm" passions of approval and disapproval (T614). In the final chapter, we will see that the transition from the violent to the calm indirect passions will be accomplished by reflection and general rules.

Although Hume does not claim that the double relation is the primary cause of love and hatred, he insists that it has a greater influence on the production of these passions than what might initially be thought (T357–458). It is worthwhile to consider the twofold association, although by the end of his analysis, Hume will admit that the double relation resolves itself into sympathy for the arousal of love and hatred (T360).

Hume begins his study of the indirect passions with pride and humility. He thinks that pride is an "original" passion and the source of many other passions. "One of the most considerable of these passions is that of love or esteem in others" (T365). But he thinks there is so great a resemblance between these passions that his discussion of love is just an "abridgment" of his treatment of pride (T329). Hume presupposes an understanding of the double relation in his brief discussion of love. One must look to pride for an explanation.

The "object" of pride is always oneself. Hume is concerned to make the point. Pride is *never* directed toward anyone but oneself. "When self enters not into consideration, there is no room either for pride or humility" (T277). When there is talk of pride in others, "'tis not in a proper sense." We love others for having praiseworthy or beautiful qualities and take pride in ourselves for being related to them (T338). The same causes which produce pride when related to oneself also produce pride, though to a lesser extent, when related to someone who is related to oneself. The object of pride, what one takes pride in, or is proud of, is oneself.

> Pride and humility, being once rais'd, immediately turn our attention to oneself, and regard that as their ultimate and final object (T278).

Hume distinguishes the *cause* from the *object* of pride and humility, "betwixt that idea, which excites them, and that to which they direct their view, when excited," and so places the impression of pride between two ideas "of which the one produces it, and the other is produced by it" (T278). The cause is divided threefold, mental and bodily qualities and objects related to oneself. In discussing these causes, Hume is able to mark a distinction between "the quality which operates on the passion, and the subject, in which the quality inheres" (T279).[1] One is proud of one's beautiful house. The cause-quality is the beauty, the cause-subject, the house. Both parts, Hume insists, are necessary for the production of pride, and both are "component" parts of the cause (T279).

Hume next draws our attention to two types of association, the familiar association of ideas, where ideas are related by resemblance, contiguity and causation, and the newly introduced association of impressions, where impressions are related only by resemblance. Both types of associations "assist" each other in the production of pride.

> Those principles, which forward the transition of ideas, here concur with those, which operate on the passions; and both uniting in one action, bestow on the mind a double impulse (T284).

It will be helpful here to briefly look ahead at Hume's chemistry of the passions (T443).[2] Resembling impressions are connected in a uniquely intimate way to which ideas present no counterpart. Ideas cannot merge into one another but are "endowed with a kind of impenetrability." They may form a compound by their conjunction but cannot unite by their mixture. On the other hand, "impressions and passions are susceptible of an entire union; and like colors, may be blended so perfectly together, that each of them may lose itself" (T366). In the transition from one idea to another, the ideas are discrete while in the transition between impressions, say, from joy to pride, "the passions are like an alcali and an acid, which, being mingled, destroy each other" (T443). It is because of the intimate tie between passions that Hume found it difficult to separate the pleasure of joy from the pleasure of pride. "They become in a manner undistinguishable" (T331).

What impressions are associated by resemblance and what ideas by similarity, proximity and causation? Looking now more closely at the cause of pride and the passion of pride itself, Hume finds that the *quality* of the cause produces pleasure or pain independent of pride and humility, a pain or pleasure "separate" from the sensation of the passion. The beauty of a house is an initial source of pleasure, independent of a second pleasure, the pleasurable pride one takes in owning it.

> We may feel joy upon being present at a feast … but 'tis only the master of the feast, who, beside the same joy, has the additional passion of self applause and vanity (T290).

Hume finds that the second property of the cause, the *subject*, is either part of oneself or something closely related to oneself, one's virtuous characteristics, or physical beauty, or beautiful objects. Pride or humility cannot be produced when the quality of a cause is placed on a subject that is unrelated to oneself. In short, the pleasure one receives from the cause is separate from the pleasure of pride, and the cause is always related to oneself.

Looking now at the passion itself, Hume discovers two properties which correspond to the properties of the cause. First, pride is "determin'd by an original and natural instinct" to have oneself for its object (T280). Commentators are in general agreement that the determination Hume is talking about is a contingent connection and not "essential" to pride (T367).[3] It is simply a matter of fact that "here the view always fixes," that pride produces the idea of self (T289). It is just the case that the mind happens to be constituted in such a way that pride causes the idea of self to arise in the proud person. Were it differently constituted, pride could have been directed at another object. The relation is natural from the "constancy" of the association. The fact can be noted and described, but not explained (T275). Hume allows the point. Why does the "view always rest" on oneself when experiencing pride? "For this I pretend not to give any reason" (T286).

> The uniting principle among our internal impressions is as unintelligible as that among external objects, and is not known to us any other way than by experience (T169).

We might accept the suggestion that the connection between pride and its object is a non-contingent relation, "that the relation to oneself is a logical aspect of pride without which it could not be pride."[4] We might accept the "conceptual requirement ... no pleasant emotion counts as pride unless its object is oneself,"[5] or "a person who enjoys his garden, but does not take pride in it, does not think of himself as: owner of the garden."[6] Hume is not comfortable with letting the relation go as purely contingent and considers this hypothesis more than once. He states, "'tis absolutely impossible" to overlook oneself when feeling proud (T280,286). One cannot possibly be feeling proud and "look beyond" oneself. The object of pride is "inseparable" from pride. One does not just happen to think of oneself moments after one feels proud.

When discussing the connection between love and motivation, Hume maintains that the desire for the happiness of someone we love and the aversion to the happiness of someone we hate necessarily constitute "the very nature" of love and hatred. They comprise their "very being and essence" (T367). But he soon rejects this view in favor of the alternative hypothesis that the relation between the passion and the desire is a contingent connection. The desire and aversion are connected with love and hatred by an "original" quality of the mind or "primary constitution of nature ... this order of things, abstractly consider'd, is not necessary" (T368). There is nothing inconceivable in the thought that a desire for misery is connected with love or a desire for happiness with hatred. We are not "necessarily determin'd" to think of the connection in one way rather than the other. "The imagination is free to conceive both sides of the question" (T95).

Hume is pleased to compare the relation between pride and its object to "the belief attending the judgments, which we form from causation" (T289). Despite Hume's sometimes forceful language, the connection he has in mind is a contingent connection. One can no more discover a priori that the impression of pride is connected with its object than one can discover from inspecting a stone that it will descend when unsupported.[7] One cannot know these things in advance of the facts.[8] On Hume's view, it would be just as intelligible to feel proud without thinking of oneself as it would be to imagine an upward rather than a downward motion of an unsupported object.

We might consider the view that the connection between pride and self is one that holds by "closer than causal ties"[9] without feeling forced to make the relation a logical one, as one discovered a priori by comparing ideas. The relations which already hold between the cause and the object of pride are contiguity and causation. One is proud of having been to a safari in Africa and one is proud of one's garden and children. If causation and contiguity are the only relations that hold between the cause and the object of pride, it would follow that the connection between pride and the idea of self is a straightforward causal connection. Association might make the idea of self more vivid or the impression of pride more intensely felt. But association cannot further strengthen the causal connection beyond which pride and its object are already associated.[10] Very simply, nature has "assign'd" the idea of self to the passion of pride, and pride "always" produces the idea of self. Pride is related to self in the same way the nerves of the nose or palate are "dispos'd ... to convey such peculiar sensations to the mind." Hume thinks his explanation of the connection requires no proof (T287).

It is open for the imagination, however, to strengthen the association between pride and the idea of self. We recall Hume's claim that the imagination is "determin'd to join ... and unite, by a new bond, such objects as have already an union in the fancy." We have seen this propensity at work on a number of occasions.[11] It is simply a natural fact that we have a tendency to further join "internal perceptions" no less than "external objects" (T170). The additional tie the imagination adds to the relations of causation and contiguity makes pride and the idea of self "not only inseparable but the same" (T367). "The object is not something separate from the pride."[12] Both are "blended so perfectly together, that each of them may lose itself, and contribute only to vary that uniform impression, which arises from the whole" (T366). The relation between pride and the idea of self thus becomes a logical relation without which pride could not be pride. Pride and the idea of self are two "aspects" of a simple impression that are separated only by a distinction of reason (T25).

The necessity of the connection between pride and the idea of self arose from the same tendency of imagination that was responsible for the necessary connection between the angles of a triangle and 180°.[13] Like the discovery of geometric equality, the relation between pride and the idea of self was not discovered analytically, by simply comparing the meanings of terms, but required the intervention of mind. It is only because the imagination derives pleasure from further uniting perceptions that pride cannot be interpreted as a simple impression that is contingently connected to its object.

The second property of pride Hume takes notice of and which he does think constitutes "the very being and essence" of the passion is its peculiar pleasantness. "Thus pride is a pleasant sensation, and humility a painful; and upon the removal of the pleasure and the pain, there is in reality no pride or humility" (T286). Comparing the two properties of the cause, a *subject* related to oneself and a *quality* which is an independent source of pleasure, with the two properties of the passion, its *object* which is oneself and its *sensation* of pleasure, the "true system" of the indirect passions becomes evident.

> That cause, which excites the passion, is related to the object, which nature has attributed to the passion; the sensation, which the cause separately produces, is related to the sensation of the passion: From this double relation of ideas and impressions, the passion is deriv'd (T286).

The object, the idea of self, is related by causation or contiguity to the subject, the idea of what belongs to self. The quality of the cause, the separate impression of pleasure, is related by resemblance to the pleasant impression of pride (T288). As Hume presents it, the transition is from the perception of a beautiful house, which gives a separate pleasure, to the pleasant sensation of pride as owner of the house. One's idea of the house is "converted" into the idea of *one's* house, and the pleasure one receives from a beautiful house resembles the pleasurable pride in owning it.

The point of the separate pleasure is not without its difficulties. Donald Davidson interprets the separate pleasure produced by the cause-quality as a generalized attitude of approval of which pride and love are particular cases.[14] Davidson is here pointing to Hume's division of the passions into "direct" and "indirect" (T276). The direct passions of joy and grief are the "immediate effects" of pain and pleasure. When the object that produces the impression of joy becomes related to oneself or others, it causes the new impression of pride or love. The idea of the cause becomes related to the idea of oneself, or another self, and the impression of joy is "transfus'd" into the impression of pride or love. They become "blended" so as to form one simple impression. How the separate joy comes to be distinguished from the pleasure of pride or love can only be explained by a distinction of reason (T25). By comparing the pleasure which an object produces when related to oneself or others with the pleasure it produces when unrelated to oneself or others, we distinguish the pleasure of joy from the pleasures of pride and love.

Hume wants to keep separate the pleasure one receives from one's virtuous mental qualities and the pleasure of pride, even when one's mind is at once both subject and object of the passion. The pleasure one receives from one's virtue is supposed to be separate from the pride. But aside from things like sunsets and seascapes and houses and gardens, pleasure-giving subjects "related to us" but not "part of ourselves," it is difficult to see how these latter causes can ever give a *separate* pain or pleasure, the pain or pleasure one receives from things which are not qualities of the mind or body. How can "beauty, strength, agility," or mental qualities like "courage, justice, integrity," be related to oneself or others in such a way as not to produce *only* pride or love? How can these be causes of joy apart from the indirect passions? It would seem that one cannot enjoy them without taking pride in them or loving others for having them. It is, after all, as Hume admits, only a "suppos'd" property of the cause that it produces a pain or pleasure independent of the passion, that it produces grief and joy independently of pride and humility, love and hatred (T286).

Davidson understands the direct passion of joy as a "generalized pleasure or approbation ... the generalized impression of approval."[15] Hume would allow that virtue and beauty give pleasure generally without admitting the pleasure to be a general impression of approval. That approval involves generality is correct, but the generality lies in the "point of view," not in the impression (T582). The kind of pleasure we *call* "moral pleasure" does not refer to a general impression of moral pleasure (T472). As Hume presents it, the moral sentiment is a "peculiar kind" of pleasure and pain, "a real pain and pleasure ... which arises from the general survey or view of any action or quality of mind" (T298,614). When Davidson claims that we can "shift – from considerations of pleasure to the attitude of approval or thinking well – without doing violence to Hume's view,"[16] the shift, as I see it, is one between two different sorts of general rules, from the rule of imagination to the rule of understanding.

We will continue to discuss the double relation but now in the context of sympathy. We will see that both the double relation and sympathy are required for the production of love and hatred. By itself, the double relation is not enough to produce these passions (T360). But Hume also insists that love and hatred cannot be produced unless sympathy and the double relation "concur" (T358). He acknowledges that both are necessary, but is concerned to determine which is the "predominant" cause. In following Hume's analysis, we will see why he concludes that sympathy is the "principal" cause of love and hatred.

## LOVE AND HATRED

Throughout, Hume appeals to the double association of impressions and ideas to account for the passions of love and hatred. But he also states that sympathy is required for love or hatred to be produced, and it is also required for pride or humility, but only to be sustained. The reason is obvious.

> As the immediate object of pride and humility is self or that identical person, of whose thoughts, actions, and sensations we are intimately conscious; so the object of love and hatred is some other person, of whose thoughts, actions, and sensations we are not conscious (T329).

Someone might feel proud from possessing a fine object or character trait without it being necessary to sympathize with the pleasure of an admirer. Sympathy is a "secondary" cause of pride. In the case of love, sympathy is the "principle" cause. It is not enough that we stand in relation to the owner of a beautiful object for love to be aroused. It is, after all, someone else that is owner and so receives the additional passion of pride over and above the pleasure we all receive from a beautiful object. What is missing is a principle of communication. For although we receive pleasure from the object, we are not conscious of the owner's pleasure. We are not conscious of his or her pride.

The "object" of love and hatred is always another person. Love is a pleasant impresssion, hatred a painful one.

> The cause of both these passions is always related to a thinking being, and that the cause of the former produce a separate pleasure, and of the latter a separate uneasiness (T331).

This sounds more like an explanation of why the object of love feels proud rather than why we love the object. That the cause of love or hatred is related to *another* person does not explain why *we* love or hate that person.

> A prince, that is possess'd of a stately palace, commands the esteem of the people upon that account; and that first, by the beauty of the palace, and secondly, by the relation of property, which connects it with him (T330).

Why do we love or "esteem"[1] the prince? Because of the pleasure *he* derives from owning a beautiful palace. Again, it is difficult to see where a lover fits into the picture. Perhaps the two-fold reason explains reasons for loving,[2] but it does not explain how we acquire the pleasant impression of love. That we are related to the prince and also, like him, take pleasure in his beautiful palace leaves out the explanation of how we become conscious of his impression of pride, of being pleased by his pleasure and not merely by what pleases him. In Hume's early discussion of love and hatred, one is uncomfortably aware of this missing component he later introduces, the required sympathy which grants us access to and thus enables us to *share* the pleasures and pains of others.

While Hume maintains that the causes of love, like the causes of pride – virtue, beauty and possessions like clothes and houses – are independent pleasure-givers, one's attention does not remain fixed on the subject-cause without passing to the idea of the object of the passion. From the impression of a house, coupled with the sensation of pleasure from its beauty, to the belief that this house belongs to Jones, and from the belief that this house belongs to Jones to the thought of Jones as owner of the house. But we still do not know how Jones feels about being the owner. The sensation of pleasure, the pleasurable pride belonging to Jones has not "become our own." Here, sympathy is required.

> We must enter into this sentiment of the proprietor, and that without such a sympathy, the idea of the agreeable objects ... would have but a feeble influence upon us (T360).

What is Hume thinking about when he writes "enter into"? From Jones' glow of pride, or from his report, or manner of report, one infers the idea or belief that Jones feels proud, an idea "resembling the original impression in force and vivacity" (T362). So the belief that Jones feels proud becomes just as vivid as Jones' pride.

> This satisfaction is convey'd to the beholder by the imagination, which produces an idea resembling the original impression in force and vivacity (T362).

Hume's account here is somewhat puzzling. According to the process of sympathy, if my belief that Jones is proud becomes so vivid as to become "the very sentiment or passion," it would follow that I receive pride from sympathy and not love.[3] Hume states that the vivid idea or belief of another's passion "acquires such a degree of vivacity, as to become the very passion itself" (T317). But what very passion does one's lively idea become – pride or love? How does the belief that Jones is proud change into the impression of love? How can sympathy with a proud person ever produce any passion other than pride? In short, how does sympathy enter into the explanation of love?

I think the reason why commentators are troubled by the problem is because they require of Hume that the spectator feels "the very same thing that others feel."[4] I don't think Hume held the view that sympathizing with someone who is anxious or having a toothache entails being anxious or having a toothache oneself.[5] Hume allows that the feelings of others "in some measure" become our feelings and may be experienced "as if" they were our own (T579). But he wants to distinguish one's sympathetically acquired feeling from *one's* feeling by directing pride and love to their proper objects. We have seen that Hume seriously considered the hypothesis that pride and love are not contingently connected with their objects, and does not clearly accept the Cartesian view that the relationship between a passion and its object is only a contingent one (T367).[6] Certainly, at the level of common sense, Hume wants to distinguish "the financier's apprehension and the sympathetic agent's apprehension."[7] Generally, commentators interpret Hume's account of sympathizing by focusing exclusively on what he says about sympathy. In raising the question of how sympathy explains the occurrence of love and hatred, it is necessary to include in the account the "double relation."[8] Hume insists on the point.

> I say then, that nothing can produce any of these passions without bearing it a double relation, viz. of ideas to the object of the passion, and of sensation to the passion itself (T333).

Before I can sympathize with Jones' pride in being owner of a house, I need to believe that Jones owns the house (T331,595). By itself, sympathy does not provide this belief. It informs me of another's state of mind but not whether it is based on a false or an unreasonable belief. If Jones shows signs of pride as if he were owner, and I do not believe that he is, the inference from his signs to the belief that Jones is proud cannot give me pleasure. In fact, Hume later tells us, the belief causes pain (T595,121). Jones is pleased by the belief that he or she owns the house, a belief that I do not share. In the context of judgment, as opposed to imagination, that is, from a reasonable point of view, one is not pleased by a fact that one does not believe exists. "The moment we perceive the falsehood of any supposition ... our passions yield to our reason without any opposition" (T416). But Hume reminds us that things do not always proceed in such a reasonable way and states that given an enthusiastic presentation of pride, we cannot help but sympathize with the pleasure others receive from qualities we do not believe them to have. There is always some degree of sympathy with the "elevated sentiments, which the proud man entertains of himself" (T595,123). While Hume claims that one's judgment does not assent to what the proud man believes, the tendency to believe what is reported, especially in a convincing manner, makes us believe that the proud man has the qualities he believes himself to have (T592,595). But this belief, Hume continues, causes pain by comparison rather than pleasure by sympathy.

> The firm persuasion he has of his own merit, takes hold of the imagination, and diminishes us in our own eyes, in the same manner, as if he were really possess'd of all the good qualities which he so liberally attributes to himself (T595).

Sympathy, however, always involves reasoning. We consider the judgment of others "as a kind of argument" for the passions they present. "These two principles of authority and sympathy influence almost all our opinions" (T321). We likewise do not take pride in the thought that others love us for our vicious qualities of character or for objects we are not in any special way related to (T322). In order for the proud person to "justify"[9] his or her pride, the quality-cause must be an independent source of pleasure, and he or she must stand in the relation of causation or contiguity to the subject-cause. Someone comes to be loved when we believe that both these conditions are met (T331). An object which produces pleasure but is not related to oneself or others cannot produce pride or love, and an object that is related by property but does not cause pleasure cannot produce these passions (T335). One must first think of the beautiful house, or see the house, and then think of Jones as owner of the house; or think of Jones, or see Jones, elated with pride, and then think of Jones' fine house. Hume's double relation is what provides this belief, without which there could be no sympathy.

Hume is saying that once this belief is established and the inference drawn from expressions of pride to the thought that Jones is proud, the thought is similar to Jones' impression of pride in its vividness, and the thought becomes the belief that Jones is proud. Additionally, the belief resembles Jones' pride in that both are pleasant impressions. The belief that Jones is proud is, itself, a pleasant belief (T362). One is pleased by the thought that another is proud. Hume wants to say that being pleased by Jones' pride is related by resemblance to loving Jones. What is experienced is love and not pride (T362).

Hume insists that being so pleased is not equivalent to feeling proud oneself. It is not pride that is felt but a pleasant sensation directed to Jones which is similar to his pride in its pleasantness. For, first, we are informed of Jones' pride, and his pride is thought to belong to Jones (T319). Secondly, we receive the belief that Jones is proud from the pleasure he receives from his possessions but are prevented from experiencing pride by the break in the relation between the subject-cause and ourselves (T359). The difference between pride and love lies in whether the subject-cause is related to oneself or another. They are related only by resembling sensations (T333). If the subject is related to oneself, the pleasure is immediately received; if to another self, mediately by sympathy. Love follows from a sympathy with the pleasure of the possessor, from the belief, or vivid and pleasant impression, that another is proud (T358). The possessor also sympathizes with the spectator's love, and what the possessor experiences is not love but a "second reflexion" of pride (T365). What follows is that a spectator sympathizes with the pleasure of pride but is prevented from feeling proud by the break in the relation between the subject-cause and himself. Hume illustrates the point in his "Fourth Experiment" to confirm the double relation.

> I suppose the virtue to belong to my companion, not to myself; and observe what follows from this alteration. I immediately perceive the

affections to wheel about, and leaving pride, where there is only one relation, viz. of impressions, fall to the side of love, where they are attracted by a double relation of impressions and ideas (T336).

Notice the claim that when the cause is transferred to another self, pride is lost. However, the relation of resembling, pleasant impressions continues to hold between the separate pleasure which virtue produces and the pleasant sensation of love. There would now seem to be some discrepancy in Hume's account. What impressions does Hume here have in mind? Is he talking about the separate pleasure virtue produces and which, by resemblance, produces love, or is it the sympathetically acquired pleasure in the belief that another is proud that is related to love? Both the separate pleasure and the pleasure from sympathy are impressions which resemble the passion of love. Which impression makes up Hume's "relation of impressions"? Which couples with love?

Hume tells us that thinking about pleasant objects, what is just "entertaining" to the imagination, is not the "principle cause" of love. The simple reflection involves only *ideas* of pleasure. They are not vivid enough to become pleasant ideas. And he goes on to say that an idea of another's pleasure has more of a tendency to become vivid than only an idea of what gives pleasure (T359). Interestingly, Hume does not mention the impression or "sentiment of pleasure" one receives when he or she "surveys" the object. Does the ommission indicate some hesitancy on Hume's part in choosing the "predominant" cause of love? Wouldn't this *impression* of pleasure be sufficient to immediately trigger love, without the need for sympathy? Hume doesn't think so. He insists, "'tis sympathy, which is properly the cause of the affection" (T359).

Although the causes of love produce pleasure independent of the passion of love, they are not primary causes of love. The ideas which influence love are "favour'd by most circumstances," such as our ideas of the beliefs and passions of others (T359). The perception of a pleasant *subject* directs one's attention to the person uniquely related to it, the *object* of love. Also, the resemblance which holds between oneself and all other persons helps in the transition from the subject to the object. "However the ideas of the pleasant wines, music, or gardens, which the rich man enjoys, may become lively and agreeable, the fancy will not confine itself to them, but will carry its view to the related objects; and in particular, to the person, who possesses them" (T359). Here is the transition from the quality of a cause, which is placed on the subject-cause, to the object of love. "The pleasant idea or image produces [love] towards the person, by means of his relation to the object." By "towards," Hume is stressing the connection between love and its object (T330). The passion of love, perhaps, "preselects"[10] its object so that it is "unavoidable" that the object "enter[s] into the original conception" (T359). But if by "enter into" we take Hume to mean having received from the proud person an "agreeable idea or impression," and are thereby pleased by the belief that he or she enjoys the pleasant objects, then sympathy is the cause of love (T359). The double relation connects the ideas of lover and object by resemblance, contiguity or causation; sympathy connects the impressions of love and pride by resemblance in their pleasantness.

In the section we have been discussing, Hume is also concerned to show that sympathy provides the basis for a "disinterested esteem for riches," one which does not rely on any expectation of benefit (T360). Unless the rich person is our friend, or at least likes us somewhat, it is hard to see on what basis we can hope to benefit from his or her riches. But Hume thinks it is "certain" that we have a high regard for the rich "even before we discover in them any such favorable disposition towards us" (T361).

It might be argued that the tendency to esteem the rich without expecting to benefit from them, and even if we would refuse if offered, is the outcome of a general rule and not sympathy. Hume tries the argument but finds "'tis impossible any custom can ever prevail in the present case" (T362). It is only on the assumption that we love the rich because of the habit we form to expect benefits from them, that we extend the habit to persons that resemble them in their wealth but from whom we expect nothing (T362). But in order to establish the rule of expectation, and then go on to extend the rule to instances which do not fall under it, it is necessary that there be some regularity in our experience of rich persons benefitting us. But experience shows that there is no such regularity. "Of a hundred men of credit and fortune I meet with, there is not, perhaps, one from whom I can expect advantage" (T362).

It is by means of sympathy, then, that we have a disinterested love for the rich, one where "our own interest is not in the least concern'd." We "enter into" the rich person's pleasure and are pleased by the belief that he or she is pleased. The idea becomes so vivid, that it becomes a pleasant impression. It is thus that we "share" their pleasure.

> Riches give satisfaction to the possessor; and this satisfaction is conveyed to the beholder by the imagination, which produces an idea resembling the original impression in force and vivacity. This agreeable idea or impression is connected with love, which is an agreeable passion. It proceeds from a thinking conscious being which is the very object of love (T362).

Were it not for sympathy, we would be unable to love others unless they possessed objects or qualities that produced pleasure only for us. We would be unable to love them for the pleasure they receive from objects or qualities they possess, objects or qualities which are pleasing to them as possessers. But it is not just our houses, or beauty, or virtue, that please us. We love others who possess the same objects or qualities that give us pride (T320).[11] Hume illustrates by having us walk through a house we do not own but observe to be designed for the sake of comfort and convenience, an observation which pleases us. He thinks the cause of the pleasure is sympathy since our interests are not in the least effected.

> This is an advantage that concerns only the owner, nor is there anything
> but sympathy, which can interest the spectator (T364).

We are not pleased by the house in the unique way the owner is pleased since we do not believe the house is ours. We do not expect the house to give us the same pride the owner receives. We are pleased by the thought that the owner is pleased, without expecting to be pleased *as* the owner is pleased.

We have seen that sympathy and the double relation are required in order to arouse love and hatred. Sympathy grants us access to the pains and pleasures of others. But we saw that by itself, sympathy could not explain why we receive love from sympathizing with another's pride, and pride from sympathizing with their love. Here the double relation was required to secure the belief that another person was related to the subject-cause of love. And the quality-cause had to be an independent source of satisfaction, so that were anyone specially related to the subject-cause, they too would feel proud. But Hume insisted that sympathy was the primary cause of love and hatred. It was required in order to explain how we became pleased by another's pleasure, and not simply by what gives pleasure generally. We found that we sympathized with the object of love and became pleased by the belief that he or she was pleased.

Sympathy expands that "narrowness of soul" Hume speaks of and gives us the ability to have concern for the feelings of others. Although we saw that sympathy was the source of a disinterested love, it does not guarantee an impartial sort of love. For while it remains open for us to love others for qualities of character that are pleasant or useful to themselves or others, we have a tendency to love them more or less according to the relations they bear to ourselves. We recall that sympathy is "very variable." But Hume wants to show that approval and disapproval do not admit of the same variation. The shift from loving and hating to approving and disapproving will result from the influence of general rules.

# CHAPTER FIVE

# General Rules and the Impartial Point of View

Although Hume thinks that sympathy is the foundation of moral evaluation, he does not think sympathy is enough to produce impartial moral judgment. The degree of felt sympathy changes according to a number of factors Hume regards as irrelevant from an impartial point of view. Changes in the relations between a sympathizer and the persons with whom he or she sympathizes; changes in degree of resemblance, space and time differences, degrees of intimacy, and partiality for ourselves and close relations alter the feeling which constitutes moral judgment.

By now we are familiar with the form of Hume's argument. The initial sympathetic judgment requires correction by reflecting on the circumstances which produce a range of sympathetic reactions. The shift is from a "violent" love and hatred to a "calm" sort of approval and disapproval, the "peculiar kind" of pleasure and pain which produces the sentiment of praise and blame. Hume tells us there are four sources of this pain and pleasure. Any mental quality that *tends* to be useful or pleasant to the person that has it, or to others, is approved of and considered virtuous. "These circumstances convey an immediate pleasure to the person who considers the object, and commands his love and approbation" (T614). Notice that Hume speaks of both "love and approbation." It is important to keep in mind just how closely the indirect passions and approval and disapproval are connected in Hume's theory of moral judgment. The same mental quality that brings about an indirect passion brings about approval and disapproval, pride and humility in self evaluation, love and hatred in the evaluation of others.[1]

Hume calls any mental quality "virtuous" which causes pride or love and any one "vicious" which causes humility or hatred (T575). In other words, any mental quality that tends to produce pleasure in oneself or others is the cause of an indirect passion. Recall that for something to act as cause, it has to produce a separate sensation which resembles the sensation of the passion and must be related to the object of the passion.

> Now, virtue and vice are attended with these circumstances. They must necessarily be placed either in ourselves or others, and excite pleasure or uneasiness; and therefore give rise to one of these four passions (T473).

It is understandable that Hume should be criticized for claiming that the causes of the indirect passions are the causes of approval and disapproval. For it is clear that we do not love whenever we approve and hate whenever we disapprove.[2] Yet for Hume, the feeling of approval *is* a calm feeling of love, one felt with little emotional intensity. It is, thus, an indirect passion but pruned of the factors that make it partial and regulated according to factors that are relevant from an impartial point of view. On the level of impartial approval, Hume would say that we love whenever we approve and hate whenever we disapprove, but on the level of ordinary likes and dislikes, there is no more sense in the claim that we love whenever we approve than in the claim that we hate whenever we disapprove. Hume reminds us that it is sometimes painful to praise the virtue of people we hate and states that only with a great mental effort do we blame the vices of people we love (T348). Hume's meaning can be better captured by saying that we do not necessarily feel love when we approve and hatred when we disapprove but we must feel one or the other, either love or hatred when we approve or love or hatred when we disapprove. He insists that any quality of mind that tends to produce pleasure in oneself or others always causes pride or love. It is due to the flexibility of Hume's associationism that he can explain the facts as they are, that there is often a conflict between our likes and our dislikes and our approvals and disapprovals. A case can be made to show that Hume does not fail to distinguish the pleasure we get from people we love but do not approve, from the pleasure we get from people we approve but do not love.[3]

What does Hume have in mind when he states that the mental quality that causes love is the mental quality that is judged to be virtuous? By "virtue" and "vice" does he mean the feelings of love and approval themselves, or the mental quality that causes them, or the person who possesses the quality? We can safely say for Hume that someone is virtuous if his mental qualities tend to be pleasant or useful to himself or others (T499,591). The person possessing the quality is the object of love and approval, whereas the quality of mind is what gives pleasure in the case of love and a particular kind of pleasure in the case of approval (T472). Hume says the mental quality that gives pleasure *is* virtuous and completely depends on the pleasure. Pain and pleasure comprise the "nature and essence" of vice and virtue (T296). Hume earlier told us that "the vice entirely escapes you as long as you consider the object" and he compared vice and virtue to qualities which are not "qualities in objects, but perceptions in the mind" (T469). A mental quality does not really inhere in a subject-cause, a person's mind (what Hume takes for granted in Book II), but is a perception in the mind that contemplates it. The "it," here, shows the work of the imagination's tendency to "spread" its perceptions onto material objects (T167). This "productive faculty," Hume writes, by "gilding and staining all natural objects with the colors, borrowed from internal sentiment, raises in a manner a new creation" (EM294). The feeling of approval is thus objectified by its being projected onto another mind.[4]

Hume states that any mental quality that tends to produce pleasure always produces pride or love. But since a virtuous mental quality is the mental quality that tends to produce pleasure, then a virtuous mental quality tends to produce pride or love (T288,575). One's approvals, however, as opposed to one's likes and dislikes, arise from the "general survey" of the quality.

> Moral distinctions depend entirely on certain peculiar sentiments of pain and pleasure, and that whatever mental quality in ourselves or others gives us a satisfaction, by the survey or reflexion, is of course virtuous; as everything of this nature, that gives uneasiness, is vicious (T574,575).

Only when a quality is "consider'd in general" does the approving and disapproving sort of sentiment emerge. Hume identifies the "peculiar kind" of pain and pleasure with the calm passion of approval and disapproval (T472,615). So, whenever one approves of $X$ one loves $X$, but when one loves $X$ one does not necessarily approve of $X$. Approval involves a particular kind of pleasure, a particular kind of love, but the pleasures of love are many and varied. The indirect passions and approval operate on two different levels. "The good qualities of an enemy are hurtful to us; but may still command our esteem and respect" (T472). By reflecting on the circumstances that surround the causes of the indirect passions, one becomes aware that love and hatred are "different to the feeling" than approval and disapproval. "The mind can easily distinguish betwixt the one and the other" (T630).

The connection between the indirect passions and moral evaluation can further be seen by considering the following passage.

> If any action be either virtuous or vicious, 'tis only as a sign of some quality or character. It must depend upon durable principles of the mind, which extend over the whole conduct, and enter into the personal character. Actions themselves, not proceeding from any constant

principle, have no influence on love or hatred, pride or humility; and consequently are never consider'd in morality (T575).

Since actions are not causes of indirect passions, they are not causes of approval and disapproval. Hume regards actions as "signs" of mental characteristics. They are "by their very nature temporary and perishing." The "external performance," he says, has no merit. "We must look within to find the moral quality."

By "durable principles," he means mental qualities like generosity, compassion and disinterestedness that usually or constantly *inhere* in a mind. The indirect passions cannot be lasting when produced by changeable mental qualities or ones that are only occasionally present (T293). We are not pleased by persons who now and again show virtue. One's pleasure is halted by the belief that their qualities of mind are not constantly related to their mind. We anticipate a change of character which "makes us little satisfy'd with the thing." Moral judgments, therefore, are made on the basis of the belief that one always has, or usually has, a quality of mind that tends to produce pleasure.

Among the conditions for impartial judgment, an observed regularity is required between a certain kind of action and its pleasant or painful consequences before one can be judged to have the tendency or "motive" to bring about such consequences; that is, before one can be said to be the "cause" of them (T411,477). Beliefs about the constant or occasional presence of a disposition to produce pain or pleasure come about as a result of observing actions that actually cause pain or pleasure. Hume's point here is that our beliefs about a person's character are not formed by relatively few observations. A person might be *hated* for performing a certain action but will not be *blamed* "if it proceeded from nothing in him, that is durable or constant" (T411).[5]

Clearly, then, Hume thought there was a close tie between the indirect passions and approval and disapproval. Sympathy is appealed to in order to account for both. In the explanation of why we love the rich, sympathy is the "principle cause," and in the explanation of why certain mental dispositions arouse pleasure or pain, sympathy is again called upon. But Hume must somehow characterize approval and disapproval in such a way as to distinguish the impartial evaluation of character from the biased passions of love and hatred. It is necessary here to introduce sympathy in order to explain the variation of our loves and hatreds "without a variation in our esteem" (T581). Let us say that changes in the degree of love and hatred result from changes in the degree of sympathetic pleasure and pain, and these latter changes result from Hume's associationism.

Hume's theory of belief is two-fold, consisting of natural and reflective belief. We recall that the difference between them reflects the operation of, and often the conflict between, two sorts of general rules: rules of imagination and rules of understanding. Let us also say that love and hatred are governed by the imagination. They are natural, unreflective indirect passions which change in emotional intensity with every change in the vivacity of ideas. Approval and disapproval, however, are stable passions which arise from reflection, from general rules of understanding, and involve a particular *manner* of conceiving ideas (EM173). One's unreflective sympathetic pains and pleasures, that is, various degrees of love and hatred, require correction if one is to be an impartial spectator. I have already outlined the first of two objections Hume raises against the doctrine of sympathy. I will restate the first objection and also state the second. I will then consider Hume's replies to determine how far the changeableness of sympathy can be reconciled with the stability of approval and disapproval.

In the *first objection*, Hume proceeds by stressing the influence of sympathy on our approvals and states that we are pleased with and approve of any mental quality that tends to promote the social good. The mental characteristic "presents the lively idea of pleasure; which idea affects us by sympathy, and is itself a kind of pleasure" (T580). But since the degree of sympathy pains and pleasures varies with the relations between oneself and the people with whom one sympathizes, it follows that approval and disapproval likewise vary along the same relations. But approval and disapproval do not vary with changing degrees of pain and pleasure.

> Nor can I feel the same lively pleasure from the virtues of a person, who lived in Greece two thousand years ago, that I feel from the virtues of a familiar friend and acquaintance. Yet I do not say, that I esteem the one more than the other (T581).

The feeling of approval is "stable" against a background of loves and hatreds. We approve of the same characteristics wherever they are found, and whenever they occur, and whoever has them. From the point of view of an impartial spectator, "they appear equally virtuous." Sympathy pleasures and pains vary but approval and disapproval do not. It would follow that sympathy is not the source of approval and disapproval. But Hume maintains that sympathy is the "chief source" of approval and disapproval. How does sympathy enter into the emergence of a unique pain and pleasure which distinguishes vice and virtue from any kind of pain and pleasure we receive from character traits?

Again challenging the thesis that sympathetic feelings form the basis of approval and disapproval, Hume places the *second objection*. He recognizes that we approve of persons who have the *tendency* to benefit society and that we continue to approve even though certain "accidents" prevent them from actually bringing about any pleasant or useful consequences.

> Virtue in rags is still virtue; and the love, which it procures, attends a man in a dungeon or a desart, where the virtue can no longer be exerted into action, and is lost to all the world (T584).

The way we become concerned with what is conducive to the welfare of others and not just to ourselves is by sympathy. But if no one were actually benefitted from someone disposed to produce benefit, there would be no feelings of pleasure to be sympathized with, and if no sympathetic feelings, then no feelings of approval (T584). How can sympathy explain our approval of a character trait that fails to bring about pleasure or utility for anyone? In reply to both objections, Hume retains the doctrine of sympathy but restrains its "partial and contradictory motions" (T489).

Let us return to the first objection. Hume proceeds with a statement about sympathy.

> When any quality, or character, has a tendency to the good of mankind, we are pleas'd with it, and approve of it; because it presents the lively idea of pleasure; which idea affects us by sympathy, and is itself a kind of pleasure (T580).

He seems to be saying that we approve of people who have the behavioral disposition to produce pleasure by sympathizing with the pleasure of persons who benefit from the disposition. There is, of course, the ambiguity here of whether we are sympathizing with the actual pleasure of persons who are actually benefitted or with the pleasure of those who would have been pleased had the disposition been realized in action. For now, let us leave aside pains and pleasures that might have been and concentrate on sympathy with actual pain and pleasure.

Notice that we sympathize with persons affected by the tendency, now realized in action, but the *object* of approval is the person who possesses it.[6] Hume's double relation requires that approval is no more to be identified with sympathetic feeling as love or hatred is to be identified with the *separate* pain or pleasure the quality of mind produces. In keeping with his theory of the double relation, Hume wants to distinguish the pains and pleasures received sympathetically from the pains and pleasures of approval and disapproval. The feeling of approval and sympathetic feeling are different whether we sympathize with persons who are affected by their own mental qualities or with others who are affected by them.

Among the causes of the indirect passions, we recall that in the case of mental qualities, when the subject-cause and object of the passion coincide – a person's mind and a person – it was hard to see how a quality of mind could be related to a mind in such a way as to produce grief or joy *independent* of an indirect passion. According to Hume's notion of the mind as "a bundle or collection of different perceptions" which are related by resemblance and causation, Hume finds no contradiction in separating a quality of mind from a mind and "breaking off all its relations, with that connected mass of perceptions, which constitutes a thinking being" (T207,233). It is only on the assumption that qualities of a mind are inseparable from a mind, or inhere in a mental substance, that the pleasure we receive from a person's mental qualities is not separate from the pleasure of love or approval (T636). Despite the "labyrinth" of personal identity in which Hume finds himself, he wants to keep the double relation intact and associate by resemblance the separate pleasure received from a mental quality with the pleasurable passion of love. And since the former pleasure "resolves itself in a great measure" into the pleasure of sympathy, it follows that sympathetic pleasure is not identified with the pleasure of love or approval (T360).[7]

Replying to the first objection, Hume stresses that sympathy by itself is inadequate for the arousal of that special pain and pleasure which characterizes impartial judgment. When operating according to the straightforward principle of vivacity, sympathetic feelings are more intense when communicated by persons spatially near to us than from persons that are placed at a distance, and are more intense when communicated from friends than from strangers (T581). As a result, our loves and hatreds are more or less intense according to the relations that hold between ourselves and the object of evaluation (T591). Immediate sympathetic feelings require correction in order to eliminate the contradictions which follow within ourselves at different times, and among each other at the same time, when each person considers the object of evaluation from their "peculiar point of view." The general point of view is what corrects the partial morality generated from the immediate sympathetic judgment.

The various degrees of pain and pleasure to which sympathy is susceptible are explainable according to the principles of association. In the situation where a sympathizer stands in the relations of resemblance, contiguity and causation to the object of love or hatred, sympathy operates in its "full perfection" and love and hatred "rise to the greatest height" (T276). It is important to see that the principle of vivacity determines the intensity of sympathetically acquired pain and pleasure, and the intensity of pain and pleasure determines the calmness or violence of love and hatred.

The relations in which a sympathizer stands to the object of love or hatred determine the vividness of the sympathizer's idea of another's pain or pleasure. And the vividness of this idea determines the extent to which the sympathizer is actually pained or pleased by the belief that another is pained or pleased. In terms of calmness and violence, love and hatred are coordinate with the vividness of the idea of another's pleasure and pain.

Hume's method of correcting biased sympathy and, therefore, biased love and hatred is thus aimed at the vividness by which the ideas of another's pain or pleasure are thought. In Book I, Hume sought to distinguish a genuine belief from sheer vivacity of conception. By reflection he discriminated causal from contingent features of causes and distinguished the unique vivacity occasioned by the causal inference from the enlivening influence of resemblance and contiguity. The reasonable judgment stayed within the scope of a causal rule. In Book III, the only relation which is relevant from an impartial point of view is the *general* resemblance that holds between all persons (T319). The general viewpoint requires that we consider only those features of a situation which would be common to any spectator. Causation, relations of time and place and *particular* resemblances are relations which bias sympathy and render love and hatred partial passions. Hume tells us that causation has a greater influence on enlivening ideas than resemblance and spatio-temporal proximity. Causation informs us, first, of the existence of a passion and, secondly, sometimes holds between oneself and the object of love and hatred. We strongly sympathize with the pain of our child even when we do not resemble him or her in any particular way, and even if he or she lives in a distant part of the world. For Hume, familial relations are a kind of causation, and love and hatred are aroused when only these relations are present. Accordingly, we sympathize more with friends than acquaintances and more with acquaintances than with strangers.

Changes in space and time relations between the spectator and the object of sympathy change also the vividness of ideas and, therefore, the degree of pleasure and pain communicated by others (T582). Sympathy is more intense when directed at persons we resemble in some particular character trait. The tendency to associate with persons similar to ourselves makes for an "easy" sympathy and increases the vividness of our idea of their pain and pleasure. The greatest partiality is directed towards oneself, "where each person loves himself better than any other single person."[8] Sympathy is thereby increased and the pains and pleasures we receive from persons whom we believe will benefit us are greater than those received from persons that promise us nothing.

Now the point of the general point of view is to overcome the contradictions that result within a system of morality where everyone's loves and hatreds count as the standard of morality. Were everyone to approve and disapprove of persons according to the extent of sympathy and, therefore, the degree of love and hatred, there would be little agreement on the evaluation of character. Appealing only to the unique set of relations that holds between each person and the object of evaluation would undermine the possibility for any reasonable discourse on the subject of evaluation, "unless they chose some common point of view, from which they might survey the object, and which might cause it to appear the same to all of them" (T591). The movement toward an impartial and interpersonal system of moral sentiments is explained by the "uneasiness" the mind feels when confronted with conflict and contradiction (T206).[9] The imagination's tendency to discover and even create in experience continuity and stability moves us out of a system of morality plagued with instability and conflict. As Hume described it, the mind moves in whatever direction promises most ease. He says it takes only a little reflection to find "relief" from those spontaneous passions which result in contradictory appraisals. The departure from an unreflective morality of discordant loves and hatreds to a common standard of approval is another convention, similar to the convention to "bestow stability" on external possessions, possessions which, again, become "fix'd and constant" (T489).[10] It is no less necessary for the maintainance of society to secure possessions by property rules than it is to stabilize evaluations by "general rules of morality." The rules Hume here has in mind are clearly the regulative rules of understanding.

> The remedy, then, is not deriv'd from nature, but from artifice; or more properly speaking, nature provides a remedy in the judgment and understanding, for what is irregular and incommodious in the affections" (T489).

The corrective judgment from understanding, then, is an artificial judgment. The sympathetic response the judgment corrects is more natural and spontaneous. But notice Hume's change of mind from "artifice" to "nature." He will be able to explain the disruptive upsurges of natural passion against the reasonable demand for moral stability by maintaining that corrective judgments as well as corrected ones ultimately rest on the vivacity of ideas, on "habit and experience" (T585).

What exactly is involved in taking the "common" point of view from which Hume hopes to find that unique impression of pleasure and pain which constitutes impartial judgment? And once viewing the moral scene from the "general survey," how does sympathy re-enter into the account of the correction of immediate sympathetic judgments?

To take the position of an impartial spectator is to exclude from consideration one's pleasure, interest and spatio-temporal location with regard to the object of evaluation. Looking at the factors of pleasure and interest, Hume writes:

> Now, in judging of characters, the only interest or pleasure, which appears the same to every spectator, is that of the person himself, whose character is examined; or that of persons, who have a connexion with him. And tho' such interests and pleasures touch us more faintly than our own, yet being more constant and universal, they counter-ballance the latter even in practice, and are alone admitted in speculation as the standard of virtue and morality. They alone produce that particular feeling or sentiment, on which moral distinctions depend (T591).

Whether we sympathize with the agent or his associates depends on whether the agent tends to be useful or pleasant to himself or others. In any case, we must "overlook" the pleasures and interests that concern only ourselves (T582). Since the concern for self and close associates is greater than the concern for strangers, it is natural that we sympathize more with persons who are already pleasant or useful to us and from whom we expect further pleasure or utility. It is rare that we love others who show no tendency to further our interest (T583). But when the step is taken to evaluate persons according to a vivid sympathy from the expectation of benefit only to ourselves or family, we run into contradictions within ourselves as our interests change and with others whose interests differ from and often conflict with our own. From the confusion and discomfort of contradiction that follows from such widespread disagreement, "we seek some other standard of merit and demerit, which may not admit of so great a variation" (T583).

We overlook our own particular set of interests and consider the interests of people associated with the person being evaluated. Hume thinks the *only* point of view from which contradictions can be overcome, and agreement reached, is from the consideration of qualities of character that tend to benefit or harm the individuals that are immediately related to the person who has them (T603). All reference to personal self interest is excluded (T472). Our interests are excluded because of the contradictions that arise among people who are not all on the receiving end of a beneficial tendency simply because they do not have the same interests as ourselves (T602).

From the point of view of what promotes the particular interest of each individual, no one mental tendency can be expected to satisfy the interests of everyone. Different qualities promote different interests. What pleases a partner displeases a competitor (T383). The same quality, therefore, is judged virtuous and vicious according to its tendency to promote some interests and not others. The discomfort that follows from contradiction "makes us form some general inalterable standard, by which we may approve or disapprove of characters and manners" (T440,603). From the point of view of what promotes the interest of all individuals, reference to one's own interest is excluded, and consideration is given only to persons who have an "immediate connexion" with the agent (T583,603). From this viewpoint, the same mental quality $q$ ceases to be virtuous and vicious. For persons with interests not forwarded by $q$ do not consider $q$ as a quality which affects themselves, or their family and friends, but consider $q$ only with respect to persons directly affected by $q$ (T582). By this means, the interests of all persons are considered and the same mental quality either promotes or does not promote the interest or pleasure of everyone. But if we ignore our interests and pleasures, and the interests and pleasures of our family and friends, and if approval and disapproval are particular pleasures and pains, then the *only* way we become pleased by what promotes the pleasure and utility of others is by sympathy (T583).

What is interesting in the account is Hume's appeal to the same system of morality which first drove us to seek something more stable.

> Being thus loosen'd from our first station, we cannot afterward fix ourselves so commodiously by any means as by a sympathy with those, who have any commerce with the person we consider (T583).

The pleasures and pains we receive sympathetically from persons who have the tendency to be pleasant or useful to themselves, or from persons who have an "immediate connexion" with them, are disinterested and impartial pleasures and pains, approval and disapproval rather than love and hatred.

> We approve of a person, who is possess'd of qualities immediately agreeable to those, with whom he has any commerce; tho' perhaps we ourselves never reap'd any pleasure from them. We also approve of one, who is possess'd of qualities, that are immediately agreeable to himself; tho' they be of no service to any mortal (T590).

The pleasures and pains we receive immediately from persons who tend to be pleasant or useful to us, or the pleasures and pains we receive sympathetically from persons closely related to the object of evaluation and to us, count as the "partial affections," love and hatred rather than approval and disapproval (T590). When we approve or disapprove, then, we sympathize with and "receive by communication" pleasures and pains which the person himself receives from his pleasant or useful qualities "as if these qualities had a tendency to our advantage or loss," or we sympathize with the pleasures and pains of persons who are likely receivers of his or her quality as if we were receiving the pleasures and pains of persons closely related to us. So the feelings acquired by sympathy are as if they were the feelings we would have were the qualities immediately pleasant or useful to us, or the feelings acquired by sympathy are as if they were the feelings we would have were we to sympathize with persons closely related to us.

Sympathy pulls us back into the situation from which reason takes us. Reason allows us to step aside from our own concerns and to consider the concerns of others, but only at the expense of bringing those concerns so "very near us ... as to give us the same pleasure and uneasiness in the characters of others, as if they had a tendency to our own advantage or loss" (T579,603). We depart from a partial point of view upon pain of contradiction in order to get a glimpse of how things would look were we placed in a partial point of view. Impartiality, in any strict sense, without any reference to oneself, either actual or sympathetic, lies outside the science of man. Hume does not try to deny this.

> In general, it may be affirm'd, that there is no such passion in human minds, as the love of mankind, merely as such, independent of personal qualities, of services, or of relation to ourself (T481).

Elsewhere Hume writes that in our evaluation of others, we "always confine our view to that narrow circle, in which any person moves, in order to form a judgment of his moral character."

> When the natural tendency of his passions leads him to be serviceable and useful within his sphere, we approve of his character, and love his person, by a sympathy with the sentiments of those, who have a more particular connexion with him (T602).

A person who departs from this partiality, "either by too great an enlargement or contraction of the affections," is judged to be vicious (T483,488).

A similar "virtuous circularity"[11] runs through Hume's discussion of justice, where the understanding redirects heedless self interest by the reflection that "self interest is much better satisfy'd by its restraint, than by its liberty" (T492). By means of an agreement that establishes the stability of possessions, self interest is restrained in its "partial and contradictory motions" (T489).

In the evaluation of character, the issue, again, is not so much between partiality and impartiality as it is between stability and instability. Hume's concern is to overcome contradictory evaluations which result from unrestrained loves and hatreds. The adoption of a general viewpoint, which involves sympathizing with the object of evaluation or with his or her associates, causes the object to "appear the same to every spectator" (T583,590). From this viewpoint, Hume thinks there can be little talk "of a right or wrong taste in morals" (T547).

Hume's reply to the *second objection* addresses the question of what is involved when mental qualities are judged according to their *tendency* to promote pleasure or utility. One's character traits are evaluated and judged vicious or virtuous irrespective of whether external circumstances prevent them from promoting pleasure or utility for anyone. According to the objection, were sympathy the basis of approval and disapproval, those feelings would occur only when tendencies to action are put into action and actually benefit or harm someone. Where a person tries but fails to bring about pleasure or utility, where the mental quality is an "imperfect means," there are no pleasant or painful feelings to be sympathized with. Consequently, there can be no feelings of approval and disapproval.

To this Hume replies, "'Tis sufficient if everything be compleat in the object itself," and says that qualities which are *fitted* to produce pleasure are pleasing to a spectator even when external conditions prevent them from producing any pleasure in the world (T584). A house that is designed for ease and comfort is pleasing although it is believed that it will never be occupied.

> A fertile soil, and a happy climate, delight us by a reflexion on the happiness which they wou'd afford the inhabitants, tho' at present the country be desart and uninhabited (T585).

Hume's answer is no mere "restatement of the problem"[12] but involves the operation of general rules at the levels of imagination and understanding. In the present context, Hume is discussing the inference from imagination. Given the impression that resembles a cause in some of its features, the idea of the effect is thought in as vivid a manner as it would be thought were all the features given.

> Where a character is, in every respect, fitted to be beneficial to society, the imagination passes easily from the cause to the effect, without considering that there are still some circumstances wanting to render the cause a compleat one. General rules create a species of probability, which sometimes influences the judgment, and always the imagination (T585).

From the perception of persons that are "dispos'd" to produce pleasure or utility, or from the belief that they are the cause of pleasure or utility, the imagination vividly thinks the idea of the effect, of the pleasure of the agent or his associates, ignoring the accidental circumstances required to complete the cause (T584). At this point, it is unclear whether Hume considers this inference reasonable or unreasonable, for one wonders in what sense an absent *accident* makes a cause incomplete. In what follows, we will see Hume's characteristic indecisiveness as to whether imagination or understanding is determinative of the impartial, sympathetic judgment. The conflict of general rules will resume, and the way we ought to judge dispositions will be challenged by the way dispositions must be judged.

Sympathizing from a general point of view is often thought to be "equivalent to *knowing* how one would feel if one were impartial."[13] According to such accounts, sympathizing with non-existent feelings involves *thinking* of, or conceiving, the sympathy that would be felt had the benevolent disposition actually benefitted someone. Again, it is not altogether clear whether Hume counts this as reasonable or unreasonable moral judgment. But the point is that it can only make sense to talk about feelings one *would* have only if the imagination merely *thought* about the sort of feelings that would be felt. But in simply thinking about sympathetic feelings, one leaves out of the account the sympathetic feelings themselves, and such feelings, occurring at the level of immediate and unreflective sympathy, always survive the reflective process of discriminating the features of causes (T585). One cannot characterize a vivid idea of another's pleasure as simply thinking about the sympathetic pleasure one would have. A vivid idea of another's pleasure is not a simple conception, but a vivid and pleasant idea that another is pleased. What is being overlooked is the "set of passions" belonging to the imagination.

> These passions are mov'd by degrees of livliness and strength, which are inferior to belief, and independent of the real existence of their objects (T585).

However, "inferior to belief" does not go to the extreme of no vividness whatsoever. For to have a vivid idea is, more often than not, to have a belief that another is pleased and to feel pleasure in the belief. There is nothing hypothetical about the matter. One becomes aware of the difference in feeling between a vivid idea and a belief after reflection, yet simple vivacity of conception always compels belief (T149,266).

Hume allows just one way in which contrary to fact descriptions of feelings legitimately describe feelings that would be felt. Initially, it is clear that if one has not gone through the process of sorting the causal from the noncausal features of a cause, it makes no sense to speak of the feelings one would have, for one has not become aware of the difference between a vivid idea and a belief. One is not aware of the persistent inference from imagination *despite* the more reasonable judgment from understanding. One cannot be in a position to believe what feeling one would have without having made the reflection and without having learned the difference, that is, without having experienced the feeling itself.

One can speak of the feeling that would be experienced when one tries by reflection but fails *entirely* to overlook the enlivening influence of, say, familial relations on one's sympathy. That one completely fails is important, for if one is experiencing the "commotion" Hume recognizes between, say, hatred and approval, then one is actually experiencing approval, however interrupted by spontaneous eruptions of passion. In this situation, approval could only be described as a feeling one would have during the moments one does not experience approval. Only if one utterly fails to experience the unique feeling of the corrected judgment, can one reflect and *think* about what feeling would be felt by recalling similar situations where one was more successful, but is now unable to feel what one merely thinks would be felt.

Moving from the other direction, does Hume allow that one may simply think about one's immediate sympathetic judgment and thus come to know how one would feel if one were not impartial? Again, we could only think about the feelings we would have were the reflective judgment able to *entirely* eradicate one's vivid idea of, say, a close relation's pain or pleasure. Is it Hume's view that one may recall situations where, for example, our especially vivid idea of the pleasure others receive from our child's disposition was completely destroyed for the sake of impartiality? Clearly not. In fact, and not contrary to fact, the *additional* vivacity our idea acquires when we sympathize with the pleasure others reap from our son's or daughter's disposition cannot be checked by the reflection that a stranger, or an enemy, with a similar disposition would also tend to be pleasant to others. Hume is thus able to explain why approval and disapproval become difficult when challenged by hatred and love (T472). He states that "sympathy varies, without a variation in our esteem." But the ups and downs of sympathy are always present, even when set against the stable moral judgment. "General rules create a species of probability, which sometimes influences the judgment, and always the imagination." A lively idea or belief is a sensation which cannot be thwarted by "mere ideas and reflections" (T184). The sympathetic moral judgment, whether it turns out to be a corrected or an immediate judgment, is one which Hume expresses counterfactually but which, he admits, does not describe the facts as they are.[14]

Hume considers it an "accident" when a tendency to promote pleasure or utility is prevented from being realized in action (T584). The tendency remains "compleat in the object" despite such factors as imprisonment or being in a desert. Yet the factors required to release the restraining factors are just the "circumstances wanting to render the cause a compleat one" (T585). The *cause* is incomplete without the accidental features while the *disposition* is complete with or without them. The cause, therefore, is twofold, a "good disposition" together with "good fortune." When the accident of bad fortune takes a turn for the better, when the restraint is relaxed, "'tis probable or at least possible" that the tendency will produce the consequences it usually produces (T313). Virtuous tendencies, then, plus good fortune possibly or probably benefit mankind (T584).

Hume thought there was no philosophical basis for the distinction between power and its exercise and reduced these concepts to probability and possibility.[15] When there is no obstacle to action – "physical impediments" like iron or "motives" like fear – one believes that a good disposition will "possibly or probably" act and produce pleasure or utility. When obstacles prevent the disposition from acting, "we conclude from past experience, that the person never will perform that action" (T312). Where an action is possible, a person has the power to act; where impossible – by a "physical [or moral] necessity" – the person has no power and never will act (T315,404). But what we take to be physical necessity is just a "determination" to infer a belief (T165). And we recall that the denial of a belief is conceivable and thus involves possible existence (T95,EU25). For this reason, Hume writes, we believe the action will *never* be performed, but we do not judge from experience that it is *impossible* for it to be performed. "Nothing we imagine is absolutely impossible" (T32). Though we believe that a disposition caught in the grip of bad fortune will never act, it is possible to conceive the opposite and imagine that the disposition will be realized in action. But Hume will soon tell us that a reasonable standard of belief ought not to be established on the basis of what is possible to conceive.

The present problem concerns the familiar question: What features among the combination of circumstances surrounding causes are essential and what features accidental? Some interesting results follow when the question is raised in reference to the account of general rules given in Book I. The circumstances external to a benevolent disposition, what Hume calls "fortune," are the superfluous features of the cause, the accidents which prevent the disposition from benefiting anyone or permit the disposition to benefit someone. We recall that when the accidental circumstances are regularly conjoined with the essential circumstances,

> they have such an influence on the imagination, that even in the absense of the latter, they carry us on to the conception of the usual effect, and give to that conception a force and vivacity, which make it superior to the mere fictions of the fancy (T148).

According to this account of rules, it would follow that even when a good disposition is not present, when presented with the sort of circumstances that usually surround the good disposition, the imagination continues to think the vivid idea of the effect, that persons will be benefitted by the disposition. The spectator does not simply *know* how he or she *would* feel, but, by reason of a vivid idea of the usual effect, is actually pleased by the belief that someone is pleased. This inference described the "first influence of general rules" which Hume prescribed ought to be regulated by general rules of understanding (T149). The inference from nonessential features to the usual effect required correction, but whatever was learned from reflecting on those features, the inference to the usual effect from features *believed* to be nonessential was made nevertheless. This sort of inference did not rest on a reasonable foundation of belief (T143). Yet, Hume found it difficult to decide what general rule ought to determine our judgments about dispositions.

According to the account of general rules in Book I, it is necessary to assume that good fortune is "frequently conjoined" with a good disposition, and bad fortune with a bad one, if the imagination is to associate fortune with disposition by resemblance and contiguity. Hume makes the assumption. Dispositions are acquired by practice, repetition and by gaining some ease in performing their corresponding actions (T422). It seems clear that without some degree of good fortune in one's external circumstances, which allows one to perform actions of a certain sort, it is unlikely that a disposition of that sort will take hold. Hume recognizes this fact and shows discomfort in calling the circumstances of fortune "accidents." Dispositions, he says, cannot be "compleat" and "effectual" without the appropriate conditions. Moreover, external circumstances may even prevent the development of a disposition (T584). When the disposition fails to act because of external circumstances, "'tis only an imperfect means." Nevertheless, if we follow the Book I account of rules, Hume thinks the inference to pleasant or painful consequences from sheer circumstance and fortune is unreasonable and recommends that we "correct this propensity by a reflection on the nature of those circumstances" (T148). The habit of inferring pleasant consequences when it is believed that a good disposition is present is extended to instances that differ from those which formed the habit. The belief that an individual is not in possession of a good disposition should halt the transition to the sort of consequences that would result were the individual in such possession. But Hume insists that the initial inference from imagination is a "natural transition, which precedes reflection and cannot be prevented by it" (T147). Presented with the circumstances that usually surround the disposition, the inference is drawn to a vivid idea of the effect, that persons will be pained or pleased by the disposition. However, by means of general rules of understanding, the "accidental circumstances" are distinguished from the "efficacious causes."

> When we find that an effect can be produc'd without the concurrence of any particular circumstance, we conclude that that circumstance makes not a part of the efficacious cause, however frequently conjoin'd with it (T149).

According to this account of general rules, good fortune, regardless of how often it may surround a good disposition, is not causally related to the disposition. From the thought of persons fortunate enough to be placed in circumstances conducive to the development of a benevolent disposition, we should not believe that they will benefit anyone unless they have the disposition. If we remind ourselves of the fellow hanging from a cliff in an iron cage, it similarly follows that the circumstances that usually surround a good disposition have as little connection with the production of pleasure and utility as does the perception of depth with descent. Both are super-fluous features and "only conjoin'd by accident," with the disposition in one case and the removal of support in the other. It would be just as unreasonable to believe that persons surrounded by leisure and opportunity have the disposition to benefit mankind as it would be to believe in our fall simply from peering over a mountain top. We should not believe that pleasant or useful consequences will exist and should not believe that such consequences are "probable or even possible" from persons who do not have the disposition to bring them about.

One is reminded that since, for Hume, the denial of a belief is conceivable and thus implies possible existence, it is possible to conceive that persons without the disposition to bring about pleasure or utility will act and bring about pleasant or useful consequences. But Hume's point is that we should not believe in the probability of an event just because we are able to conceive the event's possible occurrence. A standard of belief should not rest on the foundation of what is possible to conceive. And for Hume, the question does not concern simple conception by itself, for we have a vivid conception and thus believe in the possible or probable existence of pleasure or utility from persons who are not believed to have the benevolent disposition, but have the same luck and circumstances that usually surround persons that do. Even though such beliefs are inevitable, they should not determine a reasonable foundation of belief (T143).

If we look at the account of rules by the end of the *Treatise*, Hume seems to be saying something different. He now thinks that it would be un-reasonable to believe in the existence of pleasant or useful consequences from the good disposition by itself, without good fortune and under circumstances which prevent its operation. But we draw the inference just the same, "without considering that there are still some circumstances wanting to render the cause a compleat one" (T585). In this context, his use of "without considering" is descriptive, not prescriptive, but is shortly read prescriptively in that we ought to consider the missing circumstances before we go on to believe that pleasure or utility will exist. It would be unreasonable to believe that persons believed to be good will bring about any goodness when placed in conditions which prevent them from acting. Under such conditions, it is neither probable nor possible that any good will result and, as in the previous account, we should not establish a standard of belief based on the possibility of conceiving that pleasure or utility will exist.

Hume wants to call things like fortune and circumstance "accidents" and is yet telling us to reflect on their absence if we want to be reasonable and check the inference to the belief that consequences will exist. We ought to consider the missing circumstances required to complete the cause if we want to stop ourselves from believing the usual consequences. And it is unreasonable to continue sympathizing with pleasures and pains once we consider the circumstances preventing action and learn that there are no pleasant or painful feelings to be sympathized with.

Hume characteristically gives the argument an "oblique direction" and says that we *should* correct for the accidents of fortune and should not consider them in our approvals and disapprovals. Again, reflecting on the circumstances of the cause, fortune and disposition, "we know, that an alteration of fortune may render the benevolent disposition entirely impotent; and therefore we separate, as much as possible, the fortune from the disposition." Hume is here using "separate" prescriptively and he describes the separation as a judgment which corrects the earlier judgment to withhold belief from, and thus sympathy with, pains and pleasures that do not exist. A second reflective judgment corrects the first reflection and brings it back to the initial, unreflective belief that pains or pleasures exist. Hume is now prescribing that we continue to believe unreflectively, that we should continue to pass from a cause to an effect "without considering that there are still some circumstances wanting to render the cause a compleat one." We learn that we ought to believe the way we must believe even though we believe that the cause, the good disposition, cannot be complete without good fortune and will neither probably nor possibly produce pleasure or utility for anyone (T149,265).

How is it that we ought to believe what is unreasonable to believe and to continue sympathizing with pains and pleasures that are not believed to exist? That we do this unreflectively is understandable and is explained by the inertial tendency of imagination to extend the scope of causal rules. But once it is learned that consequences will not be produced unless the circumstances preventing action are lifted, why should we separate the fortune from the disposition? Why should we not consider the circumstances which prevent the cause from being complete?

Hume's answer is brief but points to the reasons given for departing from a moral system where each person's pleasures and interests determine their approvals. In the present case, it is because of the changeability of one's fortune and external circumstances that we are moved away from a morality of contingencies. To establish a moral system on the basis of whether fortune allows persons to exercise their dispositions would, likewise, generate contradictions. Fortune is inconstant; dispositions are permanent. They are sufficient to complete the object of evaluation (T584). Again, in order to overcome the discomfort of contradiction and to satisfy the desire for stability and cooperation, the spectator sympathizes from a general point of view (T489). Corrected sympathy, then, involves sympathizing with pains and pleasures we believe would exist had the good disposition not been hindered from action. When the disposition actually produces pleasure or utility, we sympathize to a greater extent with pains and pleasures we believe really exist, but approval and disapproval are untouched by what is believed to be the actual consequences of actions.

We recall the earlier claim that Hume talks as if no belief were involved in our evaluations according to general rules.[16] The "set of passions" belonging to the imagination involved inferences which were "inferior to belief" and "independent of the real existence of their objects," but these passions were not understood as involving no belief whatsoever. Inferences from the imagination, though expressed counterfactually – pains and pleasures the spectator would feel had others actually been pained or pleased – were not the expressions of simply thinking, or estimating,[17] or "knowing"[18] how one would feel.

Hume has it that we actually sympathize with the pains and pleasures we do not believe exist and accounts for this by the continued influence of sheer vividness even after reflection and the contingent sources of vivacity have been identified (T371,586). A vivid idea is always a believed idea. And the inference to consequences from someone believed to have the disposition to produce them, but who is presently restrained, continues to yield a vivid idea in light of the opposite judgment that no such consequences exist (T149). For Hume, a vivid idea of another's pleasure is a pleasant idea, is actually a pleasure, and is not one that merely would please us. Hume makes the point by contrasting a vivid idea with a belief.

> The seeming tendencies of objects affect the mind: and the emotions they
> excite are of a like species with those, which proceed from the real
> consequences of objects, but their feeling is different (T586).

A building that *seems* insecure is judged to be ugly even when it is believed
that it is solid and stable. A book that contains language that *would* be
difficult to pronounce is unpleasant and is judged to be written in a harsh
style. One imagines and sympathizes with the pain and discomfort it would
give were it read aloud. It is reasonable to believe that it will neither
probably nor possibly be read aloud so long as one's possession of the book
prevents others who have the disposition to read aloud (T312). Reflection
shows that we are only sympathizing with the discomfort that would exist
were a public speaker to acquire the book. The imagination, however,
thinks a vivid idea of the discomfort, "or rather feels the passion itself," in
the same way as if people were actually hearing the book read aloud and
were experiencing discomfort. The use of "as if" indicates that one has
reflected and acquired a reasonable judgment. It points to the recognition
that one is being unreasonable when one believes what will neither
probably nor possibly exist. Similarly, we feel ashamed when we see
persons act foolishly, although we believe they are unaware of their foolish
behavior.

> All this proceeds from sympathy; but 'tis of a partial kind, and views its
> objects only on one side, without considering the other, which has a
> contrary effect, and wou'd entirely destroy that emotion, which arises
> from the first appearance (T371).

It is unreasonable to believe in the existence of an effect from a cause
which we believe will never produce the effect. Experience shows that
dispositions which are under the grip of bad fortune will neither probably
nor possibly act. But we end up sympathizing with pains and pleasures we
believe will exist from dispositions believed to be under the grip of bad
fortune. The persistent belief here rests with the imagination's tendency to
extend causal rules to instances "without considering" the circumstances
necessary to complete the cause. In Book I, Hume regards this tendency as
a source of error and unreasonableness. In Book III, the same tendency
retains its unreasonable status by overlooking the circumstances of good
fortune. Yet, Hume prescribes that we ought to be *reasonable* and separate
fortune from disposition, what we ordinarily do by virtue of our
*unreasonable* nature. Hume concludes by stating that the imagination,
without the need for moral exhortation, "adheres to the general view of
things." Sympathizing with pains and pleasures which are believed not to

exist is an inevitable fact of human nature. Reflection only makes us aware that a tendency of imagination is responsible for the approval we give to the unfortunate but good disposition.

The tendency of imagination to bring order and regularity in our evaluations brought with it the belief that consequences will follow from people believed to be incapable of action. Though it was unreasonable to sympathize with pains and pleasures that were not believed to exist, the imagination sought to stabilize evaluations by separating fortune from disposition. The separation was made for the sake of regularity but resulted in unreasonable belief. The inference from dispositions to the usual effects was an unreflective judgment, made also for the sake of regularity, and also resulted in unreasonable belief. The very drive for regularity in our evaluations brought with it falsehood and unreasonableness.

Hume's theory of moral judgment concludes with the same scepticism and "manifold contradictions" as did his theory of belief and general rules at the close of Book I. Should the judgments of imagination or understanding be accepted as regulative and prescriptive? To this Hume replies "I know not what ought to be done." In an act of "blind submission," both are accepted as unavoidable operations of the mind (T269).

# CHAPTER SIX

# Conclusion

In light of the skeptical conclusion of Hume's theory of moral judgment, something more positive may be gleaned from his teachings about morality. We saw the unreasonable side of human nature contribute to the development of a number of conventions and social institutions. The rules of good breeding and the virtue of concealed pride rested on the assumption that implicit expressions of pride weakened the belief that others were proud. Yet, if our judgments were reasonable, it would make no difference how pride was expressed. Any presentation of that passion would be judged vicious. Here was an instance where Hume's reliance on the unreasonable side of human nature explained why all direct expressions of pride were condemned. People displayed "greatness" when that passion was "secretly discovered." The duty to refrain from direct expressions of pride relied on the comparative judgment, again, a judgment which expressed unreasonableness. Hume was confident that human nature would respond comparatively to an unjustified yet enthusiastic presentation of pride. Were it not for the persistent belief that another's pride is justified simply on the basis of a firm presentation, refraining from direct expressions of pride would never have become a duty.

We responded to the oversimplified view that the regulative rules always determined the impartial evaluation of character. Simple vivacity of conception challenged the judgments of understanding and, again, we were "sav'd," this time from moral skepticism. We saw Hume's wavering attitude between the claims of imagination and understanding and observed his final claim, that we *should* be reasonable and judge in accordance with our unreasonable nature. Character traits were judged virtuous regardless of whether external conditions prevented them from bringing about any goodness. Sympathizing with non-existent passions explained why "virtue in rags is still virtue." And a "sympathy with public interest," the source of approval and disapproval of just and unjust acts, likewise relied on a

134

sympathy with non-existent pleasures and pains. Were reason able to completely destroy the unreflective sympathetic judgment, the moral dimension of justice would never have developed (T371,499).

All the reason required to establish the conventions and social institutions were not to be thought superior to "human nature, however savage and uncultivated" (T522). Hume indicated that our very sense of conscience rests on the tendency of imagination to extend inductive generalizations (T551), and it was due to a "trivial" operation of imagination that theoretical and practical skepticism were circumvented. Clearly, the unreasonable side of human nature had a positive influence on the development of society and morality.

We also saw, however, that reason played a significant role in factual and moral judgment. By the general rules of understanding, factual judgments were rendered reasonable and moral judgments stable. They sustained the generalities that were already formed and protected them from the inertial tendency of imagination to extend them beyond their range of application. The regulative rules allowed us to reflect on the combination of circumstances among causes and to distinguish the accidents from the causal features. They functioned to control the initial response to infer from a vivid conception, and the difference was learned between a lively idea and a genuine judgment. If the regulative rules were not always able to correct immediate judgments, they at least made us aware of potential falsehoods, and they let us know when we were being unreasonable. The reflections of reason were themselves motivated by the passion for truth. Like the propensities of imagination, they represented a basic tendency to bring order and continuity into experience. Both were ineluctable aspects of human nature and both had their part to play in science and morals.

The present work has been an attempt to clarify Hume's theory of moral judgment as presented in *A Treatise of Human Nature*. I argued that in order to understand Hume's brief comments in Book III about the judgment of an impartial spectator, the theory of general rules in Book I provided the most explanatory interpretation. I claimed that an interpretation along the lines of general rules not only cohered with the moral theory, but also with the theory of belief and the discussion of the indirect passions in Book II.

Norman Kemp Smith has argued that it was in connection with the problems of ethics that Hume entered his general philosophy of human nature. While Kemp Smith provides evidence for this view, it is not obvious that Hume "advanced"[1] from his theory of moral evaluation to his treatment of belief. This would suppose that Hume had worked out his theory of moral judgment in Book III and then extended it to Book I, to beliefs about matters of fact. As I see it, the order of exposition must have been reversed.

The theory of belief and general rules is completely disclosed in Book I and is then extended to Book III, to the account of moral judgment. A number of remarks in the section "Of the origin of the natural virtues" point to the sections of Book I which involve belief and general rules. In his discussion of moral judgment, Hume presupposes that his readers have an understanding of the place of general rules in judgments of fact. If my reading is correct, it would be plausible to argue that while Hume may have entered his general philosophy with the particular problem of moral judgment, he proceeded with judgment in general, with an analysis of all human reason, demonstrative and then causal.

# Notes

## INTRODUCTION

1. All references to David Hume, *A Treatise of Human Nature* are to L.A. Selby-Bigge and P.H. Nidditch, Second Edition (1888; rpt. Oxford: Oxford University Press, 1978). Hereafter, I refer to the pages of this edition by the abbreviation "T" followed by the page number.
2. John A. Passmore, *Hume's Intentions* (London: Cambridge University Press, 1952), pp. 87–88.
3. All references to David Hume, *An Enquiry Concerning Human Understanding* and *An Enquiry Concerning the Principles of Morals* are to L.A. Selby-Bigge and P.H. Nidditch, Third Edition (1777; rpt. Oxford: Oxford University Press, 1975). Hereafter, I refer to the pages of this edition by the abbreviations "EU" and "EM" followed by the page number.
4. Norman Kemp Smith, *The Philosophy of David Hume*, Second Edition (1941; rpt. London: MacMillan, 1949), pp. 209–210.
5. Kemp Smith, *The Philosophy of David Hume*, p. 151.
6. For a discussion of the different senses of "reason" Hume employs in Books I & II of the *Treatise*, see Barbara Winters, "Hume on Reason," *Hume Studies*, Vol. 5, No. 1 (April 1979), p. 20. See also Houghton Dalrymple, "Kemp Smith, Hume and the Parallelism Between Reason and Morality," *Hume Studies*, Vol. 12 (April 1986), pp. 77–89.
7. Antony Flew, *David Hume, Philosopher of Moral Science* (London: Basil Blackwell, 1986), p. 156.
8. Passmore, *Hume's Intentions*, pp. 2–4. Passmore is in agreement with Kemp Smith that Hume's primary concern from the outset was with moral subjects. See Kemp Smith, pp. 12–20.
9. Of course, Hume was not the first to undertake a study of human knowledge. Among the empiricists, John Locke thought an investigation of the human understanding was necessary before one could intelligibly discourse about "very remote" subjects. See "The Epistle to the Reader" in Locke's *An Essay Concerning Human Understanding*, ed. P.H. Nidditch, second edition (1975; rpt. Oxford: Oxford University Press, 1979). George Berkeley sought to distinguish the true from the false principles of the mind in order to explain the "contradictions" and "inconsistencies" which follow when we "reflect on the nature of things." See the "Introduction" of Berkeley's *A Treatise*

*Concerning the Principles of Human Knowledge*, ed. C.M. Turbayne, first edition (New York: The Liberal Arts Press, 1957).

10. For a discussion of some similarities and differences between the *Treatise* and *Enquiries* see Chapter Eight of Nicholas Capaldi, *David Hume: The Newtonian Philosopher* (Boston, Mass.: Twayne Publishers, 1975).

11. Here I share the view of Henry D. Aiken and L.A. Selby-Bigge. See Aiken's editorial introduction in *Hume's Moral and Political Philosophy* (Darien, Conn.: Hafner Publishing Co., 1970) and Selby-Bigge's editorial introduction in *David Hume: Enquiries*.

12. Pall S. Ardal, *Passion and Value in Hume's Treatise* (Edinburgh: Edinburgh University Press, 1966), p. 126.

13. Philip Mercer, *Sympathy and Ethics* (London: Oxford University Press, 1972), p. 69.

## Part One: Hume's Analysis of Reason

### Opening Remarks

1. See James T. King, "The Place of the Language of Morals in Hume's Second Enquiry," *Hume, A Re-evaluation*, ed., Donald W. Livingston and James T. King (New York: Fordham University Press, 1976), pp. 350–352. See also Jonathan Harrison, *Hume's Moral Epistemology* (London: Oxford University Press, 1976), p. 111, Mercer, *Sympathy and Ethics*, pp. 69–73 and Ardal, *Passion and Value*, p. 5.

    Prominent in the moral epistemology of Books II&III are the claims about the impotence of pure reason in motivation and evaluation (T415,457). Criticisms which state that Hume failed to explain the correction of immediate sympathetic judgments often boil down to the objection that Hume allowed reason or reasoning to play a greater role in the moral theory than what he actually claims. The criticisms are aimed at Hume's most central doctrine according to which morality is primarily passional, not rational.

    Hume's method of correction would be pointless if the method itself were the product of understanding alone, and, accordingly, could exert no influence on modifying a passion. Nothing, says Hume, can modify "the impulse of a passion, but a contrary impulse" (T415). The contrary impulse, Hume insists, cannot arise solely from reason. On this point, see Henry David Aiken, "An Interpretation of Hume's Theory of the Place of Reason in Ethics and Politics," *Ethics*, Vol. 90 (October 1979), pp. 71–72. I depart from Aiken in that I hold the view that the method of correcting biased moral sentiments in Book III involves the same principles that govern the correction of factual judgments in Book I, i.e., the principles which underlie the theory of general rules.

2. Jonathan Harrison offers a close study of these sections in *Hume's Moral Epistemology*. See also W.D. Falk, "Hume on Practical Reason," *Philosophical Studies*, Vol. 27 (1975), pp. 1–18, and Mark Platts, "Hume and Morality as a Matter of Fact," Vol. 97 (1988), pp. 189–204.

CHAPTER ONE: REASON AND IMAGINATION

## *Distinctions of Reason*

1. Stanley Tweyman, *Reason and Conduct in Hume and his Predecessors* (The Hague: Martinus Nijhoff, 1974), p. 166. See also Tweyman's "Hume on Separating the Inseparable," *Hume and the Enlightenment*, ed. W.B. Todd (Austin: University of Texas Press, 1974), pp. 30–42. Cf. Harry M. Bracken, "Hume on the Distinction of Reason," *Hume Studies*, Vol. 10, No. 2 (November 1984).
2. See R.J. Butler, "Hume's Impressions," *Impressions of Empiricism*, ed. Godfrey Vesey (New York: St. Martin's Press, 1976), p. 128. See also Butler's "Distinctiones Rationis, Or The Cheshire Cat Which Left Its Smile Behind It," *The Aristotelian Society*, Vol. 76 (1975–76).
3. Passmore, *Hume's Intentions*, p. 110.
4. John Tienson offers a thorough account of this point in "Hume on Universals and General Terms," *Nous*, No. 18 (1984), pp. 311–330.
5. John Locke, *An essay Concerning Human Understanding*, ed. P.H. Nidditch, Second Edition (1975; rpt. Oxford: Oxford University Press, 1979), p. 411.
6. Hume's explanation of the distinction between the reasonable inference from understanding and the unreasonable inference from imagination will be considered in Chapter Two.
7. Kemp Smith, *The Philosophy of David Hume*, p. 209.
8. *Ibid.*, p. 233.
9. I owe this point to Ronald Butler who recognizes the distinction of reason between the "conceptual content" of a perception and its "feeling tone." See Butler, "Distinctiones Rationis, Or The Cheshire Cat Which Left Its Smile Behind It," p. 170.
10. Tweyman, *Reason and Conduct*, p. 165.
11. *Ibid.*

## *The Division of Reason*

1. See ch. III of Antony Flew, *Hume's Philosophy of Belief* (London: Routledge & Kegan Paul, 1961).
2. *Ibid.*, p. 53.
3. Without some understanding of Hume's views on identity, the reader is perplexed as to how identity can change without any change in its ideas. "Thus a man, who hears a noise, that is frequently interrupted and renew'd, says, it is still the same noise; tho' 'tis evident the sounds have only a specific identity or resemblance. They are not, Hume continues, "numerically" identical (T258). When we think of specific identity, we are apt to say that the identity does remain the same only if our interrupted perceptions remain precisely alike. But when philosophy informs us that interrupted perceptions, no matter how invariable, do not constitute a numerically identical object, identity has changed from specific to numerical without any change in our ideas (T201). For an object to count as numerically identical, it must meet the conditions of "invariableness and uninterruptedness." A broken series of resembling perceptions meets only the former condition. The change which occurs from specific to numerical identity, then, does not impinge on the content of perceptions but on the gaps between them. Identity,

therefore, may change without any change in our ideas.

4. See ch. III of Tweyman, *Reason and Conduct*. See also Robert F. Anderson, *Hume's First Principles* (Lincoln, Nebraska: University of Nebraska Press, 1966), pp. 59–62.

5. Farhang Zabeeh, *Hume: Precursor of Modern Empiricism* (The Hague: Martinus Nijhoff, 1960), pp. 90–91.

6. H.H. Price hesitates to attribute to Hume a clear analytic/synthetic distinction and states that it "seems" to be Hume's view that in order to know that 2+2 = 4, "you only have to know what the symbols "2," "4," "+," and "=" mean." See Price, "The Permanent Significance of Hume's Philosophy," *Philosophy*, Vol. **15** (1940), pp. 10–36. Cf. D.G.C. Macnabb, *David Hume: His Theory of Knowledge and Morality* (Hamden, Connecticut; Archon Press, 1966), pp. 43–45. See also Flew, *Hume's Philosophy of Belief*, pp. 64–67. Flew points out that it is not obvious that Hume would disagree with Kant's denial that mathematics is all analytic. The idea of "perfect" and "exact" geometric equality, Hume later states, is a "fiction" the imagination projects onto the general appearance of equal objects (T48).

7. D. Macnabb, *David Hume: His Theory of Knowledge and Morality*, p. 46.

8. Cf. John Locke, *Essay*, pp. 549–550.

## *The Standard of Equality*

1. Zabeeh offers a detailed account of Hume's ideas about logic and mathematics. See *Hume*, especially chapters three and four.

2. I discuss this matter at length in the section entitled "The Regulative Rules of the Understanding."

3. See, for example, Descartes, *Rules For The Direction Of The Mind*, Rule III, in *The Philosophical Works of Descartes*, vol. I, trans. E.S. Haldane and G.R.T. Ross (London: Cambridge University Press, 1973).

4. In support of this view see above, Chapter Five, especially my analysis of Hume's reply to "the second remarkable circumstance" (T584).

5. Hume is far from clear in drawing a distinction between numerical and geometrical equality. See Zabeeh, *Hume*, pp. 128–135 and Kemp Smith, pp. 350–354. Hume states that units of number admit of a precise comparison whereas units of space do not (T71). At (EU163) he also maintains that "the component parts of quantity and number are entirely similar." I have assumed that Hume held the view that the unit which constitutes number and the part which constitutes extention boil down to the same substantial entity. "But the unity which can exist alone, and whose existence is necessary to that of all number, is of another kind, and must be perfectly indivisible, and incapable of being resolved into any lesser unity" (T31). The simple and indivisible points, Hume shortly tells us, "necessary to that of all number," are colored and solid "impressions of atoms" which make up the compound impression of extention. "If a point be not consider'd as colour'd or tangible, it can convey to us no idea" (T38–39).

6. For an elaboration of this point see Daniel E. Flage, "Hume's Relative Ideas," *Hume Studies*, Vol. 7, No. 1 (April 1981), pp. 55–73. Flage's recognition of the distinction between positive and relative ideas in the *Treatise* (found also in the writings of Locke and Berkeley) as analogues of knowledge by acquaintance and knowledge by description, clarifies Hume's claim that one can have an idea (a relative idea) of a thousandth part of a grain of sand, even though one's mental image of it (a positive idea) in no way differs from one's mental image of the grain of sand itself.

7. Anderson correctly states that the idea of a ten thousandth part of a grain of sand is not to be considered as an image of an antecedent impression. The unit of extension is "indivisible to the eye or feeling" (T38). But he goes on to suggest that such ideas should be considered as "forms or essences merely, without regard to actuality or existence." This, however, fits ill with Hume's account since it would follow that the idea of extension, which is composed of the ideas of these units, would not exist "but if the idea of extension really can exist, as we are conscious it does, its parts must also exist" (T39). See Anderson, pp. 61–62 and Kemp Smith, p. 350. Kemp Smith and Anderson are correct to point out the difficulty. For what are we to make of Hume's assertion that the propositions of geometry and arithmetic are "discoverable by the mere operation of thought, without dependence on what is anywhere existent in the universe"? (EU25).

8. Cf. Locke, *Essay*, Book II, ch. VIII. When Locke proceeds to divide a grain of wheat with a pestle until the parts become imperceptible, the only qualities which they retain are the "primary Qualities ... Solidity, Extension, Figure, Motion, or Rest, and Number." The reduction of the grain to imperceptible parts does not take away the primary qualities. All "secondary Qualities" such as colors, sounds and tastes are nothing in the objects themselves but the various motions and figures of imperceptible primary qualities which cause in us the sensations of colors, sounds and tastes. According to Locke, "The ideas of primary Qualities of Bodies, are Resemblances of them, and their Patterns do really exist in the Bodies themselves; but the Ideas, produced in us by the Secondary Qualities, have no resemblance of them at all. There is nothing like our Ideas, existing in the Bodies themselves."

   By Hume's account, our ideas are "adequate representations of the most minute parts of extension" (T29). Parts of extension cannot be inferior to the indivisible, "minimum" idea reached by imagination. "I first take the least idea I can form of a part of extension, and being certain that there is nothing more minute than this idea, I conclude, that whatever I discover by its means must be a real quality of extension." Since the minimum cannot be conceived without its being colored and solid, the indivisible point of extension, "a real existence," consists of both "colour and solidity" (T38). For Hume, the distinction between primary and secondary qualities is only a "distinction of reason." Color and figure are "perfectly inseparable" (T25,34).

9. H.H. Price, *Hume's Theory of the External World* (London: Oxford University Press, 1940), p. 54. Price points out that Hume is in substantial agreement with Kant on the activities of the "Transcendental Imagination." Later he claims that Hume's "Inertia Principle" seems to be referring to what Kant called an "Idea of Reason." Price, pp. 16, 59. Cf. Lewis White Beck, "A Prussian Hume and a Scottish Kant," in *Essays on Kant and Hume* (New Haven: Yale University Press, 1978), pp. 111–129.

## Imaginative Supplementation

1. H.H. Price, *Hume's Theory of the External World*, p. 59.
2. *Ibid.*, p. 57.
3. See Robert Paul Wolff, "Hume's Theory of Mental Activity," in *Hume: A Collection of Critical Essays*, ed. V.C. Chappell (New York: Anchor Books, 1966), pp. 120–122.
4. The tendency to imagine a greater degree of regularity in objects and events than what has actually been observed will later explain why inductive generalizations are extended beyond the cases from which they were derived. Hume will tell us that the

tendency to over-generalize causal rules is the source of prejudice and unreasonable belief (T146).

5. My understanding of the matter has greatly been enhanced by the clarity of Price's exposition. See Price, pp. 50–59.

6. W.V. Quine, "Two Dogmas of Empiricism," in *From a Logical Point of View* (Cambridge, Massachusetts: Harvard University Press, 1980), p. 43.

7. Price, pp. 58–59.

8. *Ibid.*, p. 59.

9. It seems odd that Hume should be speaking of the "inseparable" parts of a complex idea. At the outset of the *Treatise* we are told that only simple impressions and ideas "admit of no distinction or separation" (T2). The white globe, we recall, is a simple perception. How is it, then, that the idea of an olive, a complex idea (T236), is composed of inseparable parts? Stanley Tweyman has claimed that separating the "parts" of a complex idea is no less a "distinction of reason" than separating the "aspects" of a simple idea. Although the text to which I'm referring would support this view, Tweyman also recognizes that such a reading obscures the "special role distinctions of reason play." See Tweyman's "Hume on Separating the Inseparable," pp. 32–34. Tweyman resolves the problem by recognizing Hume's equivocation on the term "simple idea." A simple idea can be taken to mean that "minimum" and "indivisible" point the imagination reaches by "proper distinctions" which "cannot be diminished without a total annihilation" (T27). Taken in this sense, the idea of a white globe is a complex idea since one can imagine the globe divided into two equal parts. Yet, Hume also calls an idea "simple" when its "aspects" (figure and color) are "perfectly inseparable" (T25). Taken in this sense, the idea of a white globe is a simple idea. Hume's reference to the idea of an olive as being complex is therefore consistent with his assertion that its taste and smell are inseparable from its color and tangibility (T237).

10. How are we to understand "conjunction in place" as the migration of tastes and smells into material bodies? In his discussion of benevolence and anger, Hume compares ideas to material objects and passions to colors, tastes and smells (T366). Ideas are impenetrable. They may form a "compound" by their conjunction, not by their "mixture." Passions, like colors may unite entirely such that "each of them may lose itself." It seems clear that the taste of an olive, together with its newly found material body, suffer no loss upon their union in the way that white may lose itself when mixed with black to form grey. Let us then allow "conjunction in place" to be the "compound" of an idea and a passion and not the blend of two passions.

## Chapter Two: General Rules

### *General Rules of the Imagination*

1. Hume's use of the term "unphilosophical" frequently has reference to the beliefs which represent common or "vulgar" opinion. See *Treatise*, pp. 150, 202. Isaac Newton, in the "Definitions and Scholium to the Definitions," *Principia*, Book I, speaks of "prejudices" which "common people" have concerning space and time, i.e., they define space and time only in relation to sensible objects. Newton then proceeds to distinguish "absolute" from "relative" space and time. See *Newton's Philosophy of Nature*, ed.

H.S. Thayer (New York: Hafner Press, 1953), p. 17. George Berkeley speaks of the "prevailing" opinion that sensible objects have a distinct existence from their being perceived. Berkeley goes on to show the contradiction involved in the common opinion. See *A Treatise Concerning the Principles of Human Knowledge* (New York: The Liberal Arts Press, 1957), pp. 24–25. John Locke finds that one of the sources of "unreasonableness" in most men is "Education and Prejudice." *Essay*, 394–395. See also *Treatise*, pp. 116–117. The beliefs which arise from education are often "contrary to reason."

2. Thomas K. Hearn has recognized the presence and influence of "general rules" in all three Books of the *Treatise* and convincingly argues that the theory of rules represents a basic ingredient in Hume's philosophy of human nature. See Hearn, "General Rules in Hume's *Treatise*," *Journal of the History of Philosophy*, Vol. 8, (October 1970), pp. 405–422 and "General Rules and the Moral Sentiments in Hume's *Treatise*," *Review of Metaphysics*, Vol. 30, (1976), pp. 57–72. Cf. Robert J. Fogelin, *Hume's Skepticism in the Treatise of Human Nature* (London: Routledge & Kegan Paul, 1985), pp. 60–63. In contrast to Hearn, Fogelin recognizes that in Hume's discussion of the "artificial" virtues an unreflective adherence to unphilosophical sorts of general rules is necessary if society is to uphold its conventions. I agree with Fogelin that Hume's account of moral judgment involves a certain amount of inevitable falsehood. See *Treatise*, pp. 584–587.

3. Kemp Smith, pp. 128, 382–388.

4. See "Of the Standard of Taste" where Hume discusses "the general rules of art" in *David Hume: Essays*, ed. Eugene F. Millar (1889; rpt. Indianapolis: Liberty Classics, 1985), p. 232.

5. Hearn, "General Rules in Hume's *Treatise*," p. 408.

6. Kemp Smith recognizes the "complication of circumstances" in which causation is at work and points out that "this is why reflective activities are indispensable." Kemp Smith, p. 385.

7. Early in the *Treatise*, Hume states that "resemblance is the most fertile source of error" (T61, 202–205).

8. John Passmore, "Hume and the Ethics of Belief," in *David Hume: Bicentenary Papers*, ed. G.P. Morice (Austin: University of Texas Press, 1977), p. 81.

## The Regulative Rules of the Understanding

1. David Hume, *The Letters of David Hume*, ed. J.Y.T. Greig (London: Oxford University Press, 1932), Vol. I, p. 23. According to Passmore, Hume's "new Scene of Thought" points to the theory of association. Passmore, p. 130. See David Hume, *An Abstract of a Treatise of Human Nature* (1740; rpt. London: Cambridge University Press, 1938), where Hume writes: "But if any thing can intitle the author to so glorious a name as that of an inventor, 'tis the use he makes of the principle of the association of ideas, which enters into most of his philosophy."

2. Kemp Smith, p. 12.

3. *Ibid.*, p. 11.

4. See *Treatise*, p. 518. "No action can be requir'd of us as our duty, unless there be implanted in human nature some actuating passion or motive, capable of producing the action." See also Knud Haakonssen, "Hume's Obligations," *Hume Studies*, Vol. 4, No. 1 (April 1978), p. 7.

5. Kemp Smith, p. 128.
6. Robert Paul Wolff, "Hume's Theory of Mental Activity," in *Hume*, ed. V.C. Chappell (New York: Anchor Books, 1966), p. 103.
7. *Ibid.*, p. 107.
8. *Ibid.*, p. 127.
9. Price, pp. 15-17.
10. Stuart Hampshire claims that Hume did not draw "any absolute distinction between the rules to which our mind conforms itself in thought and behavior, recognizing them as rules to which any thinking must conform, and mere habits and uniformities in our thought and behavior." See Hampshire's article, Hume's Place in Philosophy," in *David Hume*, A Symposium, ed. D.F. Pears (New York: Macmillan and Co., 1963), p. 7.
11. Wolff, p. 113.
12. See Jonathan Harrison, *Hume's Moral Epistemology* (London: Oxford University Press, 1976), p. 101.
13. Wolff, p. 100.
14. Kemp Smith, p. 209.
15. *Ibid.*, p. 210.
16. *Ibid.*
17. *Ibid.*
18. *Ibid.*, p. 230.
19. *Ibid.*, p. 233.
20. Price acknowledges the cognitive side of Hume's theory of belief in light of Hume's claim that "belief is more properly an act of the sensitive, than of the cogitative part of our natures" (T183). He correctly points out that Hume "does not invariably think of our beliefs as the automatic product of custom. He allows that a wise man, when he encounters $p$, can expect $r$ rather than $q$ because he has examined the situation carefully, not just because $r$ is more vivid than $q$." See Price's article, "Hume and the Ethics of Belief," in *David Hume: Bicentenary Papers*, ed. G.P. Morice (Austin: University of Texas Press, 1977), pp. 86–87.
21. Kemp Smith, p. 233.
22. See Hearn, "General Rules in Hume's *Treatise*," pp. 413–414.
23. Kemp Smith, p. 386.
24. *Ibid.*
25. See Fogelin, *Hume's Skepticism*, p. 62.
26. Passmore, *Hume's Intentions*, p. 60.

## The Conflict of General Rules

1. See, for example, Passmore, *Hume's Intentions*, p. 64 and Laird, *Hume's Philosophy of Human Nature*, p. 92. A bit further on Laird concedes that "Hume did distinguish a logical from an illogical kind of inference from experience."
2. Later in the *Treatise*, Hume seems to change his attitude and suggests that judgments of virtue and vice rest on a sympathy with feelings which are believed not to exist. It would be unreasonable to be more concerned for persons who display "greatness of mind" in the face of extreme misfortune than for those who show the usual degree of passion commonly associated with such misfortune. Yet, greatness of mind is a virtue (T370–371). See also T. 499,592.
3. Passmore wonders, "Why should we prefer regularity to irregularity? To this the only

answer can be, Hume replies, that 'the disposition and character of the person' (T150) will determine the preference. The 'vulgar' prefer caprice, 'the wise' prefer regularity. Clearly, this is question-begging." *Hume's Intentions*, p. 60.

I suggest that Passmore's question be recast: "Why *do* we prefer regularity to irregularity"? Hume opens the section "Of scepticism with regard to the senses," "What causes induce us to believe in the existence of body?" As to whether or not material objects exist, Hume continues, "that is a point, which we must take for granted" (T187). Throughout the section, one notes a general drive toward regularity. External objects "require a continu'd existence, or otherwise lose, in a great measure, the regularity of their operation" (T196). Both the common man and philosophers can't help but attribute numerical identity to what is believed to be an interrupted series of resembling perceptions. "The perplexity arising from this contradiction produces a propension to unite these broken appearances by the fiction of a continu'd existence" (T205). "Nature," writes Hume, "has not left this to our choice" (T187). It "makes us ascribe an identity to the succession" (T220).

As Hume presents it, the basic drive towards regularity and stability in our experience is the cause of much unreasonableness. But it is only by yielding to the drive that the "irregular" and "unreasonable" rules of imagination may be corrected. Hume, clearly in his sceptical mood, would side with Passmore that no logical answer can be offered which distinguishes wisdom from folly. He owns up to the contradiction. "The following of general rules is a very unphilosophical species of probability; and yet 'tis only by following them that we can correct this, and all other unphilosophical probabilities" (T150). Hume never claims to have decided by virtue of reason which persons are wise and which ones vulgar. He does no more than "make bold" to recommend philosophy. To cast aside philosophical reflection would only deprive Hume of pleasure, "and this is the origin of my philosophy" (T271).

4. See Thomas Hearn, "General Rules in Hume's *Treatise*," p. 421.
5. See Fogelin, ch. II.
6. Hume's sceptical argument concerning demonstrative and causal reason has not, for the most part, been favorably received. One commentator regards it as "one of the worst arguments ever to impose itself on a man of genius." D.C. Stove, *Probability and Hume's Inductive Scepticism* (Oxford University Press, 1973), p. 132. Even a more sympathetic reader finds the conclusion of the argument "remarkable, if not outrageous." William Edward Morris, "Hume's Scepticism About Reason," *Hume Studies*, Vol. 15, No. 1 (April 1989), p. 49. Richard Popkin offers a more charitable interpretation. Richard H. Popkin, "David Hume: His Pyrrhonism and His Critique of Pyrrhonism," *The High Road to Pyrrhonism*, ed., Richard A. Watson and James E. Force (San Diego: Austin Hill Press, Inc., 1980), pp. 107–110.

Hume's scepticism in I,iv,1 seeks to reduce all demonstrative knowledge to probability and all probability to "nothing" (T182). Regarding the first reduction, commentators are in general agreement that Hume does not provide an explanation of how we go wrong in "the most simple" (T181) operations with small numbers. Since we sometimes err when adding a great number of large numbers, we can also err in the shortest additions. Hume does not find it necessary to provide an account of the mechanics of error, of how we can be mistaken in short enumerations. One premise in his argument, not often discussed, states that since it is possible – "by gradually diminishing the numbers" – to reduce a complex calculation to a simple addition, it is "impracticable to shew the precise limits of knowledge and of probability, or discover that particular number, at which the one ends and the other begins." And he goes on to remind us that knowledge and probability are two "classes" (T68) or "kinds" (EU25) of reasoning and "cannot well run insensibly into each other" (T181). Hume's point here should be given some consideration. The question is not so much how we can make mistakes in simple operations, but to show "that particular number," or that particular operation in the mechanics of, say, addition, at which demonstrative reasoning begins to go awry, and becomes nothing more than a high degree of probability.

After reducing demonstration to probability, Hume argues that all probability is "reduc'd to nothing" (T182), to "a total extinction of belief and evidence" (T183). A number of commentators agree that Hume's argument "may not lead to Pyrrhonian doubts about the logical rules and inferences, but it does raise some doubts as to the ability of any human being ever to be positive that he is reasoning logically." See Popkin, p. 110. See also Fogelin, p. 18, who writes: "However certain or uncertain we are about our ability to calculate probabilities, if a proposition has a certain probability, that (tautologically) is the probabilitiy it has." Again, it is pointed out that the aim of Hume's argument is to reduce "*my confidence*" with each reflective judgment I make. See Morris, p. 52. These observations are clearly in line with Hume's assertion that the rules of demonstration are "certain and infallible." It is in the application of the rules that "our fallible and uncertain faculties are very apt to depart from them, and fall into error" (T180).

I agree with William Morris' view that Hume's discussion in I,iv,1 fits into the overall structure of the *Treatise*. He correctly states that in order to "understand Hume's view of the role of reason, it stands to reason that we should first figure out how to integrate "Of scepticism with regard to reason" into the picture. Only then will we be ready to move to a consideration of Hume's positive views about reason." Morris, pp. 39,58. Specifically, I have argued throughout that Hume's discussion in I,iv,1 plays an integral part in his theory of general rules.

7. See Passmore, "The Ethics of Belief," p. 86.
8. Kemp Smith, p. 386.
9. Passmore, *Hume's Intentions*, p. 60.

## PART TWO: HUME'S ANALYSIS OF SYMPATHY

### *Opening Remarks*

1. In elucidating the "meaning of 'sympathy'," Mercer holds that "the circumstances about which we sympathize with others are always unpleasant and involve some kind of suffering: it would sound odd to say that one sympathized with a person who was enjoying himself or having a good time." *Sympathy and Ethics*, p. 5. For Hume, it is clear throughout that sympathy extends to pleasures as well as to pains and to circumstances which involve "great fortune," "honourable office[s]" and, generally, "prosperity" (T370). Sympathy "makes us partake of the satisfaction of everyone that approaches us" (T358).

2. "Whoever is united to us by any connexion is always sure of a share of our love, proportioned to the connexion, without enquiring into his other qualities. Thus the relation of blood produces the strongest tie the mind is capable of in the love of parents to their children, and a lesser degree of the same affection, as the relation lessons"

(T352).

3. Hearn, "General Rules in Hume's *Treatise*," p. 422. Toward the end of his article, Hearn admits that the generalizing tendency of imagination is not always regarded by Hume as a source of error. He goes on to claim, however, that "there is still necessity here for the operation of those general rules which 'sometimes influence the judgment'." A close look at the passage Hearn refers to indicates that the understanding prescribes the inference which the imagination ordinarily makes, i.e., the imagination does not consider the "circumstances wanting to render the cause a compleat one" and "therefore we separate" those circumstances from the cause. (T585).

4. Passmore, p. 122.

### CHAPTER THREE: SYMPATHY AND JUDGMENT

## The Sympathy Mechanism

1. Mercer, pp. 26, 36. See also Terence Penelhum, *Hume* (New York: St. Martin's Press, 1975), p. 147, and Nicholas Capaldi, *David Hume: The Newtonian Philosopher* (Boston: Twayne Publishers, 1975), p. 142. Cf. Robert J. Lipkin, "Altruism and Sympathy in Hume's Ethics," *Australasian Journal of Philosophy*, Vol. 65, No.1 (March 1987), pp. 19–20.

2. "This argument involves the abandoning of every distinction between impressions and ideas except liveliness." See Passmore, p. 129 and Kemp Smith, p. 179.

3. Near the end of Book I, in the discussion on the self, Hume makes a distinction between "personal identity, as it regards our thought or imagination, and as it regards our passions, or the concern we take in ourselves" (T253). I have all along supposed that the idea of self of Book II ("as it regards our passions") refers to a "fiction" the imagination constructed in Book I. ("as it regards our thought or imagination"). As Hume describes the matter, we "feign" the new relation of "perfect identity" in order to strengthen the tie between a series of perceptions already united by causation and resemblance (T260). We have seen the cooperation of imagination on a number of occasions, the "propensity to add some new relation" to ideas which were already related by the principles of association (T237). Hume's appeal to a fictitious "idea, or rather impression of" self in Book II is not inconsistent with his claim that we have no idea of the self ("after the manner it is here explained," in Book I,) which corresponds to a "soul" or a substantial support of our perceptions (T251). We only suppose that an autobiography of our life includes the idea of a self which remains "invariable and uninterrupted." Cf. Kemp Smith, pp. 151–152, 171–173, Harrison, p. 106 and John Jenkins, "Hume's account of Sympathy – Some Difficulties," in *Philosophers of the Scottish Enlightenment*, ed. V. Hope (Edinburgh: Edinburgh University Press, 1984), pp. 91–103. For valuable discussions of Hume's ideas about the self, see Don Garrett, "Hume's Self-Doubts About Personal Identity," *The Philosophical Review*, Vol. 90, No. 3 (July 1981), pp. 337–358 and Chris Swoyer, "Hume and the Three Views of the Self," *Hume Studies*, Vol. 8, No. 1 (April 1982), pp. 43–61.

4. Cf. Passmore, *Hume's Intentions*, p. 129. Passmore claims that causal inference provides us with "no more than an idea" of the affections of others. Hume claims that the inference to another's affection yields a "lively idea" or belief (T319,105). Max Scheler, on the other hand, claims that the affections of others are given to us "not by

inference, but directly, as a sort of primary 'perception'." See ch. II of Scheler's *The Nature of Sympathy* (New Haven: Yale University Press, 1954). See also Harrison, pp. 105–106.

5. See Christopher Cherry, "Knowing, Imagining and Sympathizing," *Ratio*, Vol. 22 (1980), p. 133.

## Sympathy and Belief

1. Jonathan Harrison questions why an impression of self is necessary for sympathizing in addition to the impression which gives rise to a lively idea or belief of anothers passion. Harrison, *Hume's Moral Epistemology*, p. 106. In order to elucidate the sympathy mechanism, Hume initially assumes that the person with whom we sympathize is present before us. From the impression of "signs," the inference is made to the "reality of the passion" (T320). Now Hume thinks the causal inference "alone" is sufficient to enliven one's idea of another's passion and to make us believe in its "real existence" (T101). The inference to the idea of the passion makes the "idea approach an impression in force and vivacity" (T119). Hume would be in agreement with Harrison. The initial inference is sufficient to feel "the very passion itself" (T317). See also (T576) where Hume writes that from observing the "effects" of passion the inference is made to the cause, "and forms such a lively idea of the passion, as is presently converted into the passion itself." The impression of self is called upon not so much to get sympathy going but to further increase the degree of felt sympathy when contiguity and resemblance hold between a sympathizer and the person sympathized with. "Contiguity and resemblance have an effect much inferior to causation; but still have some effect, and augment the conviction of any opinion, and the vivacity of any conception" (T110). When the initial causal inference is made, and resemblance, contiguity and causation are also present, the idea of the affections of others are conceived "in the strongest and most lively manner" (T318). Here, sympathy operates in its "full perfection" (T320).

2. See Ronald J. Butler, "The Inaugural Address: T and Sympathy," *The Aristotelian Society*, Vol. 49 (1975), p. 11.

3. Ardal, p. 49.

4. Ronald Butler argues that Hume's analysis of causation is designed to deny the distinction between causal language and the language of signs. Butler, p. 10. See also Ardal who considers the inference from words to emotion a straightforward causal inference. Ardal p. 42.

5. Butler, p. 11.

6. A number of passages indicate that Hume was clear to distinguish the causal relation from the propensities which govern the transition from the impression of a cause to the idea of an effect. See especially the "Sixth" and "Seventh Experiment" to confirm the theory of the "double relation" (T338–346). See also Hume's discussion of the effects of contiguity in space and time (T427–438).

7. Butler, p. 11-12.

8. That Hume founds a duty to conceal expressions of pride, to show "a reserve and secret doubt," which indicates the virtue of "decency" and "good breeding," rests upon his confidence throughout that "so little are men govern'd by reason" (T312,598). For a defense of this view see Fogelin, pp. 63, 144–145.

*Sympathy and Comparison*

1. Brief discussions of Hume's principle of comparison may be found in Mercer, pp. 32–33 and Ardal, pp. 59–60. See also Alfred B. Glathe, *Hume's Theory of the Passions and of Morals* (Berkeley and Los Angeles, California: University of California Press, 1950), pp. 56–58 and John B. Stewart, *The Moral and Political Philosophy of David Hume* (Westport, Connecticut: Greenwood Press, 1973), 72–73.

2. When it is *believed* that persons have the qualities they attribute to themselves, one's response is sympathy rather than comparison (T595–596).

3. It is unreasonable to compare our mental qualities with the qualities of others, when we do not believe that others have the qualities they believe themselves to have.

4. See Ardal, p. 60.

5. Hume's argument proceeds from two premises. First, any vast object, like an ocean, or a great number of objects, like an army, excites the emotion of "admiration." Second, this emotion increases or diminishes by the increase or decrease of the extension or number. Hume concludes, "every part, then, of extension, and every unite of number has a separate emotion attending it, when conceiv'd by the mind." But from the fact that we experience awe from viewing a mountain or a fleet of soldiers, it does not follow that we experience any emotion at all whenever we think of, or look at, a molehill or an individual soldier. It would be plausible to argue that some "threshold" is required in the dimension of the extension or number of objects before the admiration sets in. I owe this insight to Professor Martin Tamny who has recognized, along with others, Hume's appeal to "a fallacy of division." See also Glathe, p. 57.

6. "Those, who are acquainted with the metaphysical part of optics, and know how we transfer the judgments and conclusions of the understanding to the senses, will easily conceive this whole operation" (T375).

7. Comparison is "directly contrary" to the generalized sympathy required for judging qualities of character and the actions which display them from a general point of view (T581,593). From the general viewpoint, the consideration of good qualities, "as they really are in themselves," produces love. From one's "peculiar" viewpoint, the same qualities, when compared with our own, produce humility. When sympathy becomes mixed with a "tacit" comparison, the good qualities of others produce respect, the bad qualities, contempt. There is always a "mixture" of pride in contempt and humility in respect. "In changing the point of view, tho' the object may remain the same, its proportion to ourselves entirely alters" (T390). The comparative judgment is a source of bias which requires correction by the reflection that one's own external possessions or internal qualities neither augment nor diminish in value when compared with the possessions or qualities of others. "A man of sense and merit is pleased with himself, independent of all foreign considerations: But a fool must always find some person, that is more foolish, in order to keep himself in good humour with his own parts and understanding" (T596).

8. In the section "Of the mixture of benevolence and anger with compassion and malice," Hume carefully considers why sympathy with another's pain and suffering sometimes produces hatred and contempt, and sometimes love and kindness (T381–389). For valuable discussions on this point see Ardal. pp. 62–67 and T.A. Roberts, *The Concept of Benevolence* (London: The Macmillan Press, 1973), 75–98.

9. The method of correcting immediate sympathetic and comparative responses is thus ultimately aimed at the the principle of vivacity. The violence and calmness of the

passions, Hume later writes, "keep pace" with variations in the vivacity of ideas (T424).


## CHAPTER FOUR: PASSION AND JUDGMENT

### *The Indirect Passions*

1. Kemp Smith shortly emphasizes "the closeness of the connexion between Hume's theory of the passions and his ethical teachings." Kemp Smith, p. 160. Ardal argues throughout that there is, indeed, a very close relation between the indirect passions and the evaluation of character. I am in substantial agreement with Ardal and have greatly profited from his *Passion and Value*.
2. See Mercer, pp. 45–48, Harrison, pp. 100–103, Haakonssen, p. 8 and Bricke, p. 24.
3. Ardal, p. 129, correctly points out that the indirect passions and approval and disapproval are not to be identified with sympathetic consciousness. Mercer also sees sympathy as the "medium" of moral judgment. Mercer, p. 45. Cf. Ingemar Hedenius, *Studies in Hume's Ethics* (rpt. from Adolph Phalen in Memoriam, Uppsala and Stockholm, 1937), pp. 461-67.
4. Here I follow Kemp Smith in taking the calm passions to be "modes of approval and disapproval." Kemp Smith, p. 167. "The reflective impressions may be divided into two kinds, viz. the calm and the violent. Of the first kind is the sense of beauty and deformity in action, composition and external objects. Of the second are the passions of love and hatred, grief and joy, pride and humility" (T276). The distinction between calm and violent passions is "vulgar and specious." Just as impressions and ideas may approach one another in point of vivacity, so the calm passions may acquire great emotional intensity while the violent ones "may decay into so soft an emotion, as to become, in a manner, imperceptible" (T276). Approval and disapproval, Hume later states, is an "imperceptible" love and hatred (T614), "a general calm determination of the passions, founded on some distant view or reflexion" (T583). Hume's scattered remarks on the calm passions have received a number of interpretations. I basically agree with Thomas Hearn's reading that a calm passion is a corrected passion based on reflection and general rules. See Hearn, "General Rules and the Moral Sentiments in Hume's *Treatise*," pp. 57–72. See also Rachael M. Kydd, *Reason and Conduct in Hume's Treatise* (New York: Russell & Russell, 1964), ch. 5.
5. See Hearn, "General Rules and the Moral Sentiments in Hume's *Treatise*, pp. 62–68. Cf. Mary Warnock, "The Justification of Emotions," *Proceedings of the Aristotelian Society*, Vol. 31 (1957), pp. 43–58."
6. I am in agreement with Ardal who claims that "Hume's statements make sense only if there is a strict parallel between the principles accounting for the origin of the indirect passions and those accounting for the origin of approval and disapproval of persons." Ardal, p. 112.
7. "We do not infer a character to be virtuous, because it pleases" (T471).
8. As I see it, by taking on a corrective or regulative status, general rules of understanding do not thereby cease to be *causal* rules. Had Hume argued for a logical or a-priori status of corrective judgments, different in *kind* from ordinary causal reasoning, he would have been able to avoid the skeptical conclusion, i.e., an endless series of corrective judgments where each, Hume makes sure to note, is "of the same kind" as the preceding, and which eventually reduces all belief to complete uncertainty. General

rules of understanding, although they function to control initial inferences, are "founded only on probability." Corrective judgments rest on "the very same principles" as does the initial inference from an impression to an idea. See *Treatise*, "Of scepticism with regard to reason" and "Rules by which to judge of causes and effects." Cf. Hearn, "General Rules and the Moral Sentiment," pp. 64–71 and Mercer, p. 69.

9. Reasoning, demonstrable or causal, does not produce any "sensible emotion." The calm passions, likewise, "produce little emotion in the mind." Hume concludes, "Whenever any of these passions are calm, and cause no disorder in the soul, they are very readily taken for the determinations of reason, and are suppos'd to proceed from the same faculty, with that, which judges of truth and falsehood." "Metaphysicians," therefore, come to believe that reason, and not a calm passion, is in "combat" with a "violent" passion. When the passions are the "slave" of reason, it is believed that reason by itself has motivated the will to action. Hume points out the oversight. "What we call strength of mind, implies the prevalence of the calm passions above the violent" (T418). See *Treatise*, "Of the influencing motives of the will." I think it can fairly be said for Hume that beliefs may be opposed to each other, and so may passions, but a belief alone, the outcome of a single relation between an impression and an idea, and separate from a "double relation" of impressions and ideas, cannot produce the indirect passions of love or hatred and, therefore, cannot motivate action. Beliefs are "languid" or "lively," passions, "calm" or "violent," and volitions, "weak" or "strong." The motivational continuum of strength and weakness is never applied by Hume to the vivacity of ideas but only to the calm/violent continuum, without there being any correspondence between motivational strength and emotional intensity (T418–422).

10. Commentators often speak of a "non-moral" or "pre-moral" stage in the development of moral evaluation. See Annette Baier, "Frankena and Hume on Points of View," *Monist*, Vol. 64 (1981), p. 347 and Carole Stewart, "The Moral Point of View," *Philosophy*, Vol. 51 (1976), p. 178. Nicholas Capaldi also describes a "conversion of non-moral characteristics into peculiarly moral sentiments" in "Hume's Theory of the Passions," p. 187. Excellent responses to this view may be found in F.A. Hayek, "The Legal and Political Philosophy of David Hume," in *Hume: A Collection of Critical Essays*, pp. 335–360 and David Fate Norton, "Hume's Moral Psychology: Motives and the Artificial Virtues," pp. 1–26. I see no such period, as Hume presents it, where mankind is placed in a "non" or "pre-moral" condition. See *Treatise* pp. 483–484 and 488–489. See also (T493) where Hume writes, "Philosophers may, if they please, extend their reasoning to the suppos'd state of nature; provided they allow it to be a mere philosophical fiction, which never had, and never could have any reality." See also ch. 10 of Flew, *David Hume: Philosopher of Moral Science*.

11. For a criticism of the "limitations" (T290) Hume adds to his general theory of pride, see Robert W. Burch, "Hume on Pride and Humility," New Scholasticism, Vol. 49 (1975), pp. 177–188.

12. See Altmann, p. 123. As far as I know, Altmann is the only commentator of Hume's theory of sympathy who argues that the sympathy mechanism remains intact in the second *Enquiry*.

## Pride and Humility

1. Hume is assuming the common view that qualities inhere in an "unknown something." Philosophers realize that we have "no idea of substance, distinct from that of a

collection of particular qualities ... that are united by the imagination, and have a particular name assigned to them, by which we are able to recall, either to ourselves or others, that collection" (T16). See also T219–225, "Of the ancient philosophy."

2. See David Hume, *A Dissertation on the Passions* in *The Philosophical Works of David Hume*, ed. T.H. Green and T.H. Grose (London, 1874), Vol. 4, p. 143.

3. See, for example, D.F. Pears, "Hume's Theory of the Passions," in David Hume: A Symposium, pp. 37–40.

4. Ardal, pp. 23–24.

5. Annette Baier, "Hume's Analysis of Pride," *The Journal of Philosophy*, Vol. 75 (1978), p. 29.

6. Amelie Oksenberg Rorty, "From Passions to Emotions and Sentiments," *Philosophy*, Vol. 57 (1982), p. 168.

7. See Anthony Kenny, *Action, Emotion and Will* (London: Routledge & Kegan Paul, 1963), pp. 23–25.

8. Cf. Baier, "Hume's Analysis of Pride." Baier thinks that Hume's simple empiricist analysis of causation in Book I is "at odds with" the account offered in Book II. In Book II, "he does not think we have to wait and see what idea the passion of pride introduces as its object ... since we know in advance that 'to this emotion she (nature) has assigned a certain idea, viz. that of self'."

9. *Ibid.*, p. 29. Baier suggests that the relationship is "special."

10. See Donald Davidson, "Hume's Cognitive Theory of Pride" in *Essays on Actions and Events* (Oxford: Oxford University Press, 1980), p. 283.

11. See below, "The Standard of Equality" and "Imaginative Supplementation."

12. Ardal, p. 23.

13. See below, "The Division of Reason."

14. Davidson, pp. 280–281. Cf. Baier, pp. 30–31.

15. Davidson, p. 283. Cf. Baier, p. 35.

16. Davidson, p. 281.

## Love and Hatred

1. Esteem is a "species" of love and hatred (T357). They are the "same passions, and arise from like causes ... but where this pleasure is severe and serious, the passion which arises from the pleasure, is more properly denominated esteem than love" (T608).

2. Davidson omits the sympathy mechanism in his propositional account of Hume's indirect passions but emphasizes the role the "double relation" plays. He points out that loving is "loving for a reason, rather than simply loving." The subject-cause of love (virtue, beauty, a palace) is related to another person. So, the state of mind that causes love is the belief that the prince owns a beautiful palace. The belief that a palace is beautiful will not cause love unless it is believed that the prince owns the palace. See Davidson, "Hume's Cognitive Theory of Pride," pp. 278–279.

3. See Tweyman, *Reason and Conduct*, pp. 160–162. What is communicated is not pride but a lively idea of the pleasure Jones receives from his house.

4. See Barry Stroud, *Hume* (London: Routledge & Kegan Paul, 1977), pp. 196–198 and John J. Jenkins, "Hume's Account of Sympathy – Some Difficulties," in *Philosophers of the Scottish Enlightenment*, ed. V. Hope (Edinburgh: Edinburgh University Press, 1984), pp. 91–94.

5. See Mercer, p. 35.

6. *Ibid.*
7. *Ibid.*
8. For a close look at Hume's theory of the double association of impressions and ideas, see Baier, "Hume's Analysis of Pride," Davidson, "Hume's Cognitive Theory of Pride" and Altmann, "Hume on Sympathy."
9. Pride may be challenged, "either on the ground that the subject that is supposed to be valuable does not in fact have the value it is believed to have, or because the proud person is mistaken in thinking that the subject is in a special way related to him." See Ardal, "Hume and Davidson on Pride," *Hume Studies*, Vol. 40 (November 1989), p. 391.
10. See Baier, "Hume's Analysis of Pride," p. 29.
11. "The same qualities, in all cases, produce both pride and love, humility and hatred; and the same man is always virtuous or vicious, accomplish'd or despicable to others, who is so to himself" (T589). See also T331–332. The same qualities also produce "vanity or the desire of reputation." It would be absurd to display the qualities which make us proud, if pride and love were not produced by the same qualities.

## CHAPTER FIVE:
### GENERAL RULES AND THE IMPARTIAL POINT OF VIEW

1. See Ardal, pp. 111–114.
2. Mercer, p. 49.
3. Harrison, p. 101.
4. Further discussions on the process of projection or objectification may be found in Mackie, *Hume's Moral Theory*, pp. 71–72 and Stroud, *Hume*, pp. 184–186. See also John McDowell, "Projection and Truth in Ethics" (The Lindley Lecture, University of Kansas, 1987).
5. See T347, "Difficulties solv'd," where Hume claims that a "condition" of love and hatred is that the pleasure and pain we receive from persons "arise knowingly; and with a particular design and intention ... by the intention we judge of the actions, and according as that is good or bad, they become causes of love or hatred." See also T411–412, 477, 575. Cf. Bernard Wand, "A Note on Sympathy in Hume's Moral Theory," *The Philosophical Review*, Vol. 64 (April 1955), pp. 275–279.
6. Ardal attributes to Ingemar Hedenius the view that Hume identifies approval and disapproval with sympathetic consciousness. Ardal, p. 130. Though Hedenius seriously considers this position, he proceeds to advance several reasons in favor of the interpretation that sympathy and moral consciousness are "different psychic states," and suggests that Hume's treatment of the social virtues should be interpreted according to the theory of the "double relation." Hedenius, pp. 460–468.
7. It is often recognized that the moral sentiment has a "tenuous ... relation with real occurrent sympathetically communicated feeling." See Annette Baier, "Frankena and Hume on Points of View," pp. 344–345.
8. According to the "double relation," the "object" of love is "always" another person (T330). It is plausible to interpret this passage as involving "selfishness" (T486), or "great partiality in our own favour" (T321), or the "concern for our private interest" (T480) rather than the indirect passion of love. "When we talk of self-love, 'tis not in a proper sense" (T329).

9. "Nothing is more certain from experience, than that any contradiction either to the sentiments or passions gives a sensible uneasiness, whether it proceeds from without or from within ... the mind must be uneasy in that situation, and will naturally seek relief from the uneasiness" (T205–206).

10. See Carole Stewart, "The Moral Point of View," p. 178.

11. See Hearn, "General Rules in Hume's *Treatise*," p. 413. Hearn is referring to Nelson Goodman's remark in *Fact, Fiction, and Forecast* (Cambridge, Massachusetts, 1955), p. 67.

12. See Mackie, pp. 72, 124. Mackie recognizes the tendency of imagination to extend causal rules but regards the "objectification theory" as more explanatory.

13. See Mercer, p. 69 and Harrison pp. 101, 109. Cf. John Bricke, "Hume, Motivation and Morality," pp. 13–14, who claims, quite correctly, that the "objective standpoint" is not to be considered as a viewpoint of "some hypothetical ideal agent."

14. See Roderick Firth's excellent discussion of ideal observer theories, "Ethical Absolutism and the Ideal Observer," *Philosophy and Phenomenological Research*, Vol. 12, No. 3 (March 1952), 317–345."

15. See Ardal, "Some Implications of the Virtue of Reasonableness in Hume's *Treatise*," *Hume: A Re-elevaluation*," pp. 93–94.

16. Ardal recognizes that beliefs of imagination are involved in evaluation but disagrees with Hume that such beliefs are to be characterized as "inferior to belief." See Ardal, *Passion and Value*, pp. 124–125. I have tried to clarify Hume's remarks concerning the matter which, admittedly, are not made clearly.

17. Harrison, p. 101.

18. Mercer, p. 69.

## CHAPTER SIX: CONCLUSION

1. Kemp Smith, pp. 12–20, 44–46.

# Bibliography

Aiken, Henry D. "An Interpretation of Hume's Theory of the Place of Reason in Ethics and Politics." *Ethics* Vol. **90** (October 1979), pp. 66–80.

Aiken, Henry D., ed. *Hume's Moral and Political Philosophy*. Darien, Conn.: Hafner Publishing Co., 1970.

Altmann, R.W. "Hume on Sympathy." *Southern Journal of Philosophy*, Vol. **18** (1980), pp. 123–136.

Anderson, Robert F. *Hume's First Principles*. Lincoln, Nebraska: University of Nebraska Press, 1966.

Ardal, Pall S. *Passion and Value in Hume's Treatise*. Edinburgh: Edinburgh University Press, 1966.

Ardal, Pall S. "Some Implications of the Virtue of Reasonableness in Hume's *Treatise*." In *Hume: A Re-evaluation*, pp. 91–106. Edited by Donald W. Livingston and James T. King. New York: Fordham University Press, 1976.

Ardal, Pall S. "Hume and Davidson on Pride." *Hume Studies*, Vol. **15**, No. 2 (November 1989), pp. 387–394.

Baier, Annette. "Frankena and Hume on Points of View." *Monist*, Vol. **64** (1981), pp. 342–358.

Baier, Annette. "Hume's Analysis of Pride." *The Journal of Philosophy*, Vol. **75** (1978), pp. 27–40.

Berkeley, George. *A Treatise Concerning the Principles of Human Knowledge*. Edited with an Introduction by Colin M. Turbayne. New York: The Liberal Arts Press, Inc., 1957.

Bracken, Harry M. "Hume on the 'Distinction of Reason'." *Hume Studies*, Vol. **10**, No. 2 (November 1984), pp. 89–108.

Bricke, John. "Hume's Volitions." In *Philosophers of the Scottish Enlightenment*, pp. 70–90. Edited by V. Hope. Edinburgh: Edinburgh University Press, 1984.

Bricke, John. "Hume, Motivation and Morality." *Hume Studies*, Vol. **14**, No. 1 (April 1988), pp. 1–24.

Burch, Robert W. "Hume on Pride and Humility." *New Scholasticism*, Vol. **49** (1975), pp. 177–188.

Butler, Ronald J. "Hume's Impressions." In *Impressions of Empiricism*, pp. 122–136. Edited by Godfrey Vesey. New York: St. Martin's Press, 1976.

Butler, Ronald J. "Distinctiones Rationis, Or The Cheshire Cat Which Left Its Smile Behind It." *Proceedings of the Aristotelian Society*, Vol. **76** (1975), pp. 165–176.

Butler, Ronald J. "The Inaugural Address: T and Sympathy." *Proceedings of the Aristotelian*

*Society*, Vol. **49** (1975), pp. 1–20.

Capaldi, Nicholas. *David Hume: The Newtonian Philosopher*. Boston, Mass.: Twayne Publishers, 1975.

Cherry, Christopher. "Knowing, Imagining and Sympathizing." *Ratio*, Vol. **22** (1980), pp. 133–144.

Cherry, Christopher. "Nature, Artifice and Moral Approbation." *Proceedings of the Aristotelian Society*, Vol. **76** (1975), pp. 264–282.

Cherry, Christopher. "Hume's Theory of the Passions." In *Hume: A Re-evaluation*, pp. 172–190. Edited by Donald W. Livingston and James T. King. New York: Fordham University Press, 1976.

Dalrymple. Houghton. "Kemp Smith, Hume and the Parallelism Between Reason and Morality." *Hume Studies*, Vol. **12**, No. 1 (April 1986), pp. 77–91.

Davidson, Donald. "Hume's Cognitive Theory of Pride." In *Essays on Actions and Events*, pp. 277–290. Oxford: Oxford University Press, 1980.

Descartes, Rene. *The Philosophical Works of Descartes*. Translated by Elizabeth S. Haldane and G.R.T. Ross. In Two Volumes. Cambridge: Cambridge University Press, 1973.

Falk, W.D. "Hume on Practical Reason." *Philosophical Studies*, Vol. **27** (1975), pp. 1–18.

Firth, Roderick. "Ethical Absolutism and the Ideal Observer." *Philosophy and Phenomenological Research*, Vol. **12**, No. 3 (March 1952), pp. 317–345.

Flew, Antony. *Hume's Philosophy of Belief*. London: Routledge & Kegan Paul, 1961.

Flew, Antony. *David Hume: Philosopher of Moral Science*. Oxford: Basil Blackwell, 1986.

Fogelin, Robert J. *Hume's Skepticism in the Treatise of Human Nature*. London: Routledge & Kegan Paul, 1985.

Gardiner, P.L. "Hume's Theory of the Passions." In *David Hume: A Symposium*, pp. 31–42. Edited by D.F. Pears. New York: St. Martin's Press, 1966.

Garrett, Don. "Hume's Self-Doubts About Personal Identity." *The Philosophical Review*, Vol. **90**, No. 3 (July 1981), pp. 337–358.

Glathe, Alfred B. *Hume's Theory of the Passions and of Morals*. University of California Publications in Philosophy, Vol. **24**. Berkeley and Los Angeles: University of California Press, 1950.

Haakonssen, Knud. "Hume's Obligations." *Hume Studies*, Vol. **14**, No. 1 (April 1978), pp. 7–17.

Harrison, Jonathan. *Hume's Moral Epistemology*. Oxford: Clarendon Press, 1976.

Hayek, F.A. "The Legal and Political Philosophy of David Hume." In *Hume: A Collection of Critical Essays*, pp. 335–360. Edited by V.C. Chappell. New York: Anchor Books, 1966.

Hearn, Thomas K. "General Rules in Hume's *Treatise*." *Journal of the History of Philosophy*, Vol. **8** (1970), pp. 405–422.

Hearn, Thomas K. "General Rules and the Moral Sentiment in Hume's *Treatise*." *Review of Metaphysics*, Vol. **30** (1976), pp. 57–72.

Hedenius, Ingemar. *Studies in Hume's Ethics*. Uppsala and Stockholm, 1937.

Hudson, W.D., ed. *The Is/Ought Question*. London: Macmillan and Co., 1969.

Hume, David. *A Treatise of Human Nature*. Edited with an Analytical Index by L.A. Selby-Bigge. Oxford: Oxford University Press, 1888; reprint ed., Oxford: Oxford University Press, 1978.

Hume, David. *Enquiries Concerning Human Understanding and Concerning the Principles of Morals*. Edited with Introduction, Comparative Table of Contents and Analytical Index by L.A. Selby-Bigge. Oxford: Oxford University Press, 1777; reprint ed., Oxford: Oxford University Press, 1975.

Hume, David. *Essays: Moral, Political and Literary*. Edited with a Foreward, Notes and Glossary by Eugene F. Miller. Indianapolis, Indiana: Liberty Classics, 1985: reprinted from *The Philosophical Works of David Hume*. Edited by T.H. Green and T.H. Grose, four vols. London: Longmans, 1889.

Hume, David. *The Letters of David Hume*. Edited by J.Y.T. Grieg. Oxford: The Clarendon Press, 1932.

Jenkins, John J. "Hume's Account of Sympathy – Some Difficulties." In *Philosophers of the Scottish Enlightenment*, pp. 91–104. Edited by V. Hope. Edinburgh: Edinburgh University Press, 1984.

Kenny, Anthony. *Action, Emotion and Will*. London: Routledge & Kegan Paul, 1963.

Kydd, Rachael M. *Reason and Conduct in Hume's Treatise*. New York: Russell & Russell, 1964.

Laird, John. *Hume's Philosophy of Human Nature*. London: Methuen & Co., 1932.

Lipkin, Robert J. "Altruism and Sympathy in Hume's Ethics." *Australasian Journal of Philosophy*, Vol. **65**, No. 1 (March 1987), pp. 18–32.

Locke, John. *An Essay Concerning Human Understanding*. Edited with an Introduction by Peter H. Nidditch. Oxford: Oxford University Press, 1975.

Mackie, J.L. *Hume's Moral Theory*. London: Routledge & Kegan Paul, 1980.

Macnabb, D.G.C. *David Hume: His Theory of Knowledge and Morality*. Hamden, Conn.: Archon Books, 1966.

McDowell, John. "Projection and Truth in Ethics." The Lindley Lecture, University of Kansas (October 21, 1987), pp. 1–14.

Mercer, Philip. *Sympathy and Ethics*. Oxford: Oxford University Press, 1972.

Morris, William Edward. "Hume's Scepticism About Reason." *Hume Studies*, Vol. **15**, No. 1 (April 1989), pp. 39–58.

Norton, David F. "Hume's Common Sense Morality." *Canadian Journal of Philosophy*, Vol. **5**, No. 4 (December 1975), pp. 523–543.

Passmore, J.A. *Hume's Intentions*. Cambridge: Cambridge University Press, 1952.

Passmore, J.A. "Hume and the Ethics of Belief." In *David Hume*: Bicentenary Papers, pp. 77–92. Edited by G.P. Morice. Austin, Texas: University of Texas Press, 1977.

Penelhum, Terence. *Hume*. New York: St. Martin's Press, 1975.

Platts, Mark. "Hume and Morality as a Matter of Fact." *Mind*, Vol. **97** (April 1988), pp. 189–204.

Popkin, Richard H. "David Hume: His Pyrrhonism and His Critique of Pyrrhonism." in *The High Road to Pyrrhonism*, pp. 103–132. Edited by Richard A. Watson and James E. Force. San Diego: Austin Hill Press, Inc., 1980.

Price, H.H. *Hume's Theory of the External World*. Oxford: Oxford University Press, 1940.

Price, H.H. "The Permanent Significance of Hume's Philosophy." In *Human Understanding*: Studies in the Philosophy of David Hume, pp. 5–33. Edited by Alexander Sesonske and Noel Fleming. Belmont, California: Wadsworth Publishing Co., 1965).

Raphael, D.D. "Hume's Critique of Ethical Rationalism." In *Hume and the Enlightenment*, pp. 14–29. Edited by William B. Todd. Edinburgh: Edinburgh University Press, 1974.

Roberts, T.A. *The Concept of Benevolence*. London: The Macmillan Press, 1973.

Rorty, Amelie O. "From Passions to Emotions and Sentiments." *Philosophy*, Vol. **57** (1982), pp. 159–172.

Scheler, Max. *The Nature of Sympathy*. New Haven, Conn.: Yale University Press, 1954.

Smith, Norman Kemp. *The Philosophy of David Hume*. London: Macmillan and Co., 1949.

Stewart, Carole. "The Moral Point of View." *Philosophy*, Vol. **51** (1976), pp. 177–187.

Stewart, John B. *The Moral and Political Philosophy of David Hume*. New York: Columbia University Press, 1963; reprint ed., Westport, Conn.: Greenwood Press, 1973.

Stroud, Barry. *Hume*. London: Routledge & Kegan Paul, 1977.

Swoyer, Chris. "Hume and the Three Views of the Self." *Hume Studies*, Vol. **8**, No. 1 (April 1982), pp. 43–61.

Thayer, H.S., ed. *Newton's Philosophy of Nature*. Introduction by John Herman Randall, Jr. New York: Hafner Press, 1953.

Tienson, John. "Hume on Universals and General Terms." *Nous*, Vol. **18** (1984), pp. 311–330.

Tweyman, Stanley. *Reason and Conduct in Hume and his Predecessors*. The Hague: Martinus Nijhoff, 1974.

Tweyman, Stanley. "Hume on Separating the Inseparable." In *Hume and the Enlightenment*, pp. 30–41. Edited by W. Todd. Edinburgh: Edinburgh University Press, 1974.

Wand, Bernard. "Hume's Account of Obligation." In *Hume*: A Collection of Critical Essays, pp. 308–334. Edited by V.C. Chappell. New York: Anchor Books, 1966.

Wand, Bernard. "A Note on Sympathy in Hume's Moral Theory." *Philosophical Review*, Vol. **64** (April 1955), pp. 275–279.

Winters, Barbara. "Hume on Reason." *Hume Studies*, Vol. **5**, No. 1(April 1979), pp. 20–35.

Wolff, Robert P. "Hume's Theory of Mental Activity." In *Hume*: A Collection of Critical Essays, pp. 99–128. Edited by V.C. Chappell. New York: Anchor Books, 1966.

Zabeeh, Farhang. *Hume*: Precursor of Modern Empiricism. The Hague: Martinus Nijhoff, 1960.

# Index

159

# ARCHIVES INTERNATIONALES D'HISTOIRE DES IDÉES
*
# INTERNATIONAL ARCHIVES OF THE HISTORY OF IDEAS

1.  E. Labrousse: *Pierre Bayle*. Tome I: *Du pays de foix à la cité d'Erasme*. 1963; 2nd printing 1984     ISBN 90-247-3136-4
    *For* Tome II *see below under Volume 6*.
2.  P. Merlan: *Monopsychism, Mysticism, Metaconsciousness*. Problems of the Soul in the Neoaristotelian and Neoplatonic Tradition. 1963; 2nd printing 1969
    ISBN 90-247-0178-3
3.  H.G. van Leeuwen: *The Problem of Certainty in English Thought, 1630–1690*. With a Preface by R.H. Popkin. 1963; 2nd printing 1970     ISBN 90-247-0179-1
4.  P.W. Janssen: *Les origines de la réforme des Carmes en France au 17$^e$ Siècle*. 1963; 2nd printing 1969     ISBN 90-247-0180-5
5.  G. Sebba: *Bibliographia Cartesiana*. A Critical Guide to the Descartes Literature (1800–1960). 1964     ISBN 90-247-0181-3
6.  E. Labrousse: *Pierre Bayle*. Tome II: *Heterodoxie et rigorisme*. 1964
    ISBN 90-247-0182-1
7.  K.W. Swart: *The Sense of Decadence in 19th-Century France*. 1964
    ISBN 90-247-0183-X
8.  W. Rex: *Essays on Pierre Bayle and Religious Controversy*. 1965
    ISBN 90-247-0184-8
9.  E. Heier: *L.H. Nicolay (1737-1820) and His Contemporaries*. Diderot, Rousseau, Voltaire, Gluck, Metastasio, Galiani, D'Escherny, Gessner, Bodmer, Lavater, Wieland, Frederick II, Falconet, W. Robertson, Paul I, Cagliostro, Gellert, Winckelmann, Poinsinet, Lloyd, Sanchez, Masson, and Others. 1965     ISBN 90-247-0185-6
10. H.M. Bracken: *The Early Reception of Berkeley's Immaterialism, 1710–1733*. [1958] Rev. ed. 1965     ISBN 90-247-0186-4
11. R.A. Watson: *The Downfall of Cartesianism, 1673–1712*. A Study of Epistemological Issues in Late 17th-Century Cartesianism. 1966     ISBN 90-247-0187-2
12. R. Descartes: *Regulæ ad Directionem Ingenii*. Texte critique établi par Giovanni Crapulli avec la version hollandaise du 17$^e$ siècle. 1966     ISBN 90-247-0188-0
13. J. Chapelain: *Soixante-dix-sept Lettres inédites à Nicolas Heinsius (1649-1658)*. Publiées d'après le manuscrit de Leyde avec une introduction et des notes par B. Bray. 1966     ISBN 90-247-0189-9
14. C. B. Brush: *Montaigne and Bayle*. Variations on the Theme of Skepticism. 1966
    ISBN 90-247-0190-2
15. B. Neveu: *Un historien à l'Ecole de Port-Royal*. Sébastien le Nain de Tillemont (1637-1698). 1966     ISBN 90-247-0191-0
16. A. Faivre: *Kirchberger et l'Illuminisme du 18$^e$ siècle*. 1966
    ISBN 90-247-0192-9
17. J.A. Clarke: *Huguenot Warrior*. The Life and Times of Henri de Rohan (1579-1638). 1966     ISBN 90-247-0193-7
18. S. Kinser: *The Works of Jacques-Auguste de Thou*. 1966     ISBN 90-247-0194-5
19. E.F. Hirsch: *Damião de Gois*. The Life and Thought of a Portuguese Humanist (1502-1574). 1967     ISBN 90-247-0195-3
20. P.J.S. Whitemore: *The Order of Minims in 17th-Century France*. 1967
    ISBN 90-247-0196-1
21. H. Hillenaar: *Fénelon et les Jésuites*. 1967     ISBN 90-247-0197-X

# ARCHIVES INTERNATIONALES D'HISTOIRE DES IDÉES
## *
# INTERNATIONAL ARCHIVES OF THE HISTORY OF IDEAS

22. W.N. Hargreaves-Mawdsley: *The English Della Cruscans and Their Time, 1783-1828.* 1967                                                ISBN 90-247-0198-8
23. C.B. Schmitt: *Gianfrancesco Pico della Mirandola (1469-1533) and his Critique of Aristotle.* 1967                                       ISBN 90-247-0199-6
24. H.B. White: *Peace among the Willows.* The Political Philosophy of Francis Bacon. 1968                                                   ISBN 90-247-0200-3
25. L. Apt: *Louis-Philippe de Ségur.* An Intellectual in a Revolutionary Age. 1969
                                                                             ISBN 90-247-0201-1
26. E.H. Kadler: *Literary Figures in French Drama (1784- 1834).* 1969
                                                                             ISBN 90-247-0202-X
27. G. Postel: *Le Thrésor des prophéties de l'univers.* Manuscrit publié avec une introduction et des notes par F. Secret. 1969           ISBN 90-247-0203-8
28. E.G. Boscherini: *Lexicon Spinozanum.* 2 vols., 1970          Set ISBN 90-247-0205-4
29. C.A. Bolton: *Church Reform in 18th-Century Italy.* The Synod of Pistoia (1786). 1969
                                                                             ISBN 90-247-0208-9
30. D. Janicaud: *Une généalogie du spiritualisme français.* Aux sources du bergsonisme: [Félix] Ravaisson [1813-1900] et la métaphysique. 1969          ISBN 90-247-0209-7
31. J.-E. d'Angers: *L'Humanisme chrétien au 17ᵉ siècle.* St. François de Sales et Yves de Paris. 1970                                       ISBN 90-247-0210-0
32. H.B. White: *Copp'd Hills towards Heaven.* Shakespeare and the Classical Polity. 1970                                                    ISBN 90-247-0250-X
33. P.J. Olscamp: *The Moral Philosophy of George Berkeley.* 1970
                                                                             ISBN 90-247-0303-4
34. C.G. Noreña: *Juan Luis Vives (1492-1540).* 1970             ISBN 90-247-5008-3
35. J. O'Higgens: *Anthony Collins (1676-1729), the Man and His World.* 1970
                                                                             ISBN 90-247-5007-5
36. F.T. Brechka: *Gerard van Swieten and His World (1700- 1772).* 1970
                                                                             ISBN 90-247-5009-1
37. M.H. Waddicor: *Montesquieu and the Pilosophy of Natural Law.* 1970
                                                                             ISBN 90-247-5039-3
38. O.R. Bloch: *La Philosophie de Gassendi (1592-1655).* Nominalisme, matérialisme et métaphysique. 1971                                    ISBN 90-247-5035-0
39. J. Hoyles: *The Waning of the Renaissance (1640-1740).* Studies in the Thought and Poetry of Henry More, John Norris and Isaac Watts. 1971     ISBN 90-247-5077-6
    *For Henry More, see also below under Volume 122 and 127.*
40. H. Bots: *Correspondance de Jacques Dupuy et de Nicolas Heinsius (1646-1656).* 1971                                                       ISBN 90-247-5092-X
41. W.C. Lehmann: *Henry Home, Lord Kames, and the Scottish Enlightenment.* A Study in National Character and in the History of Ideas. 1971          ISBN 90-247-5018-0
42. C. Kramer: *Emmery de Lyere et Marnix de Sainte Aldegonde.* Un admirateur de Sébastien Franck et de Montaigne aux prises avec le champion des calvinistes néerlandais.[Avec le texte d'Emmery de Lyere:] *Antidote ou contrepoison contre les conseils sanguinaires et envinemez de Philippe de Marnix Sr. de Ste. Aldegonde.* 1971
                                                                             ISBN 90-247-5136-5

# ARCHIVES INTERNATIONALES D'HISTOIRE DES IDÉES
*
# INTERNATIONAL ARCHIVES OF THE HISTORY OF IDEAS

64. G. Planty-Bonjour: *Hegel et la pensée philosophique en Russie (1830-1917).* 1974
ISBN 90-247-1576-8
65. R.J. Brook: *[George] Berkeley's Philosophy of Science.* 1973    ISBN 90-247-1555-5
66. T.E. Jessop: *A Bibliography of George Berkeley.* With: *Inventory of Berkeley's Manuscript Remains* by A.A. Luce. 2nd revised and enlarged ed. 1973
ISBN 90-247-1577-6
67. E.I. Perry: *From Theology to History.* French Religious Controversy and the Revocation of the Edict of Nantes. 1973    ISBN 90-247-1578-4
68. P. Dibbon, H. Bots et E. Bots-Estourgie: *Inventaire de la correspondance (1631–1671) de Johannes Fredericus Gronovius* [1611–1671]. 1974
ISBN 90-247-1600-4
69. A.B. Collins: *The Secular is Sacred.* Platonism and Thomism in Marsilio Ficino's *Platonic Theology.* 1974    ISBN 90-247-1588-1
70. R. Simon (éd.): *Henry de Boulainviller. Œuvres Philosophiques, Tome II.* 1975
ISBN 90-247-1633-0
*For Œvres Philosophiques, Tome I see under Volume 58.*
71. J.A.G. Tans et H. Schmitz du Moulin: *Pasquier Quesnel devant la Congrégation de l'Index.* Correspondance avec Francesco Barberini et mémoires sur la mise à l'Index de son édition des Œuvres de Saint Léon, publiés avec introduction et annotations. 1974    ISBN 90-247-1661-6
72. J.W. Carven: *Napoleon and the Lazarists (1804–1809).* 1974    ISBN 90-247-1667-5
73. G. Symcox: *The Crisis of French Sea Power (1688–1697).* From the *Guerre d'Escadre* to the *Guerre de Course.* 1974    ISBN 90-247-1645-4
74. R. MacGillivray: *Restoration Historians and the English Civil War.* 1974
ISBN 90-247-1678-0
75. A. Soman (ed.): *The Massacre of St. Bartholomew.* Reappraisals and Documents. 1974    ISBN 90-247-1652-7
76. R.E. Wanner: *Claude Fleury (1640-1723) as an Educational Historiographer and Thinker.* With an Introduction by W.W. Brickman. 1975    ISBN 90-247-1684-5
77. R.T. Carroll: *The Common-Sense Philosophy of Religion of Bishop Edward Stillingfleet (1635-1699).* 1975    ISBN 90-247-1647-0
78. J. Macary: *Masque et lumières au 18ᵉ [siècle].* André-François Deslandes, Citoyen et philosophe (1689-1757). 1975    ISBN 90-247-1698-5
79. S.M. Mason: *Montesquieu's Idea of Justice.* 1975    ISBN 90-247-1670-5
80. D.J.H. van Elden: *Esprits fins et esprits géométriques dans les portraits de Saint-Simon.* Contributions à l'étude du vocabulaire et du style. 1975   ISBN 90-247-1726-4
81. I. Primer (ed.): *Mandeville Studies.* New Explorations in the Art and Thought of Dr Bernard Mandeville (1670-1733). 1975    ISBN 90-247-1686-1
82. C.G. Noreña: *Studies in Spanish Renaissance Thought.* 1975    ISBN 90-247-1727-2
83. G. Wilson: *A Medievalist in the 18th Century.* Le Grand d'Aussy and the Fabliaux ou Contes. 1975    ISBN 90-247-1782-5
84. J.-R. Armogathe: *Theologia Cartesiana.* L'explication physique de l'Eucharistie chez Descartes et Dom Robert Desgabets. 1977    ISBN 90-247-1869-4
85. Bérault Stuart, Seigneur d'Aubigny: *Traité sur l'art de la guerre.* Introduction et édition par Élie de Comminges. 1976    ISBN 90-247-1871-6

# ARCHIVES INTERNATIONALES D'HISTOIRE DES IDÉES
*
# INTERNATIONAL ARCHIVES OF THE HISTORY OF IDEAS

86. S.L. Kaplan: *Bread, Politics and Political Economy in the Reign of Louis XV*. 2 vols., 1976                                                                    Set ISBN 90-247-1873-2
87. M. Lienhard (ed.): *The Origins and Characteristics of Anabaptism / Les débuts et les caractéristiques de l'Anabaptisme*. With an Extensive Bibliography / Avec une bibliographie détaillée. 1977                                          ISBN 90-247-1896-1
88. R. Descartes: *Règles utiles et claires pour la direction de l'esprit en la recherche de la vérité*. Traduction selon le lexique cartésien, et annotation conceptuelle par J.-L. Marion. Avec des notes mathématiques de P. Costabel. 1977      ISBN 90-247-1907-0
89. K. Hardesty: *The 'Supplément' to the 'Encyclopédie'*. [Diderot et d'Alembert]. 1977
                                                                      ISBN 90-247-1965-8
90. H.B. White: *Antiquity Forgot*. Essays on Shakespeare, [Francis] Bacon, and Rembrandt. 1978                                                       ISBN 90-247-1971-2
91. P.B.M. Blaas: *Continuity and Anachronism*. Parliamentary and Constitutional Development in Whig Historiography and in the Anti-Whig Reaction between 1890 and 1930. 1978                                                    ISBN 90-247-2063-X
92. S.L. Kaplan (ed.): *La Bagarre*. Ferdinando Galiani's (1728-1787) 'Lost' Parody. With an Introduction by the Editor. 1979                                   ISBN 90-247-2125-3
93. E. McNiven Hine: *A Critical Study of [Étienne Bonnot de] Condillac's [1714-1780] 'Traité des Systèmes'*. 1979                                       ISBN 90-247-2120-2
94. M.R.G. Spiller: *Concerning Natural Experimental Philosphy*. Meric Casaubon [1599-1671] and the Royal Society. 1980                                 ISBN 90-247-2414-7
95. F. Duchesneau: *La physiologie des Lumières*. Empirisme, modèles et théories. 1982
                                                                      ISBN 90-247-2500-3
96. M. Heyd: *Between Orthodoxy and the Enlightenment*. Jean-Robert Chouet [1642-1731] and the Introduction of Cartesian Science in the Academy of Geneva. 1982
                                                                      ISBN 90-247-2508-9
97. James O'Higgins: *Yves de Vallone* [1666/7-1705]: *The Making of an Esprit Fort*. 1982                                                             ISBN 90-247-2520-8
98. M.L. Kuntz: *Guillaume Postel* [1510-1581]. Prophet of the Restitution of All Things. His Life and Thought. 1981                                   ISBN 90-247-2523-2
99. A. Rosenberg: *Nicolas Gueudeville and His Work (1652-172?)*. 1982
                                                                      ISBN 90-247-2533-X
100. S.L. Jaki: *Uneasy Genius: The Life and Work of Pierre Duhem* [1861-1916]. 1984
                                     ISBN Hb 90-247-2897-5; Pb (1987) 90-247-3532-7
101. Anne Conway [1631-1679]: *The Principles of the Most Ancient Modern Philosophy*. Edited and with an Introduction by P. Loptson. 1982       ISBN 90-247-2671-9
102. E.C. Patterson: *[Mrs.] Mary [Fairfax Greig] Sommerville* [1780-1872] *and the Cultivation of Science (1815-1840)*. 1983                          ISBN 90-247-2823-1
103. C.J. Berry: *Hume, Hegel and Human Nature*. 1982                ISBN 90-247-2682-4
104. C.J. Betts: *Early Deism in France*. From the so-called 'déistes' of Lyon (1564) to Voltaire's 'Lettres philosophiques' (1734). 1984           ISBN 90-247-2923-8
105. R. Gascoigne: *Religion, Rationality and Community*. Sacred and Secular in the Thought of Hegel and His Critics. 1985                             ISBN 90-247-2992-0

# ARCHIVES INTERNATIONALES D'HISTOIRE DES IDÉES
*
# INTERNATIONAL ARCHIVES OF THE HISTORY OF IDEAS

106. S. Tweyman: *Scepticism and Belief in Hume's 'Dialogues Concerning Natural Religion'*. 1986                    ISBN 90-247-3090-2
107. G. Cerny: *Theology, Politics and Letters at the Crossroads of European Civilization.* Jacques Basnage [1653-1723] and the Baylean Huguenot Refugees in the Dutch Republic. 1987                    ISBN 90-247-3150-X
108. Spinoza's: *Algebraic Calculation of the Rainbow & Calculation of Changes.* Edited and Translated from Dutch, with an Introduction, Explanatory Notes and an Appendix by M.J. Petry. 1985                    ISBN 90-247-3149-6
109. R.G. McRae: *Philosophy and the Absolute.* The Modes of Hegel's Speculation. 1985
                    ISBN 90-247-3151-8
110. J.D. North and J.J. Roche (eds.): *The Light of Nature.* Essays in the History and Philosophy of Science presented to A.C. Crombie. 1985          ISBN 90-247-3165-8
111. C. Walton and P.J. Johnson (eds.): *[Thomas] Hobbe's 'Science of Natural Justice'.* 1987                    ISBN 90-247-3226-3
112. B.W. Head: *Ideology and Social Science.* Destutt de Tracy and French Liberalism. 1985                    ISBN 90-247-3228-X
113. A.Th. Peperzak: *Philosophy and Politics.* A Commentary on the Preface to Hegel's *Philosophy of Right.* 1987          ISBN Hb 90-247-3337-5; Pb ISBN 90-247-3338-3
114. S. Pines and Y. Yovel (eds.): *Maimonides* [1135-1204] *and Philosophy.* Papers Presented at the 6th Jerusalem Philosophical Encounter (May 1985). 1986
                    ISBN 90-247-3439-8
115. T.J. Saxby: *The Quest for the New Jerusalem, Jean de Labadie* [1610-1674] *and the Labadists (1610-1744).* 1987                    ISBN 90-247-3485-1
116. C.E. Harline: *Pamphlets, Printing, and Political Culture in the Early Dutch Republic.* 1987                    ISBN 90-247-3511-4
117. R.A. Watson and J.E. Force (eds.): *The Sceptical Mode in Modern Philosophy.* Essays in Honor of Richard H. Popkin. 1988                    ISBN 90-247-3584-X
118. R.T. Bienvenu and M. Feingold (eds.): *In the Presence of the Past.* Essays in Honor of Frank Manuel. 1991                    ISBN 0-7923-1008-X
119. J. van den Berg and E.G.E. van der Wall (eds.): *Jewish-Christian Relations in the 17th Century.* Studies and Documents. 1988                    ISBN 90-247-3617-X
120. N. Waszek: *The Scottish Enlightenment and Hegel's Account of 'Civil Society'.* 1988
                    ISBN 90-247-3596-3
121. J. Walker (ed.): *Thought and Faith in the Philosophy of Hegel.* 1991
                    ISBN 0-7923-1234-1
122. Henry More [1614-1687]: *The Immortality of the Soul.* Edited with Introduction and Notes by A. Jacob. 1987                    ISBN 90-247-3512-2
123. P.B. Scheurer and G. Debrock (eds.): *Newton's Scientific and Philosophical Legacy.* 1988                    ISBN 90-247-3723-0
124. D.R. Kelley and R.H. Popkin (eds.): *The Shapes of Knowledge from the Renaissance to the Enlightenment.* 1991                    ISBN 0-7923-1259-7
125. R.M. Golden (ed.): *The Huguenot Connection.* The Edict of Nantes, Its Revocation, and Early French Migration to South Carolina. 1988          ISBN 90-247-3645-5

# ARCHIVES INTERNATIONALES D'HISTOIRE DES IDÉES
## *
## INTERNATIONAL ARCHIVES OF THE HISTORY OF IDEAS

126. S. Lindroth: *Les chemins du savoir en Suède*. De la fondation de l'Université d'Upsal à Jacob Berzelius. Études et Portraits. Traduit du suédois, présenté et annoté par J.-F. Battail. Avec une introduction sur Sten Lindroth par G. Eriksson. 1988
ISBN 90-247-3579-3
127. S. Hutton (ed.): *Henry More (1614-1687)*. *Tercentenary Studies*. With a Biography and Bibliography by R. Crocker. 1989          ISBN 0-7923-0095-5
128. Y. Yovel (ed.): *Kant's Practical Philosophy Reconsidered*. Papers Presented at the 7th Jerusalem Philosophical Encounter (December 1986). 1989       ISBN 0-7923-0405-5
129. J.E. Force and R.H. Popkin: *Essays on the Context, Nature, and Influence of Isaac Newton's Theology*. 1990          ISBN 0-7923-0583-3
130. N. Capaldi and D.W. Livingston (eds.): *Liberty in Hume's 'History of England'*. 1990
ISBN 0-7923-0650-3
131. W. Brand: *Hume's Theory of Moral Judgment*. A Study in the Unity of *A Treatise of Human Nature*. 1992          ISBN 0-7923-1415-8

KLUWER ACADEMIC PUBLISHERS – DORDRECHT / BOSTON / LONDON